OXFORD WORLD'S CLASSICS

PRINCIPLES OF HUMAN KNOWLEDGE
AND
THREE DIALOGUES

GEORGE BERKELEY was born in Kilkenny, in Ireland, in 1685. He entered Trinity College Dublin in 1700 and was elected a Fellow in 1707. The *Principles of Human Knowledge* was published in 1710 and the *Three Dialogues* in 1713. He moved to London and became a member of the literary circles of his day, numbering Pope, Swift, Gay, and Addison amongst his friends. He toured the Continent as chaplain to the Earl of Peterborough, 1713–14, and as tutor to the son of the Bishop of Clogher, 1716–20. During this latter period he wrote the *De Motu*. He returned to academic life in Dublin until he became Dean of Derry in 1724.

Desiring to found a new civilization free of European decadence, he obtained a promise of money from the government to establish a college in Bermuda. In 1728 he married Anne Forster and sailed for America. When the government finally refused to pay the money, they returned to England in 1731, and the following year he published *Alciphron*. In 1734 he became Bishop of Cloyne and published the *Analyst*, which concerned mathematics and infinitesimals. Plans for improving the state of Ireland were the subject of *The Querist*, 1735–7. In America he had acquired a peculiar fascination with the healing power of tar-water. In *Siris* (1744) he discusses those powers, Platonistic metaphysics, and the Trinity.

He retired to Oxford in 1752 and died there on 14 January 1753, and was buried in Christ Church Cathedral. He was survived by his wife and three children.

HOWARD ROBINSON is Soros Professor of Philosophy at the Eötvös Loránd University in Budapest and Reader in the Department of Philosophy at Liverpool University. He is author of *Matter and Sense* (Cambridge: Cambridge University Press, 1982) and *Perception* (London: Routledge, 1994); editor, with John Foster, of *Essays on Berkeley* (Oxford: Clarendon Press, 1985) with Raymond Tallis of *The Pursuit of Mind* (Manchester: Carcanet, 1991), with Henry Blumenthal of *Aristotle and the Later Tradition* (Oxford: Clarendon Press, 1991), and of *Objections* ... ... :d: Clarendon Press, 1993).

OXFORD WORLD'S CLASSICS

*For over 100 years Oxford World's Classics have brought
readers closer to the world's great literature. Now with over 700
titles—from the 4,000-year-old myths of Mesopotamia to the
twentieth century's greatest novels—the series makes available
lesser-known as well as celebrated writing.*

*The pocket-sized hardbacks of the early years contained
introductions by Virginia Woolf, T. S. Eliot, Graham Greene,
and other literary figures which enriched the experience of reading.
Today the series is recognized for its fine scholarship and
reliability in texts that span world literature, drama and poetry,
religion, philosophy and politics. Each edition includes perceptive
commentary and essential background information to meet the
changing needs of readers.*

OXFORD WORLD'S CLASSICS

—

GEORGE BERKELEY

Principles of Human Knowledge

and

Three Dialogues

—

Edited with an Introduction and Notes by
HOWARD ROBINSON

OXFORD
UNIVERSITY PRESS

OXFORD

UNIVERSITY PRESS

Great Clarendon Street, Oxford OX2 6DP

Oxford University Press is a department of the University of Oxford.
It furthers the University's objective of excellence in research, scholarship,
and education by publishing worldwide in

Oxford New York

Athens Auckland Bangkok Bogotá Buenos Aires Calcutta
Cape Town Chennai Dar es Salaam Delhi Florence Hong Kong Istanbul
Karachi Kuala Lumpur Madrid Melbourne Mexico City Mumbai
Nairobi Paris São Paulo Singapore Taipei Tokyo Toronto Warsaw

with associated companies in Berlin Ibadan

Oxford is a registered trade mark of Oxford University Press
in the UK and in certain other countries

Published in the United States
by Oxford University Press Inc., New York

British Library Cataloguing in Publication Data

Data available

Library of Congress Cataloging in Publication Data
Berkeley, George, 1685–1753.
[Treatise concerning the principles of human knowledge]
Principles of human knowledge; and, Three dialogues / edited with
introduction by Howard Robinson.
p.   cm.
Includes bibliographical references.
1. Knowledge, Theory of.   2. Idealism.   3. Soul.   I. Robinson,
Howard.   II. Berkeley, George, 1685–1753.   Three dialogues.
III. Title.   IV. Title: Three dialogues.
B1331.B47   1996   192—dc20   95–10469

ISBN–13: 978–0–19–283549–9
ISBN–10: 0–19–283549–1

8

Printed in Great Britain by
Clays Ltd, St Ives plc

To John and Helen Foster,
Rachel, Gerard, Richard, Alice, and Kitty

CONTENTS

Editor's Introduction   ix

Note on the Texts   xxxviii

Select Bibliography   xxxix

A Chronology of George Berkeley   xli

PRINCIPLES OF HUMAN KNOWLEDGE   I

THREE DIALOGUES   97

Explanatory Notes   209

Index   233

EDITOR'S INTRODUCTION

i. *The Texts and their Philosophy*

Berkeley is generally regarded as the inventor of subjective idealism; that is, of the theory that the physical world exists only in the experiences minds have of it. This is one version of the doctrine that *reality is wholly mental*: the other version is *pan-psychism* (which is from the Greek, meaning 'everything-mind-ism'). *Pan-psychism* holds that there are minds in everything. So the kitchen table has a mind, or is composed of minds, or is run through with the presence of mind in some other way. Pan-psychism accepts the autonomous existence of objects outside creatures that we normally think of as possessing minds, but says that these other things, contrary to general belief, also have consciousness in them, in some way or other. Amongst major philosophers, Leibniz and, perhaps, Spinoza are pan-psychists. Berkeley's idealism restricts mind to the usual list of humans, God, animals, and whatever other spirits there may commonly be thought to be, and says that everything else—the intrinsically non-mental—exists only as features of the experience of these minds.

This seems to be a very bizarre view, but, as we shall see, it arises naturally out of the philosophy and science of the seventeenth century. That science was articulated philosophically by John Locke in his *Essay Concerning Human Understanding*. Because it articulated the new knowledge in a fairly discursive style, it found a ready audience. But Berkeley, unlike Locke, was not a discursive thinker; he dealt in crisp and purportedly decisive abstract arguments. This meant that, in his first exposition of idealism in the *Principles*, his shocking doctrine was stated rather too nakedly and without the scene-setting that might have made it acceptable. Consequently, it was simply dismissed as eccentric. The *Dialogues* are his attempt to present his doctrine in a more persuasive way. In the *Dialogues*, therefore, he personifies the debate that leads from the fashionable scientific philosophy of

Locke to his own idealism in two characters. One, *Hylas* (the name is derived from the Greek for *matter*) defends the scientific view of the material world as existing independently of the mind; the other, *Philonous* (from the Greek *lover of mind*) defends idealism. The *Dialogues* are masterpieces of both literature and philosophy. The style is almost perfectly lucid and the debate proceeds with something as close to the dynamic of a real argument between intelligent and sympathetic interlocutors as one could hope to capture in the written word. There are few long speeches and the dialogue has a natural to-and-fro quality. Hylas' thoughts follow a natural development and, in the course of the dialogues, he makes every objection that might reasonably have occurred to an opponent of Berkeley's. In short, Hylas is as far from the tedious sycophants who constitute Socrates' opponents in most of Plato's dialogues as one could hope to get. This is because in Plato's dialogues the discussion is usually between master and student: Hylas and Philonous are, in all except the outcome of the argument, friends and equals. Because the *Dialogues* are more accessible than the *Principles*, it is from the perspective of the *Dialogues* that most of this Introduction is written. But almost all the arguments find a place in both sources.

ii. *Historical Background*

George Berkeley was born at Kilkenny on 12 March 1685. His grandfather had gone to Ireland after the Restoration of 1660 and his father was a gentleman farmer. He entered Trinity College Dublin in 1700, took his BA in 1704 and was elected a Fellow in 1707. There he developed his system in the notes now published as the *Philosophical Commentaries* and published his first work, *Essay Towards a New Theory of Vision* in 1709. This remained the standard theory of vision until the mid-nineteenth century. In 1710 he was ordained priest in the Anglican Church and published the *Principles of Human Knowledge*. Because this was thought merely peculiar in intellectual circles in London, he wrote the *Three Dialogues* and published them in London in 1713. Both volumes were motivated by Berkeley's resistance to the 'new philosophy' of the seventeenth century.

This new philosophy was, roughly, the philosophical articulation of the new science of the period. Isaac Newton (1642–1727) was the greatest scientist of the age, and John Locke (1632–1704) the philosopher most crucial in turning Newtonian science into a philosophy, but many other philosophers and scientists, including Descartes (1596–1650), Malebranche (1638–1715), Galileo (1564–1642), and Boyle (1627–91) helped form and popularize the new ideas. Most of the modern thinkers—with the important exception of the Cartesians—were atomists. Atomists not only believed that bodies are made from minute particles, they also held that the particles, and the bodies made from them, possess only primary, and not secondary qualities. Descartes, though rejecting atomism, agreed that bodies really only possessed primary qualities. This means that, in themselves, bodies possess size, shape, motion, and impenetrability, but not colour, sound, taste, hardness, or smell.[1] These latter qualities are said to be dependent on the senses—colour is, so to speak, generated in the mind through the eye, sound through the mechanism of hearing, etc. But the secondary qualities are a vital component of the world as we experience it. It follows that the world of experience is very different from the world as science discovers it really to be. And not merely are they different qualitatively, but they are located in different realms. Because the things of which we are immediately aware really do possess secondary qualities, and because secondary qualities exist only 'in the mind', then what we are aware of are 'ideas in the mind', not objects in the external world. The ideas of which we are aware are, indeed, held to represent, and, in respect of primary qualities, resemble, objects in the world, but, nevertheless, they also constitute a 'veil of perception' standing between the perceiver and the external world. So the *phenomenal* or *experiential* realm, on the one hand, is differ-

---

[1] The classic philosophical statement of the distinction is in John Locke's *An Essay Concerning Human Understanding*, 2. 8.

ent from the *real* or *external* world investigated by science, on the other.

The term 'idea' as coined by Locke and used by Berkeley does not have its normal sense—a fact much remarked upon by Locke's contemporaries. We think of ideas as creatures of the intellect, as things that are *thought*: indeed 'idea' is very close to 'concept'. Locke, however, defined an idea as 'whatever is the *object* of the understanding when a man thinks' and included sensations and sensory images amongst ideas: indeed, not merely did he include them, they became the paradigm ideas, for ideas are treated as sensory, or quasi-sensory, images. Traditional Aristotelian and scholastic philosophy had distinguished between two kinds of objects of mental life. On the one hand, there are forms or species, which are universals, and so appropriate for intellect and thought: these are, roughly, what we would call 'concepts'. On the other hand, there are *phantasms*, which are the objects for sensory perception, and are particular sensory images or sense-data. Locke's adoption of the term 'idea' for all mental objects signalled his determination to assimilate these two groups— the intellectual and the sensory—to each other, and to make the sensory the model for both. (Why he did this we shall see in section (vii).)

Once one has accepted that one is directly aware of ideas in the mind, in the sense just explained, not of external things, it becomes pressing to prove that there really are any external things at all. To dramatize the possibility that there may be no external world, Descartes suggested that our experience could be the product of an evil demon whose intention was to deceive us. He then tried to refute such sceptical possibilities by proving, a priori, the existence of a good God; such a God, he argued, would not deceive us, nor allow us to be deceived, in something so fundamental as our belief in an external world. But Descartes's way of proving the existence of God— the *ontological argument*—did not command general acceptance, even amongst theists. Locke's response to scepticism was hardly more helpful. He was robustly anti-sceptical in spirit, but had little to offer in the way of argument against the sceptic. Although none of the major figures of seventeenth-century philosophy were sceptics, the new philosophy was always tainted, if not with espousing scepticism explicitly, at least with having no convincing refutation of it and, hence, encouraging it amongst its readers. This potential for scepticism came to fruition in a major philosopher slightly later, with David Hume (1711–76).

Closely connected to the fear of scepticism was a fear of materialism and atheism. The mechanistic and, hence, determinist view of the physical world that went with atomism made it difficult to understand how immaterial spirits, such as the soul or God, were related to the physical world: in particular it was thought difficult to understand how there could be causal interaction between a material and an immaterial substance. Descartes's attempt to make the interaction of mind and body scientifically respectable by saying that it took place in a particular part of the brain—namely the pineal gland—conspicuously failed to address the problem. The unease felt about interaction suggested that a materialist theory of the mind would be preferable. And just as the mechanistic view of the body threatened to squeeze out the immaterial soul or mind, so Newton's rigorously determinist laws of motion left God little to do in the cosmos at large. The response was deism, according to which God sets the world in motion, but then it runs without His support or intervention. Atheism is the next step. These tendencies had already borne fruit in the materialist philosophy of Thomas Hobbes (1588–1679).

iii. *Berkeley's Philosophical Task*

We can see common sense as clinging to two principles. One is that we are directly aware of physical objects and the other is that physical objects are independent of us and exist outside our minds. The new philosophy made it impossible to hold both these principles in their natural sense. If we are directly aware of ideas in our minds and not of the external world, then our naïve realist understanding of perception cannot be maintained. The new philosophers, typified by Locke, therefore abandoned naïve realism in favour of representative realism. Berkeley, by contrast, was determined to hold on to the idea that we are directly aware of the physical world itself, whilst accepting that what we are aware of must be mind-dependent ideas. He was, therefore, forced to conclude that

the physical world consists essentially of ideas in our minds—
that its *esse* is *percipi*: for material objects, *to be* is *to be
perceived*. So instead of abandoning direct realism, Berkeley
preferred to abandon the principle of the mind-independence
of the physical world. At least, he modified it. The mind
independence of objects, according to Berkeley, is not absolute, but relative. A physical object, unlike a hallucinatory one,
is not dependent on the perception of any given person, and,
in that sense, is mind-independent. But he denies that anything exists outside all minds taken together. The physical
world consists of those patterns of experience that are available to all: so metaphysical mind-independence is not needed
to guarantee objectivity.

But if the world is just experience, then there is a problem
about the origin of experience, for it can no longer be
explained by the interaction of the subject and the mind-
independent physical world. The natural alternative explanation is that God, instead of creating a mind-independent
world which then produces experience in us, produces the
experience directly, and these experiences are deemed to constitute the physical world. On this scheme, we are directly
acquainted with the physical world, so removing the barrier
which made scepticism a temptation, and God is made essential to the existence of the world at every moment.

iv. *Perception and the World:*
The Philosophical Options

Before considering Berkeley's arguments for his idealism, it
would be helpful to have a rough taxonomy of the various
accounts of the relation between perception and the physical
world that have appeared in modern philosophy. There are at
least eight such theories, and they mark out the ground from
naïve realism, through different kinds of representative realism, to idealism. The two forms of realism that have already
been mentioned are:

(1*a*) *Naïve or direct realism*. This is supposed to be the
theory of untutored common sense, and it holds that in
normal perception we are aware only of mind-independent

physical objects and their mind-independent properties. So if, in normal perception, I seem to see a red patch, then the red expanse of which I am aware is the surface of a physical object in public space: it is *not* simply some idea or sense-datum in my mind.

(2*b*) *Scientific or Lockean representative realism*. This is the view attributed in section (ii) to the 'new philosophy': the external world possesses only primary qualities, the secondary being properties of ideas; but the primary qualities of external things do resemble those of ideas. So if I accurately perceive a red square, the external object will be square in the way I perceive it to be; but its redness consists only in the fact that it has the power to cause in me the sensation of red; red-as-I-see-it exists only in the mind's eye.

I have called these (1*a*) and (2*b*) because there are two positions so far not mentioned, one of which is an attenuated kind of direct realism and the other a richer kind of representationalism which fall between them on the spectrum of options. The attenuated version of direct realism is not a very plausible theory, but Hylas seems to defend it at one point in the argument, and it has had more recent supporters. It is

(1*b*) *Primary quality direct realism*. This theory is a compromise between naïve and representative realism. It says that the secondary qualities of which we are aware exist only in our minds, but *the very instances* of the primary qualities of which we are aware are external. So if I am aware of a square patch of red, the red is a feature of an 'idea', but the squareness is the contour of an external physical thing. This is a very odd theory, because it would seem that the shape must be the shape *of the red patch*, so if the red is in the mind, that particular instance of shape must be so too. Hylas might be defending *primary quality direct realism* on page 126 of the *Three Dialogues*. (See note to this passage.) The richer form of representative realism is

(2*a*) *Simple representative realism*. We are directly aware only of 'ideas in the mind', but the external physical world resembles these ideas in respect of both primary and secondary qualities. Both ideas and external things can be, for example, red and square in just the same way. Visual ideas are like coloured photographs of a coloured world.

There are two other more attenuated forms of representative realism which were not explicitly developed until after Berkeley's death, but against which some of his arguments can be employed.

(3) *Structural representative realism.* The primary qualities that external objects possess cannot be said to resemble those qualities as found in ideas. What they have in common is purely formal or structural. This may mean no more than that they can be described in the same mathematical way.

(4) *Kantian or 'barely representative' realism.* Nothing, or virtually nothing, can be said about the nature of the mind-independent world, except that it is, in some sense, responsible for the world of experience.

All these forms of realism can be subdivided according to how they stand on a further issue. I have been talking about the external world in terms of the kind of qualities it is supposed to possess, but physical objects are *substances* and there is the question of what there is to a substance in addition to its qualities—if anything. That there is an extra something seems to follow from the thought that qualities and other properties *belong* to some*thing* and that this something is not itself just a bundle of qualities, but a deeper 'thinginess'. Because of its mysteriousness, not everyone agrees that one needs this extra. Indeed, although Locke wrote a long chapter on substance (*Essay*, 2. 23) and talked extensively about the *substratum* which is over and above qualities, scholars cannot agree whether he was for it or against it!

So all the above forms of realism can be distinguished into a version in which the external world consists of sensible qualities which belong to some further *substratum* or *substance*—the unknown extra that owns the qualities—and a version which has the external objects consisting entirely of qualities. This distinction is relevant to our concerns because Berkeley discusses the idea that matter possesses a sub-stratum, as well as the question of what qualities matter is supposed to possess.

There remain the two principal forms of non-realism, as articulated by Berkeley and Hume.

(5) *Berkelian idealism.* There is nothing to the physical world except our experience and its patterns. This ordering of experience is sustained directly by God.

(6) *Sceptical or Humean phenomenalism.* There is nothing to the physical world except experience and its patterns, and there is no good reason to look for an explanation of why there should be such ordered experiences: their existence is just a brute fact.

Although some of these positions were not explicitly for-mulated until after Berkeley's day, there are arguments that can be deployed against all except (5), Berkeley's own posi-tion, in the texts in this book. Berkeley can, therefore, be read as trying to eliminate all the above options other than his own. First, he seeks to refute naïve realism, then the forms of representative realism, discrediting the notion of *material substratum* on the way: then to show that God is required for the system. This is, in effect, the structure of the *Three Dia-logues*. At the centre of such a strategy is the refutation of the realism that is common to (1)–(4). This Berkeley attempts in two radically different ways. One way is to examine the con-cept of matter and discover that it lacks any proper content. The essence of this strategy is to enquire what properties mind-independent matter is supposed to possess and to show that it could not possess any of them. This is a natural part of the attacks on naïve and representative realism, for it is by arguing that neither primary nor secondary qualities nor a residual substratum could be mind-independent that he re-futes the theories of perception and the theories of the physi-cal world that are contained in (1)–(4). The second strategy against matter is radically different and philosophically more esoteric. It starts *not* primarily from reflecting on the content of the concept of matter, but from reflecting on the nature of thought—on what it is for something to be, or be the content of, an idea—and concluding that there cannot be a concept or idea of anything essentially independent of mind. It is this strategy of which Berkeley was most proud and which greatly impressed Hume.[2] It is expressed in the attack on abstract ideas and the supposed proof that one cannot conceive of the unperceived. At its core lies the theory that thoughts are merely images—that is, they are not essentially different from sense-contents and sensations. Berkeley wants to rest a knock-down demonstration of idealism on the foundation of this theory of thought, but, as we shall see, this conception of thought is so confused and inadequate that Berkeley has to fall back on the more lucid and commonsensical arguments that constitute his more general attack on matter. This is why it is the mass of arguments that make up his criticisms of the other theories and of particular conceptions of matter that have more usually impressed his more modern readers, and why it has been a puzzle for many commentators how the attack on abstraction is supposed to relate to the proof of idealism.

v. *The Main Argument of the* Three Dialogues

a. Against the externality of secondary qualities. First I shall consider the less esoteric argument of the *Three Dialogues*. The *Dialogues* were written to make the doctrine and the argument of the *Principles* more accessible. The *Principles* starts from Berkeley's more or less novel theory of concepts—his attack on 'abstract ideas'—and approaches the notions of matter and mind-independence with that novel theory very much in mind. The *Three Dialogues*, by contrast, starts from the kind of arguments against naïve realism that would have been familiar to his readers and seeks to show that these arguments develop naturally into arguments against representative realism, and, hence, against realism in

---

[2] Hume said that Berkeley's dismissal of abstract ideas was 'one of the greatest and most valuable discoveries that has been made of late years in the republic of letters'; *Treatise of Human Nature*, 1. 7.

general. The attack on abstract ideas is invoked where helpful, but it is not the cornerstone that it is meant to be in the
Principles.

In the *Three Dialogues* Berkeley attacks every one of our
eight options except (5)—his own form of idealism—more or
less in the order I number them. After an initial exchange on
the dangers of scepticism, Hylas and Philonous agree that
'sensible things' consist of 'sensible qualities', such as 'lights,
colours, figures, sounds, tastes, odours'. Philonous sets out to
prove that all these sensible qualities and, hence, all sensible
things are mind-dependent. To do this he mainly uses three
arguments that would have been familiar to, and accepted by,
the 'modern minded' amongst his readers. Two of these are
still amongst the stock-in-trade philosophical arguments
against naïve realism. The first is the *argument from illusion*,
which concludes from the fact that objects look (or sound, or
feel, etc.) different to different observers or to the same
observer at different times, whilst not themselves changing,
that what one is directly aware of in those varied 'looks'
cannot be the objects themselves. The second is the *causal
argument*, which argues from the fact that our experiences
are caused at the end of a chain of events that runs from
the object to the sense organ and then the brain, to the conclusion that the immediate objects of those experiences must
also be caused at the end of the process and so be 'in the
mind' or 'in the head'; they, therefore, cannot be identical
with the objects in the external world that initiated the causal
chain. The third argument, which is of ancient origin, does
not have the same modern currency as the other two and is
less familiar. It might be called the *assimilation argument*.
Certain mental contents are incontrovertibly subjective, so
that it makes no sense to suggest that they might exist extra-
mentally. There are, for example, no thoughts, emotions,
pains, or sensations outside of minds. One way of showing
that sensible qualities are subjective would be to show that
they are essentially interconnected with one of these necessarily subjective elements and so assimilate the sensible
quality to the subjective one. Berkeley follows a line of argument dating at least from Aristotle, which asserts that certain

sensible qualities are essentially connected to pleasure and pain. An example of this strategy is his treatment of heat. An intense degree of heat is a very great pain, so intense heat can be assimilated to pain and so does not exist in the external world.[3] I mention this now largely ignored strategy because it will feature in the crucial question, to be discussed later, of whether 'an idea can be like nothing but an idea'.

I cannot deal satisfactorily here with the still controversial question of whether these, and similar arguments against naïve realism are successful.[4] As they were the common currency of the day, Berkeley's claim to fame rests, not on them, but on the idealist developments he makes from them. One point is, however, worth making. On pages 112–25 of the *First Dialogue* he applies the above arguments to secondary qualities, and concludes 'Colours, sounds, tastes, in a word, all those termed *secondary qualities*, have certainly no existence without the mind.' Berkeley is here making an exaggerated claim. All that the arguments, even if sound, justify one in concluding is that those instances of secondary qualities *of which one is immediately aware* exist only in the mind: they do not, that is, refute (2*a*) above, *simple representative realism*, according to which both primary and secondary qualities belong both to ideas in the mind and to the external objects the ideas represent. In making this confusion, Berkeley is simply following Locke, who had used similar arguments against the objectivity of secondary qualities. Both Locke and Berkeley, that is, confuse arguments which, if successful, show that the immediate objects of our awareness are subjective, with proofs that secondary qualities are *per se* subjective.[5] In the case of secondary qualities this is, perhaps, an understandable mistake, because secondary qualities play such a central role

---

[3] I discuss this argument in the note to *Dialogues*, p. 112.

[4] I argue that, contrary to current belief, the arguments are successful in *Perception* (London: Routledge, 1994).

[5] In *Essay*, 2. 8. 21 Locke argues that the perception of primary qualities does not vary with subjective conditions, as perception of secondaries does, and that this shows the former to exist externally and the latter in the mind.

in constituting the immediate objects of our awareness. But, as we shall see when considering primary qualities, the error is more gross than that; for it appears to involve the principle that, if a kind of quality is proved to exist in the mind, it follows that it does not also exist outside the mind, and this is question-begging.

b. Against the externality of primary qualities. Believing himself to have disposed of secondary qualities, Berkeley can be read as then considering the bizarre option (1*b*); that we are directly aware of external primary qualities, though not of secondary. He has no difficulty refuting this by using the same arguments as he had used to refute the objectivity of secondary qualities, and similarly proceeds to conclude that primary qualities exist only in the mind. He is thereby misled into thinking that he has disposed of the forms of representative realism contained in (2*a*), (2*b*), and (possibly) (3). Locke's mistaken interpretation of these arguments is, therefore, easily turned against his own philosophy. It is not until late on in the first dialogue, after an interesting digression, that Hylas realizes that representationalism is still available. The digression contains three arguments that all involve backtracking on his concession that no sensible qualities exist externally. Two of these arguments merit comment.

In one of these, Hylas suggests that if one distinguishes between the *act* and the *object* of perception one can see that the former is subjective and the latter—which includes the sensible qualities—is not. This is a strategy widely used by modern philosophers. They argue that perceiv*ing* is something we *do* and the *objects* of perception are things we do it to. The psychological state is the act and the object is out in the world: such terms as 'idea' only serve to conflate these two poles of perception. A proper discussion of this point would take us into the more sophisticated reaches of the philosophy of perception, but Philonous' response is not without force. He replies that perceptual *experience*—as opposed to, for example, the act of turning one's head to look—is entirely involuntary and the act–object distinction cannot be applied where the will is not involved.

The other interesting argument in the digression comes from Hylas' suggestion that sensible qualities can be looked on in either of two ways: they can be considered either as modes of sensation which could not exist outside the mind; or as modes of a material substratum. This does nothing to answer directly the arguments already employed against mind-independent sensible qualities, and faces also the problem of giving some literal sense to 'substratum' and its task of 'underlying' or 'supporting' qualities. Berkeley argues that one can make sense of an unknown, such as substratum is meant to be, only if one can set it in a known relation to something known. An example of this might be that I can form an idea of Smith's father, though I do not know him, because I know Smith and understand the relation 'being the father of'. Substratum supposedly stands in relation to known sensible qualities, but that relation—'underlying' or 'supporting'—is itself metaphorical—not 'as your legs support your body'. So there are not two knowns and one unknown, but two unknowns and only one known. This is essentially Berkeley's objection to all those forms of realism that make material substance consist of more than qualities alone.

The digression ends when Hylas realizes that he should be defending a representative realism involving qualities alone, so picking the argument up where it should have left off after the attack on naïve realism.

To speak the truth, Philonous, I think there are two kinds of objects, the one perceived immediately, which are likewise called *ideas*; the other are real things or external objects perceived by the mediation of ideas, which are their images and representations. Now I own, ideas do not exist without the mind; but the latter sort of objects do. I am sorry I did not think of this distinction sooner ... (pp. 142–3)

Philonous glosses this, saying: 'you will have our ideas, which alone are immediately perceived, to be pictures of external things ...' Philonous makes two important responses: (i) He asks how we could ever come to know about the objects behind the pictures. In the case of normal pictures, we can perceive both picture and object with the same degree of directness, but in the case of ideas and things only the ideas are directly available in experience. Our knowledge of objects, therefore, would have to be 'by some internal faculty of the soul, as reason or memory'. Hylas here admits 'I do not find I can give you any good reason for' believing in objects, but in the second dialogue he comes near to the natural reply by saying that the external world causes, and thereby explains, our ideas. That they provide such an explanation would be a reason for believing in external objects.

Berkeley's response to this suggestion brings into play one of the most contentious of his anti-realist claims. He argues that only minds are real causal agents, so the postulation of an external world could never explain anything. He backs this up by an appeal to introspection. We know from experience that our volitions can cause things, but that ideas are passive: we see the white blob touch the red blob and the red blob then moves, and we see such things regularly, but see no *making* or *causing* connecting the white and the red ideas. Berkeley's position would have seemed much weaker if he had concentrated on tactile, rather than visual cases. The feeling of being pressed and the feeling of motion that is associated with it do not seem to be merely contingently connected—it seems to be part of the nature of the one that it tends to lead to the other. Even if this is so (which is not clear) the Berkelian need not worry. The feeling of being pushed is still a *feeling* and, hence, a mental state. To say that causal power in the world is like a feeling of pressure except that it is outside of mind seems hardly better than saying it is like an extra-mental act of will. Phenomenological judgements in these areas are very difficult to evaluate, but it is plausible for a Berkelian to argue that saying something is like what you feel when you feel yourself being pushed, except that it is not a sensation, is no better than saying that something is like yellow, but not a colour. (ii) His second response is to deny that there could be anything in the external world which was *like* anything presented in an idea: 'nothing but an idea could be like an idea'. If this is correct then no kind of representative realism which allows the representation to tell us anything about what the thing represented is *like*, will be possible: this would certainly rule out (2*a*) and (2*b*) which claim that ideas and the world share certain positive qualities. It would probably permit (4), for that makes no claims about the nature of the physical world: whether it allows (3) will depend on whether structural features are 'likenesses' in the sense covered by this argument (whatever that sense exactly may be).

c. *That 'an idea can be like nothing but an idea'*. When applied to *perceptual* ideas, this principle seems, at first sight, both sophistical and question-begging. On the ordinary, non-philosophical sense of 'idea', where it means *thought* or *concept*, it is plausible to say that nothing outside the mind could be like an idea, for things like bits of thoughts cannot float around in the external world. But Berkeley is using 'idea' in Locke's way, to mean anything with which the mind concerns itself directly, which includes perceptual contents as well as intellectual contents. And it seems simply to beg the question against the representative realist to assert as a principle that the extra-mental world could not be like our perceptual contents.

The situation for Berkeley's argument is not, however, as bad as this suggests. It is true, not only that nothing extra-mental could be like a thought, but also that nothing extra-mental could be like a sensation. As I pointed out when discussing the *assimilation argument* above, there can be no pains, itches, or tactile sensations, or anything like them, in the external world. Berkeley has to show, therefore, that all perceptual 'ideas' fall into this category: in particular, he has to show that colour patches are just as much mere sensations as twinges and feelings. His attack on visual depth (which is discussed in (vii)) is part of such a strategy. It can be carried further by a thought-experiment. Imagine someone born blind, who was given, by direct cortical stimulation, visual sensations. Given that these were not so ordered as to map onto his picture of the world gained through the other senses, would there be anything about them which made them seem any different in status from other sensations? Although this is speculative, it seems reasonable to guess that they would seem to be 'in the head' and no more apparently external than aches and throbs. It is the kind of structure that normal visual experience possesses, rather than its intrinsic nature, that makes it natural to read its contents as external.[6] If our visual experience were chaotic and accidental, even that feature of it that we identify as visual shape would have no apparent claim to greater objectivity than any other feature of the sensation.

If these considerations have force, then the external world would not be like our ideas of it and so would have to be something the nature of which (if it has one) is hidden from us. This conception of physical reality is one that was developed after Berkeley, but there are arguments in our texts which are relevant to it.

Hylas suggests that we have no other conception of matter than as that which causes experience. If developed systematically, this would lead to the conception of the physical world as the formal structure of causal laws that explain the phenomena: that is, as a version of (3), *structural representative realism*. Berkeley admits that there could be things of which we do not know the intrinsic nature (pp. 164–5), so his only direct objection to this attenuated realism is the claim that causation is essentially connected with will and, hence, mental.[7] In desperation Hylas attenuates matter further: 'I at present understand by *matter* neither substance nor accident, thinking nor extended being, neither cause, instrument, nor occasion, but something entirely unknown, distinct from all these' (p. 163). This conception is reminiscent of Kant's *noumenon*, in that it is wholly negative: matter has become a mere place-holder (not literally, for Hylas concedes that *place* has been shown to be mental). Philonous has little difficulty persuading Hylas that this idea is entirely empty. Having done this, each of (1) to (4) has been disposed of to Berkeley's satisfaction.

---

[6] For the classic exposition of this account of externality, see Hume's *Treatise*, 1. 4. 2.

[7] This is the only argument apart from those to be considered in the next section by which he argues that the very idea of extra-mental existence is defective.

vi. *Mites, Men, and Objective Space*

There is an argument that Berkeley uses against the objectivity of physical space which is not, I think, taken seriously by
most commentators, but which I believe has more force than
is generally appreciated. Berkeley argues that because things
look bigger to a mite than to a human and there is no clear
sense in which one of them perceives the 'right' size, then
there is no fact about the size and, therefore, no such thing
as real or objective size, and so no such thing as mind-
independent spatial dimensions.

The first objection to this argument that springs to mind is
that measurement can pick out real size and that, irrespective
of how it looks to mite or man, an object will have a specific
measurable size; for example, being two inches long. But this
will achieve nothing unless we can give objectivity to units of
measurement, and an inch is a long distance to a mite and a
small one to a human, so in agreeing that an object is two
inches long the mite and the man have only an illusion of
agreement. There is agreement on the relative sizes of the
object and an inch on a ruler, but no agreement about the
absolute size of either. It seems that subjects of radically
different sizes can agree on the *relative* sizes of objects, but
not on their intrinsic dimensions. The response to this is obvious, namely that size is a relative matter and agreeing on the
relative dimensions of things is agreeing on their actual dimensions. The matter is not, however, quite so simple. It can
be proved that a purely formal definition of space, in terms,
say, of Cartesian co-ordinates and axes, is not a complete
representation of the nature of space.[8] As well as such formal
features, there must be something intuitive and qualitative,
like the way that extension presents itself experientially in
vision. But it is in respect of this qualitative feature that things
look many times larger to the mite: relative sizes are pre-
served, but the qualitative interpretations of dimensions are
not. If such an interpretation is essential to any real space,
as I have claimed it is, then there is a problem. The physical world in which things cannot all double in size—as

---

[8] John Foster shows this in *The Case For Idealism*, 73–88.

they can when one moves from a human world to a mite's—is an abstraction created by measurement from the various worlds of experience, which are the ultimate constituents of reality. This is a line of argument that I think merits further investigation.[9]

vii. The Principles *and Abstraction*

The feature of *The Principles* on which I want to concentrate is Berkeley's theory of thought. This is to be found in the attack on abstract ideas in the Introduction, and in section 23, where he argues that we cannot form the idea of an extramental object. (This argument also occurs in *Dialogues*, pp. 139–40.) Berkeley's purpose is to demystify our understanding of thought.

Thoughts and their contents possess two strictly distinct but closely connected properties. First, thoughts possess intentionality, which means that they are *about* things other than themselves: my thoughts are about elephants or books, which are not themselves simply events in my mind. Second, most thought contents possess generality. All our concepts, except those strictly used to name or indicate particular objects, express features, such as being red or being human, which an indefinite number of things might possess. *Being about things* and *being general* are mysterious properties, in the sense that they are peculiar to mind and are not possessed by physical particulars in their own right. The classical and medieval preoccupation with forms and universals was precisely concerned with the generality of thought and with how the world had to be so that it could match the generality found in thought—that is, how the world had to be so that thoughts could be true of it. This concern spawned a whole class of general or potentially general entities, such as forms, universals, essences, and sensible species. Nominalists—of

[9] In a sense it has already received such investigation, for Foster's argument in pt. 3 of *The Case for Idealism* can be regarded as a very sophisticated development of Berkeley's point. Physical space requires an intuitive element, but what this element is actually like must be a function of the nature of experience, not of some mind-independent reality.

whom Ockham is the most notorious—denied the reality of
generality in the world, somehow wanting generality to be
spun by language, and by the seventeenth century nominalists
had gained the day with regard to supposed generality in the
external world, but some, such as Descartes, still accepted
generality as an intrinsic feature of mental life. British philosophers—including both Hobbes and Locke—were determined that absolutely everything real had to be wholly
particular. This leaves a problem for the undoubted generality
of thought. The particulars that were agreed to constitute
thought were images, conceived of as colour patches, sounds,
etc. Thus there was no essential difference between thought
and sensation. Locke tried to solve the problem of generality
by invoking abstract general ideas, which, sometimes at least,
he treats as abstract general *images*. So the idea of triangle is
an image which is, at the same time, every specific kind of
triangle—isosceles, rectangle, scalene, etc.—and none in particular. Berkeley has no difficulty showing that there is no
sense in the idea of such an image. His alternative theory is
that a thoroughly particular image becomes general by *representing* or *standing for* some class of images. From the point
of view of the subject, this happens by his *selectively attending*
to the relevant feature of the image. So, though I am imaging
an equilateral triangle, I take it as representing all triangles by
selectively attending just to the fact that it has three sides, and
ignoring their relative proportions, its size, colour, etc.

This explains why Berkeley thought his attack on abstraction refuted the belief in mind-independent reality. If we can
have genuine ideas only of those features which are literally
realized in images, such as red or square, or are names for
collections of such ideas (such as 'apple') then *being mind-
independent*, *being unperceived*, or *material substance* will not
be genuine ideas, for no idea can literally possess these features: all ideas can occur in hallucinations and no hallucination can literally possess such characteristics. Nor can they
be names for a collection of ideas, unless one agrees to give
these concepts their Berkelian gloss.

His theory of thought explains what otherwise can seem the
rather strange argument in section 23. Berkeley appears to be

arguing that you cannot form the idea of something unthought of, for once you form such an idea its object is, *ipso facto*, thought of.

To make out [that the objects of your thought may exist without the mind], it is necessary that you conceive them existing unconceived or unthought of, which is a manifest repugnancy. When we do our utmost to conceive the existence of external bodies, we are all the while only contemplating our own ideas.

Put in this way, the argument feels sophistical: all you need is a distinction between the *thought* and its *object*, and though the former is in the mind, the latter is not. This distinction is what we mean by the *intentionality* of thought. The theory of thought found in the introduction to the *Principles* undermines such an appeal to intentionality. If everything thinkable can be realized in an image as a feature of it, then the concepts of mind-independent matter, and mind-independence, *simpliciter*, should be so realizable. But, necessarily, such things cannot be properties of images, which are essentially mental, so we cannot have ideas of them.

It is at this point that the argument about visual distance, which had been the main topic of the *New Theory of Vision*, Berkeley's first book, becomes important. It is natural to suggest that we are directly aware of distance in sight, because things *look to be* out in front of us and some of them *look to be* further away than others: so these visual ideas do seem really to represent the property of externality and mind-independence. Berkeley argues against this suggestion that distance is not a real visual phenomenon because it is 'a line turned end on to the eye'. If we consider visual space on the left–right and up–down axes, then a space of, say, two inches is represented by an area in which a two-inch visual object— an extent of colour—could be present to awareness. For these axes, that is, a spatial distance is something in which a visual phenomenon is presented. But this is not so for depth. If one object is two inches *behind* another then the space between them is invisible, in the sense that something placed there cannot be seen. The line is end-on to the eye in the sense that no spatial extent is directly visible in depth. Our sense of depth comes only from a learnt association between certain visual experiences and the fact that we have to *reach out* to touch the more distant objects. It is this correlation between touch and vision that creates the experience of depth, not something intrinsic to vision.

The objection from intentionality, however, is not adequately dealt with merely by disparaging our perception of depth. No theory of thought can operate without a distinction between the thought, considered as a psychological episode, and what the thought is about. Berkeley does not deny that I can now think of myself as existing yesterday, and that I can think of your mind and what might be in it: but neither past time nor other minds and their contents can be features of the current image with which I am thinking. If a current episode of thought could not be *about* something outside that episode, then we would be stuck in a solipsism of the present moment; that is, we could have no thought of anything but the current contents of our own consciousness.

Berkeley does implicitly take notice of these problems, for, as we have seen, he does have a doctrine of representation whereby an idea can stand for others. As we shall see, his account of this is seriously inadequate.

Berkeley's claim that particular ideas stand for other ideas is the source of the doctrine of *associationism*, which was to be the principle empiricist account of meaning and thought until the end of the nineteenth century. Associationists explained thought and meaning by saying that the meaning of a mental episode consisted in its association with other mental episodes which tended to occur in close proximity to it. For example, the word 'red' means the colour red because the word tends to summon up an image of the colour. Hume applies this idea to explain our attribution of necessity to causal relations: because we have often seen events of type F followed by events of type G, whenever we see an F our minds immediately form an idea of G, and so we think them necessarily connected.

A fatal flaw with associationism can be exposed by noticing an ambiguity in the notion of association. An association can be either *objective* or *subjective* in the following way. It might just be a matter of fact that certain ideas tended to occur together, or it might be the case that the subject *noticed* these associations and so actively *thought of them* as associated. In so far as we are trying to understand the *experience* of meaningful thought, it must be the latter that is intended, for the bare occurrence of correlations would not alone constitute the experience of meaning. Berkeley certainly meant the subjective association when he talked of *attending to* the triangularity of a particular triangle and ignoring its other features. But to allow that one can subjectively see an idea as representing others and that one can attend to some feature of an idea reimports the original problem of generality. For what is it for one idea to represent others to a subject, if it is not only for them to be objectively associated? Making an association between particular ideas cannot consist in having another wholly particular idea or image. It would seem to be for them to be brought under a concept, where a concept is an inherently general kind of entity. And the kind of attention involved in selectively attending to the triangularity of a particular idea is not a mere focusing on a spatial region of the idea, it is the focusing on a conceptual feature of the image, and this presupposes, it does not analyse, the possession of concepts.

Even if we were to ignore these difficulties with Berkeley's nominalism, the doctrine of the association of ideas cannot overcome the problems with intentionality raised by section 23. If my current idea can mean the other ideas with which it is associated, then I am no longer trapped in a solipsism of the present moment, for my current idea can mean other ideas with which my experience associates it. But I am still a solipsist, for no association can be made in my experience between an idea of mine and an idea of yours, for I never experience the latter. For Berkeley, the fundamental form by which ideas represent one another is through resemblance, not simply by brute contingent association, like cause and effect, which need possess no similarity. So one triangle can represent all triangles. I can, therefore, think of something similar to my current idea and impute it either to my own past or to your mind. These other times and other minds are intelligible because they are like—or at least strongly ana-

xxxii   *Introduction*

logous to—the present moment and my own mind. Intentionality is, for Berkeley, therefore, a matter of association and,
primarily, of resemblance.

It is at this point that the argument based on the nature of
thought ceases to be autonomous. If the present red, square
idea can represent other ideas that are square, why cannot it
represent square as it occurs in the external, physical world?
Once there is allowed to be 'intentionality by resemblance',
then qualities in the world similar to those in the mind should
be amongst the things one can intend. At this point the principle that 'an idea can be like nothing but an idea' (s. 8)
becomes essential to the argument, for only by appeal to that
principle can it be denied that images can represent external
qualities that resemble them. But the same principle was essential to the attack on representative realism. 'Nothing but
an idea can be like an idea' turns out to be the corner-stone of
both of Berkeley's argumentative strategies, and the nominalist argument loses any independent force.

viii. *Salvaging Berkeley on Abstraction*

Berkeley's remarks on abstraction are not as completely mis-
conceived as the above may suggest. Imagism as a theory of
what concepts *are* is hopeless, but an imagist approach to *what
we can conceive of*—that is, to the contents of concepts—is
not open to the same objections, and captures more directly
the spirit of empiricism. It is empiricism freed from the concern to be nominalist. Imagism as a theory of the *content* of
concepts, rather than of the nature of concepts themselves
could be expressed as follows:

> The only properties that we can conceive of as they are in
> themselves are ones that can be presented in, or con-
> structed from features presented in, experience.

Clearly not all concepts could have their contents represented
in images in this way. For example, logical connectives, such
as 'and', 'or', and 'if . . . then', do not have that kind of content—though ultra-empiricists have tried such moves as
equating the sense of 'or' with a feeling of uncertainty at the
back of the neck! And one would probably need something

like analogy to carry one from a grasp on one's own experience to giving sense to something as being another mind and its contents, for the property of *belonging to someone else* could not be directly imaged. But it is intuitively plausible to claim that the fundamental properties of the world must be like something *in themselves*. And if we cannot experience certain properties directly—as we cannot the properties of electrons or, if the defence given above of the principle that 'an idea can be like nothing but an idea' is sound, the properties of the mind-independent world in general, then we cannot know what those properties—electrons, or the external world in general—are like in themselves. We can then either think of them on analogy with what we experience by constructing models to interpret them, or can try to treat their concepts on analogy with the logical connectives, as ideas used to structure and relate elements that have the more full-blooded imageable content.

For reasons that it is not possible to give here, it has proved difficult to make progress clarifying even this modest empiricism, but it does express the ambition of empiricism more accurately than the attempt, with which it is confused in Berkeley, to give a reductive imagistic account of concepts themselves.

ix. *The Case for Theistic Idealism*

This completes Berkeley's case against physical realism, but it leaves open the choice between his theistic idealism and the sceptical phenomenalism of Hume, that is, between options (5) and (6). The plain fact is that Berkeley does not seriously consider the sceptical possibility that our experience may come—and come in ordered patterns—without any cause. It seems obvious to him—as it does to common sense—that such things are not acceptable as brute facts. Similarly, he does not consider Hume's radical empiricist principle that what is probable or improbable can only be based on experience, so there can be nothing improbable in the fact that experience just happens to come, and come in patterns; this cannot be improbable, on Humean principles, because experience shows us it happens that way. The difference between

Berkeley and Hume is that Berkeley is implicitly accepting
that there are a priori probabilities relevant to matters of
fact—that is, that considerations of what is possible can be
enough on their own to influence probability, without further
information about how things actually work. This is too difficult a question to investigate here.[10]

In general, Berkelian idealism differs from sceptical
phenomenalism in its attitude towards *spirit* and its powers.
The full version of Berkeley's famous maxim is *esse est percipi
vel percipere*: perceiv*ers* exist as well as the perceiv*ed*. Because they are not objects of awareness, but agents, spirits and
their activities are not ideas. A full-blown empiricism, therefore, that says that only ideas are intelligible has a problem
with spirit. In his early notebooks Berkeley considered the
theory that there are only ideas and, hence, considered what
we think of as the Humean thesis that the self is only a
collection of ideas. Berkeley, however, thought that he could
hold on to spirit and its powers—acts of understanding and
of will—because, though not captured in ideas, they are
captured by consciousness. Berkeley would have rejected
Hume's claim that

when I enter most intimately into what I call *myself*, I always stumble
upon some particular perception or other . . . I never catch *myself* at
any time without a perception, and never can observe anything but
the perception. (*Treatise*, 1. 4. 6)

because there is a conscious experience of acting, as opposed
to merely undergoing, and of the enduring unity of the self.
Berkeley has often been criticized for inconsistency in refus-
ing to allow that matter is intelligible though not an idea,
whilst spirit is allowed, though not an idea. There is no inconsistency, however, because he does argue that consciousness
makes spirit available to us in a way that it cannot make
matter: though there are no ideas of spirit or its activities,
there are what Berkeley calls 'notions'. In short, Berkeley

[10] It is dealt with a little more fully in Robinson, 'The General Form of
the Argument for Berkeleian Idealism', in Foster and Robinson (eds.),
Essays on Berkeley (Oxford: Clarendon Press, 1985), 163–86.

believes that experience presents us with its agent and his activities, as well as with its objects, though the agent side of the divide is more elusive than the object side. As with the issue of a priori probabilities, it is not possible to pursue here the arguments between Hume and Berkeley, which remain live issues. But the Humean has great difficulty explaining the unity of the self, both through time, and, more crucially, at a time: what is it that constitutes the experienced unity of my current thoughts, emotions, and perceptions from different senses, if not that they are all given to a single subject? The difference between ideas floating into the mind and controlled thought is also difficult to explain if there is no such thing as agency or will.

x. *Berkeley's Influence*

In a sense, Berkeley's main influence has been just the opposite of what he intended. Instead of saving religion and common sense from atheism and scepticism, Berkeley is seen as providing the stepping-stone from Locke's scientific realism to Hume's radical empiricism and scepticism: Hylas' verdict on Berkeley's system has, for the most part, been followed by history, both in Berkeley's own day, and since. There are a variety of reasons for this. First, there are those, such as Hume, who think there is an actual inconsistency between Berkeley's strict empiricist criterion of meaning and allowing in spirits and their activities. We have seen that Berkeley was ready to meet this objection, but it continues to be used; (for example, by A. D. Lindsay in the introduction to the old Everyman edition of the *Principles* and *Dialogues*). If one shares this feeling, then Berkeley will merely be clearing the way for Hume's consistent statement of empiricism. Second, there was the powerful influence of John Stuart Mill. Mill described physical objects as 'the permanent possibilities of sensation' and, reasonably, regarded this as equivalent to Berkeley's understanding of the physical. Mill was the vital link between eighteenth-century empiricism and the twentieth-century, more positivistic, versions of it (as represented by Bertrand Russell, A. J. Ayer, and the Vienna Circle) and his advocacy of Berkeley turned the Anglican bishop into the officially approved forerunner of modern radical empiricism and phenomenalism. In a famous article, Sir Karl Popper suggests that Berkeley be seen as the precursor of both Ernst Mach, the proto-logical positivist, and of Albert Einstein, thus adopting Berkeley into a modern scientific empiricism that was completely unconcerned with his spiritual objectives. Third, the ethos of both Christianity and common sense has proved resolutely Johnsonian. Dr Johnson claimed to refute Berkeley by kicking a stone to prove that the world was *real* and *solid*, and though no one—probably not even Johnson—thought this a serious argument, it represents a perennial feeling about the system, and one that makes it, as a matter of psychological fact, generally unbelievable by those who are supposed to find it most congenial. Radical empiricists, on the other hand, find the mixture of reductionism and a hint of scepticism extremely attractive. Fourth, there is a matter of *Zeitgeist*. The Enlightenment, and the scientific age that followed it, were not the time for a religious metaphysic—especially an idealist one—to commend itself to advanced thinkers. As a plain matter of history, therefore, Berkeley occupied a place in a process that was more receptive of certain of his ideas than of others. This is no doubt why the more spiritual Berkeleian ethos found an echo in those philosophers who were reacting against the Enlightenment, namely certain Hegelian idealists. The Hegelian tradition, represented in Britain most notably by F. H. Bradley, took Berkeley's attack on matter as conclusive and agreed with him that Absolute Mind was in control of the universe. They did not conceive of that mind as an independent spiritual substance, as did Berkeley. It was more like a Humean bundle composed of all the experiences that make up the total idealist universe: except that, for the Hegelians, unlike Hume, a bundle is more than the sum of its parts, and so has a principle of unity or identity in its own right, which is lacking in Hume's conception.

If Berkeley's defence of orthodox religion is to have its day, that day has not yet come. But there are modern philosophers, such as John Foster and Timothy Sprigge, who defend idealist philosophies that owe much to Berkeley. The processes against which Berkeley struggled, however, grow stronger, and the need for his insights grows greater, not less.[11]

[11] The stream of philosophical orthodoxy has always run against Berkeley's religious metaphysic, but its influence against the current has not been negligible. C. S. Lewis credits Berkeley with a major role in his reconversion to Christianity and Cardinal Newman admitted a debt to him in the development of his own empiricist Catholicism. I suspect that Berkeley's influence in private religious resistance to the metaphysical mischief of the Enlightenment is greater than the secular public consensus reveals.

NOTE ON THE TEXTS

The *Principles* was published twice in Berkeley's lifetime; first in Dublin in 1710 (this is known as *A*), second in London in 1734, together with the *Three Dialogues* (edition *B*). The *Three Dialogues* were published three times; 1713 (*A*), 1725 (*B*), 1734 (*C*). The texts used here are the 1734 versions, as found in volume ii of the complete *Works*, edited by A. A. Luce and T. E. Jessop (London, 1948–57). In the Notes I have drawn attention to those differences between the editions that may be of philosophical interest.

SELECT BIBLIOGRAPHY

The standard edition of Berkeley is *Works of George Berkeley, Bishop of Cloyne*, edited by A. A. Luce and T. E. Jessop in 7 vols. (London: Nelson, 1948–57). An elegant and brief introduction is the excellent volume in the 'Past Masters' series, J. O. Urmson, *Berkeley* (Oxford: Oxford University Press, 1982).

Longer and more difficult monographs are:

Bennett, J., *Locke, Berkeley, Hume: Central Themes* (Oxford: Oxford University Press, 1971).

Dancy, J., *Berkeley: An Introduction* (Oxford: Basil Blackwell, 1987).

Grayling, A. C., *Berkeley: The Central Arguments* (London: Duckworth, 1986).

Pitcher, G., *Berkeley* (London: Routledge & Kegan Paul, 1977).

Tipton, I. C., *Berkeley: The Philosophy of Immaterialism* (London: Methuen, 1974).

Warnock, G. J., *Berkeley* (Harmondsworth: Pelican, 1953).

Winkler, K. P., *Berkeley: An Interpretation* (Oxford: Oxford University Press, 1989).

Useful collections of articles include:

Foster, J., and Robinson, H. (eds.), *Essays on Berkeley* (Oxford: Oxford University Press, 1985).

Martin, C. B., and Armstrong, D. M. (eds.), *Locke and Berkeley* (London: Macmillan, 1968).

Sosa, E. (ed.), *Essays on the Philosophy of George Berkeley* (Dordrecht: Reidel, 1987).

Turbayne, C. (ed.), *Berkeley: Critical and Interpretative Essays* (Manchester: Manchester University Press, 1982).

Modern defences of idealism can be found in:

Foster, J., *The Case for Idealism* (London: Routledge & Kegan Paul, 1982).

Robinson, H., 'The General Form of the Argument for Berkelian Idealism', in Foster and Robinson (eds.).

Sprigge, T., *The Vindication of Absolute Idealism* (Edinburgh: Edinburgh University Press, 1983).

A more accessible version of Foster's argument can be found in his 'The Succinct Case for Idealism', in H. Robinson (ed.), *Objections to Physicalism* (Oxford: Clarendon Press, 1993). Also relevant is the final chapter of H. Robinson, *Matter and Sense* (Cambridge: Cambridge University Press, 1982).

A CHRONOLOGY OF
GEORGE BERKELEY

1685   Berkeley born in County Kilkenny, 12 March.

1696   Enters Kilkenny College.

1700   Enters Trinity College Dublin.

1702   Elected a scholar of Trinity College.

1704   Receives his BA. Death of John Locke.

1707   Elected a Fellow of Trinity College. Develops his system over the next three years, as found in the notebooks now called the *Philosophical Commentaries*.

1709   Publishes the *Essay Towards a New Theory of Vision*.

1710   Ordained priest in the Church of Ireland; publishes the *Principles of Human Knowledge*.

1711   Birth of David Hume.

1712   Publishes *Passive Obedience*.

1713   First visit to England; publishes *Three Dialogues*. As chaplain to the Earl of Peterborough, he visits Paris until the following year.

1716–20   Travels in France and Italy as tutor to the son of the Bishop of Clogher.

1720   The 'South Sea Bubble' helps to disillusion Berkeley with Europe and leads to his plans for a college in the New World.

1721   *De Motu*, written the previous year in France, published in Britain.

1724   Appointed Dean of Derry; birth of Immanuel Kant.

1726   Grant of £20,000 promised by the government for the college in the New World.

1728   Marries Anne Forster and sails to Virginia.

1728–31   Lives in Newport, Rhode Island, waiting for the grant to be paid, preaching and writing *Alciphron*.

1731   Learning that the money will not be paid, he returns to England.

1732   Publishes *Alciphron*.

1733   Publishes *Theory of Vision Vindicated and Explained*.

1734	Consecrated Bishop of Cloyne; publishes *Analyst*. Berkeley lives in Cloyne, attending to the affairs of his diocese and working for the improvement of the state of Ireland, until 1752.
1735	Publishes *Defence of Freethinking in Mathematics*.
1735-7	The three parts of *The Querist* published in succeeding years.
1739	Hume's *Treatise on Human Nature* published.
1744	Publishes *Siris*.
1752	Leaves Cloyne for Oxford, to see his son through University.
1753	Dies in Oxford, 14 January; buried in Christ Church Cathedral. He is survived by his wife and three children.

PRINCIPLES OF
HUMAN KNOWLEDGE

ANALYTICAL CONTENTS

(by section numbers)

Introduction: Attack on Abstract Ideas

1–2   Philosophy, instead of bringing serenity, brings disturbance and doubt;

3–5   This must be due to false principles, which will be investigated;

6–9   Fundamental false principle is doctrine of abstract ideas;

10   That can abstract spatial parts but not logical features;

11   Locke on abstraction as differentiating us from animals;

11–12   Berkeley's own account of generality;

13–14   Locke's own account and the difficulty of abstracting;

15–16   Berkeley's account of generality developed;

17–21   The errors are caused by taking all words to name ideas;

22–5   Looking behind words to ideas will avoid error.

Part I: The Main Text

1–33   Initial statement of the arguments for idealism, of which the most important elements are:

3, 6, 10, 22–4: various forms of the psychological appeal that we cannot form the idea—that is, an image—of an object independent of perception (22–3 constitutes the major *argument* of this form).

7: That it is a contradiction that an idea should exist in an unperceiving substance;

8: That an idea can be like nothing but an idea;

9–15: Attack on Lockean representationalism and the primary–secondary quality distinction;

10: Cannot conceive primary without secondary;

11: Great, small, swift, and slow are relative, therefore mind-dependent;

12: Number is relative, so mind-dependent;

13: Unity is relative, so mind-dependent;

14–15: Argument from illusion equally effective against both kinds of qualities;

16–17: Emptiness of calling matter a *substratum*;

18: Argument from hallucination;

19–20: That the hypothesis of a mind-independent world is idle;

25: The inactivity of ideas;

26–7: Spirit as the cause of ideas;

27–8: The nature of spirit;

29–33: The difference between veridical ideas and others, and the role of God in this.

34–84 Seventeen objections to his theory and the answers to them.

34–40: (1) 'All that is real and substantial in nature is banished out of the world';

41: (2) That there is a great difference between a real thing and an idea of it;

42–4: (3) That we see things at a distance outside of us: Berkeley's account of depth;

45–8: (4) That Berkeley's theory has things being constantly created and destroyed;

49: (5) If extension and figure exist in the mind then the mind is extended and shaped;

50: (6) His theory undermines explanatory value of the corpuscularian philosophy;

51–3: (7) It is absurd to replace natural causes with spirits;

54–5: (8) That the whole world believes in matter and could hardly be mistaken;

56: (9) That there is a need to explain this error;

58–9: (10) That it is inconsistent with certain truths of philosophy and mathematics;

60–6: (11) It leaves no point to the mechanisms of nature. Berkeley replies by giving ideas a role as *signs* not as *causes*;

67–72. (12) That matter as a substance without accidents could still exist, perhaps as an occasion for God's giving us ideas;

73–6: *Digression* on the motives for believing in material substance;

77–8: (13) Matter might possess qualities wholly unknown to us;

79: (14) That there is no contradiction in matter, even if we do not know what it means;

80: (15) Matter could be 'an unknown *somewhat*';

81: (16) That it is sufficiently distinguished from nothing by bare idea of *existence*;

82–4: (17) That scripture requires the existence of material substance.

85–134 Positive consequences of Berkeley's doctrine:

85–96: (1) Refuting errors consequent on a belief in matter, especially connected with scepticism, fatalism, and atheism;

97–117: (2) Clarification of various scientific concepts which had been confused by being treated as abstract ideas:

98: (*a*) Nature of time;

103–9: (*b*) Concept of attraction;

110–17: (*c*) Absolute space and motion;

118–34: (3) Clarification of mathematical concepts confused by the doctrine of abstract ideas:

119–22: (*a*) Numbers as signs, not abstract objects;

123–34: (*b*) Problems with the supposed infinite divisibility of extension and with infinitesimals.

135–56 The nature and role of spirits:

135–8: There is no idea of spirit;

139–40: This does not make it insignificant, because we have a *notion*;

141: Natural immortality of the soul;

142–5: Spirits wholly unlike ideas, but are known to others through their role in producing ideas;

146–50: God is plainly knowable by the ideas He produces;

151–4: The problem of evil;

155–6: Inexcusability of atheism and conclusion.

THE PREFACE*

What I here make public has, after a long and scrupulous inquiry, seem'd to me evidently true, and not unuseful to be known, particularly to those who are tainted with scepticism, or want a demonstration of the existence and immateriality of GOD, *or the natural immortality of the soul. Whether it be so or no, I am content the reader should impartially examine. Since I do not think myself any farther concerned for the success of what I have written, than as it is agreeable to* truth. *But to the end* this *may not suffer, I make it my request that the reader suspend his judgment, till he has once,* at least, *read the whole through with that degree of attention and thought which the subject matter shall seem to deserve. For as there are some passages that, taken by themselves, are very liable (nor could it be remedied) to gross misinterpretation, and to be charged with most absurd consequences, which, nevertheless, upon an entire perusal will appear not to follow from them: so likewise, though the whole should be read over, yet, if this be done transiently, 'tis very probable my sense may be mistaken; but to a thinking reader, I flatter myself, it will be throughout clear and obvious. As for the characters of novelty and singularity, which some of the following notions may seem to bear, 'tis, I hope, needless to make any apology on that account. He must surely be either very weak, or very little acquainted with the sciences, who shall reject a truth, that is capable of demonstration, for no other reason but because it's newly known and contrary to the prejudices of mankind. Thus much I thought fit to premise, in order to prevent, if possible, the hasty censures of a sort of men, who are too apt to condemn an opinion before they rightly comprehend it.*

INTRODUCTION*

1. Philosophy being nothing else but the study of wisdom and truth, it may with reason be expected, that those who have spent most time and pains in it should enjoy a greater calm and serenity of mind, a greater clearness and evidence of knowledge, and be less disturbed with doubts and difficulties than other men. Yet so it is we see the illiterate bulk of mankind that walk the high-road of plain, common sense, and are governed by the dictates of Nature, for the most part easy and undisturbed. To them nothing that's familiar appears unaccountable or difficult to comprehend. They complain not of any want of evidence in their senses, and are out of all danger of becoming *sceptics*. But no sooner do we depart from sense and instinct to follow the light of a superior principle, to reason, meditate, and reflect on the nature of things, but a thousand scruples spring up in our minds, concerning those things which before we seemed fully to comprehend.* Prejudices and errors of sense do from all parts discover themselves to our view; and endeavouring to correct these by reason we are insensibly drawn into uncouth paradoxes, difficulties, and inconsistences, which multiply and grow upon us as we advance in speculation; till at length, having wander'd through many intricate mazes, we find ourselves just where we were, or, which is worse, sit down in a forlorn scepticism.

2. The cause of this is thought to be the obscurity of things, or the natural weakness and imperfection of our understandings. It is said the faculties we have are few, and those designed by Nature for the support and comfort of life, and not to penetrate into the inward essence and constitution of things.* Besides, the mind of man being finite, when it treats of things which partake of infinity, it is not to be wondered at, if it run into absurdities and contradictions; out of which it is impossible it should ever extricate itself, it being of the nature of infinite not to be comprehended by that which is finite.

3. But perhaps we may be too partial to ourselves in placing the fault originally in our faculties, and not rather in the wrong use we make of them. It is a hard thing to suppose, that right deductions from true principles should ever end in consequences which cannot be maintained or made consistent. We should believe that God has dealt more bountifully with the sons of men, than to give them a strong desire for that knowledge, which He had placed quite out of their reach. This were not agreeable to the wonted, indulgent methods of Providence, which, whatever appetites it may have implanted in the creatures, doth usually furnish them with such means as, if rightly made use of, will not fail to satisfy them. Upon the whole, I am inclined to think that the far greater part, if not all, of those difficulties which have hitherto amused philosophers, and blocked up the way to knowledge, are entirely owing to ourselves. That we have first raised a dust, and then complain, we cannot see.

4. My purpose therefore is, to try if I can discover what those principles are, which have introduced all that doubtfulness and uncertainty, those absurdities and contradictions into the several sects of philosophy;* insomuch that the wisest men have thought our ignorance incurable, conceiving it to arise from the natural dulness and limitation of our faculties. And surely it is a work well deserving our pains, to make a strict inquiry concerning the first principles of *human knowledge*, to sift and examine them on all sides: especially since there may be some grounds to suspect that those lets and difficulties, which stay and embarrass the mind in its search after truth, do not spring from any darkness and intricacy in the objects, or natural defect in the understanding, so much as from false principles which have been insisted on, and might have been avoided.

5. How difficult and discouraging soever this attempt may seem, when I consider how many great and extraordinary men have gone before me in the same designs: yet I am not without some hopes, upon the consideration that the largest views are not always the clearest, and that he who is short-sighted will be obliged to draw the object nearer, and may, perhaps, by a close and narrow survey discern that which had escaped far better eyes.

6. In order to prepare the mind of the reader for the easier conceiving what follows, it is proper to premise somewhat, by way of introduction, concerning the nature and abuse of language. But the unravelling this matter leads me in some measure to anticipate my design, by taking notice of what seems to have had a chief part in rendering speculation intricate and perplexed, and to have occasioned innumerable errors and difficulties in almost all parts of knowledge. And that is the opinion that the mind hath a power of framing *abstract ideas* or notions of things. He who is not a perfect stranger to the writings and disputes of philosophers, must needs acknowledge that no small part of them are spent about abstract ideas. These are in a more especial manner, thought to be the object of those sciences which go by the name of Logic and Metaphysics, and of all that which passes under the notion of the most abstracted and sublime learning, in all which one shall scarce find any question handled in such a manner, as does not suppose their existence in the mind, and that it is well acquainted with them.

7. It is agreed on all hands, that the qualities or modes of things do never really exist each of them apart by itself, and separated from all others, but are mixed, as it were, and blended together, several in the same object. But we are told, the mind being able to consider each quality singly, or abstracted from those other qualities with which it is united, does by that means frame to itself abstract ideas. For example, there is perceived by sight an object extended, coloured, and moved: this mixed or compound idea the mind resolving into its simple, constituent parts, and viewing each by itself, exclusive of the rest, does frame the abstract ideas of extension, colour, and motion. Not that it is possible for colour or motion to exist without extension: but only that the mind can frame to itself by *abstraction* the idea of colour exclusive of extension, and of motion exclusive of both colour and extension.

8. Again, the mind having observed that in the particular extensions perceived by sense, there is something common and alike in all, and some other things peculiar, as this or that figure or magnitude, which distinguish them one from another; it considers apart or singles out by itself that which is common, making thereof a most abstract idea of extension,

which is neither line, surface, nor solid, nor has any figure or
magnitude but is an idea entirely prescinded from all these. So
likewise the mind by leaving out of the particular colours
perceived by sense, that which distinguishes them one from
another, and retaining that only which is common to all,
makes an idea of colour in abstract which is neither red,
nor blue, nor white, nor any other determinate colour. And
in like manner by considering motion abstractedly not only
from the body moved, but likewise from the figure it describes, and all particular directions and velocities, the abstract idea of motion is framed; which equally corresponds to
all particular motions whatsoever that may be perceived by
sense.

9. And as the mind frames to itself abstract ideas of qualities or modes, so does it, by the same precision or mental
separation, attain abstract ideas of the more compounded
beings, which include several coexistent qualities. For
example, the mind having observed that Peter, James, and
John resemble each other, in certain common agreements of
shape and other qualities, leaves out of the complex or compounded idea it has of Peter, James, and any other particular
man, that which is peculiar to each, retaining only what is
common to all; and so makes an abstract idea wherein all the
particulars equally partake, abstracting entirely from and cutting off all those circumstances and differences, which might
determine it to any particular existence. And after this manner it is said we come by the abstract idea of *man* or, if you
please, humanity or human nature; wherein it is true, there is
included colour, because there is no man but has some colour,
but then it can be neither white, nor black, nor any particular
colour; because there is no one particular colour wherein all
men partake. So likewise there is included stature, but then it
is neither tall stature nor low stature, nor yet middle stature,
but something abstracted from all these. And so of the rest.
Moreover, there being a great variety of other creatures that
partake in some parts, but not all, of the complex idea of *man*,
the mind leaving out those parts which are peculiar to men,
and retaining those only which are common to all the living
creatures, frameth the idea of *animal*, which abstracts not only

from all particular men, but also all birds, beasts, fishes, and insects. The constituent parts of the abstract idea of animal are body, life, sense, and spontaneous motion. By *body* is meant, body without any particular shape or figure, there being no one shape or figure common to all animals, without covering, either of hair or feathers, or scales, &c. nor yet naked: hair, feathers, scales, and nakedness being the distinguishing properties of particular animals, and for that reason left out of the *abstract idea.* Upon the same account the spontaneous motion must be neither walking, nor flying, nor creeping, it is nevertheless a motion, but what that motion is, it is not easy to conceive.

10. Whether others have this wonderful faculty of *abstracting their ideas*, they best can tell: for myself I find indeed I have a faculty of imagining, or representing to myself the ideas of those particular things I have perceived and of variously compounding and dividing them. I can imagine a man with two heads or the upper parts of a man joined to the body of a horse. I can consider the hand, the eye, the nose, each by itself abstracted or separated from the rest of the body. But then whatever hand or eye I imagine, it must have some particular shape and colour. Likewise the idea of man that I frame to myself, must be either of a white, or a black, or a tawny, a straight, or a crooked, a tall, or a low, or a middle-sized man. I cannot by any effort of thought conceive the abstract idea above described. And it is equally impossible for me to form the abstract idea of motion distinct from the body moving, and which is neither swift nor slow, curvilinear nor rectilinear; and the like may be said of all other abstract general ideas whatsoever. To be plain, I own myself able to abstract in one sense, as when I consider some particular parts or qualities separated from others, with which though they are united in some object, yet, it is possible they may really exist without them. But I deny that I can abstract one from another, or conceive separately, those qualities which it is impossible should exist so separated; or that I can frame a general notion by abstracting from particulars in the manner aforesaid. Which two last are the proper acceptations of *abstraction.* And there are grounds to think most men will acknowledge

themselves to be in my case. The generality of men which are simple and illiterate never pretend to *abstract notions*. It's said they are difficult and not to be attained without pains and study. We may therefore reasonably conclude that, if such there be, they are confined only to the learned.

11. I proceed to examine what can be alleged in defence of the doctrine of abstraction, and try if I can discover what it is that inclines the men of speculation to embrace an opinion, so remote from common sense as that seems to be. There has been a late deservedly esteemed philosopher, who, no doubt, has given it very much countenance by seeming to think the having abstract general ideas is what puts the widest difference in point of understanding betwixt man and beast. 'The having of general ideas (*saith he*) is that which puts a perfect distinction betwixt man and brutes, and is an excellency which the faculties of brutes do by no means attain unto. For it is evident we observe no footsteps in them of making use of general signs for universal ideas; from which we have reason to imagine that they have not the faculty of *abstracting* or making general ideas, since they have no use of words or any other general signs. *And a little after.* Therefore, I think, we may suppose that it is in this that the species of brutes are discriminated from men, and 'tis that proper difference wherein they are wholly separated, and which at last widens to so wide a distance. For if they have any ideas at all, and are not bare machines (as some would have them) we cannot deny them to have some reason. It seems as evident to me that they do some of them in certain instances reason as that they have sense, but it is only in particular ideas, just as they receive them from their senses. They are the best of them tied up within those narrow bounds, and have not (as I think) the faculty to enlarge them by any kind of *abstraction.*' *Essay on Hum. Underst.*, b. 2. c. 11. sects. 10 and 11. I readily agree with this learned author, that the faculties of brutes can by no means attain to *abstraction*. But then if this be made the distinguishing property of that sort of animals, I fear a great many of those that pass for men must be reckoned into their number. The reason that is here assigned why we have no grounds to think brutes have abstract general ideas, is that we

observe in them no use of words or any other general signs; which is built on this supposition, to wit, that the making use of words, implies the having general ideas. From which it follows, that men who use language are able to abstract or generalize their ideas. That this is the sense and arguing of the author will further appear by his answering the question he in another place puts. 'Since all things that exist are only particulars, how come we by general terms?' *His answer is*, 'Words become general by being made the signs of general ideas.' *Essay on Hum. Underst.*, b. 3. c. 3. sect. 6. But it seems that a word becomes general by being made the sign, not of an abstract general idea but, of several particular ideas, any one of which it indifferently suggests to the mind. For example, when it is said *the change of motion is proportional to the impressed force*, or that *whatever has extension is divisible*; these propositions are to be understood of motion and extension in general, and nevertheless it will not follow that they suggest to my thoughts an idea of motion without a body moved, or any determinate direction and velocity, or that I must conceive an abstract general idea of extension, which is neither line, surface nor solid, neither great nor small, black, white, nor red, nor of any other determinate colour. It is only implied that whatever motion I consider, whether it be swift or slow, perpendicular, horizontal or oblique, or in whatever object, the axiom concerning it holds equally true. As does the other of every particular extension, it matters not whether line, surface or solid, whether of this or that magnitude or figure.

12. By observing how ideas become general, we may the better judge how words are made so. And here it is to be noted that I do not deny absolutely there are general ideas, but only that there are any *abstract general ideas*: for in the passages above quoted, wherein there is mention of general ideas, it is always supposed that they are formed by *abstraction*, after the manner set forth in sects. 8 and 9. Now if we will annex a meaning to our words, and speak only of what we can conceive, I believe we shall acknowledge, that an idea, which considered in itself is particular, becomes general, by being made to represent or stand for all other particular ideas of the

same sort. To make this plain by an example, suppose a geom-
etrician is demonstrating the method, of cutting a line in two
equal parts. He draws, for instance, a black line of an inch in
length, this which in itself is a particular line is nevertheless
with regard to its signification general, since as it is there used,
it represents all particular lines whatsoever; for that what is
demonstrated of it, is demonstrated of all lines or, in other
words, of a line in general. And as that particular line becomes general, by being made a sign, so the name *line* which
taken absolutely is particular, by being a sign is made general.
And as the former owes its generality, not to its being the sign
of an abstract or general line, but of all particular right lines
that may possibly exist, so the latter must be thought to derive
its generality from the same cause, namely, the various particular lines which it indifferently denotes.

13. To give the reader a yet clearer view of the nature of
abstract ideas, and the uses they are thought necessary to, I
shall add one more passage out of the *Essay on Human Understanding*, which is as follows. '*Abstract ideas* are not so
obvious or easy to children or the yet unexercised mind as
particular ones. If they seem so to grown men, it is only
because by constant and familiar use they are made so. For
when we nicely reflect upon them, we shall find that general
ideas are fictions and contrivances of the mind, that carry
difficulty with them, and do not so easily offer themselves, as
we are apt to imagine. For example, does it not require some
pains and skill to form the general idea of a triangle (which is
yet none of the most abstract comprehensive and difficult) for
it must be neither oblique nor rectangle, neither equilateral,
equicrural, nor scalenon, but *all and none* of these at once. In
effect, it is something imperfect that cannot exist, an idea
wherein some parts of several different and *inconsistent* ideas
are put together. It is true the mind in this imperfect state has
need of such ideas, and makes all the haste to them it can, for
the conveniency of communication and enlargement of
knowledge, to both which it is naturally very much inclined.
But yet one has reason to suspect such ideas are marks of our
imperfection. At least this is enough to shew that the most
abstract and general ideas are not those that the mind is first

and most easily acquainted with, nor such as its earliest knowledge is conversant about', b. 4. c. 7. sect. 9. If any man has the faculty of framing in his mind such an idea of a triangle as is here described, it is in vain to pretend to dispute him out of it, nor would I go about it. All I desire is, that the reader would fully and certainly inform himself whether he has such an idea* or no. And this, methinks, can be no hard task for anyone to perform. What more easy than for anyone to look a little into his own thoughts, and there try whether he has, or can attain to have, an idea that shall correspond with the description that is here given of the general idea of a triangle, which is, *neither oblique, nor rectangle, equilateral, equicrural, nor scalenon, but all and none of these at once*?

14. Much is here said of the difficulty that abstract ideas carry with them, and the pains and skill requisite to the forming them. And it is on all hands agreed that there is need of great toil and labour of the mind, to emancipate our thoughts from particular objects, and raise them to those sublime speculations that are conversant about abstract ideas. From all which the natural consequence should seem to be, that so difficult a thing as the forming abstract ideas was not necessary for *communication*, which is so easy and familiar to all sorts of men. But we are told, if they seem obvious and easy to grown men, *It is only because by constant and familiar use they are made so*. Now I would fain know at what time it is, men are employed in surmounting that difficulty, and furnishing themselves with those necessary helps for discourse. It cannot be when they are grown up, for then it seems they are not conscious of any such pains-taking; it remains therefore to be the business of their childhood. And surely, the great and multiplied labour of framing abstract notions, will be found a hard task for that tender age. Is it not a hard thing to imagine, that a couple of children cannot prate together, of their sugar-plumbs and rattles and the rest of their little trinkets, till they have first tacked together numberless inconsistencies, and so framed in their minds *abstract general ideas*, and annexed them to every common name they make use of?

15. Nor do I think them a whit more needful for the *enlargement of knowledge* than for *communication*. It is I know

a point, much insisted on, that all knowledge and demonstration are about universal notions, to which I fully agree: but then it doth not appear to me that those notions are formed by *abstraction* in the manner premised; *universality*, so far as I can comprehend not consisting in the absolute, positive nature or conception of anything, but in the relation it bears to the particulars signified or represented by it: by virtue whereof it is that things, names, or notions, being in their own nature *particular*, are rendered *universal*. Thus when I demonstrate any proposition concerning triangles, it is to be supposed that I have in view the universal idea of a triangle;* which ought not to be understood as if I could frame an idea of a triangle which was neither equilateral nor scalenon nor equicrural. But only that the particular triangle I consider, whether of this or that sort it matters not, doth equally stand for and represent all rectilinear triangles whatsoever, and is in that sense *universal*. All which seems very plain and not to include any difficulty in it.

16. But here it will be demanded, how we can know any proposition to be true of all particular triangles, except we have first seen it demonstrated of the abstract idea of a triangle which equally agrees to all? For because a property may be demonstrated to agree to some one particular triangle, it will not thence follow that it equally belongs to any other triangle, which in all respects is not the same with it. For example, having demonstrated that the three angles of an isosceles rectangular triangle are equal to two right ones, I cannot therefore conclude this affection agrees to all other triangles, which have neither a right angle, nor two equal sides. It seems therefore that, to be certain this proposition is universally true, we must either make a particular demonstration for every particular triangle, which is impossible, or once for all demonstrate it of the *abstract idea of a triangle*, in which all the particulars do indifferently partake, and by which they are all equally represented. To which I answer, that though the idea I have in view whilst I make the demonstration, be, for instance, that of an isosceles rectangular triangle, whose sides are of a determinate length, I may nevertheless be certain it extends to all other rectilinear triangles,

of what sort or bigness soever. And that, because neither
the right angle, nor the equality, nor determinate length of the
sides, are at all concerned in the demonstration. It is true, the
diagram I have in view includes all these particulars, but then
there is not the least mention made of them in the proof of the
proposition. It is not said, the three angles are equal to two
right ones, because one of them is a right angle, or because the
sides comprehending it are of the same length. Which sufficiently shews that the right angle might have been oblique,
and the sides unequal, and for all that the demonstration have
held good. And for this reason it is, that I conclude that to be
true of any obliquangular or scalenon, which I had demonstrated of a particular right-angled, equicrural triangle; and
not because I demonstrated the proposition of the abstract
idea of a triangle. And here it must be acknowledged that a
man may consider a figure merely as triangular, without attending to the particular qualities of the angles, or relations of
the sides. So far he may abstract: but this will never prove,
that he can frame an abstract general inconsistent idea of a
triangle. In like manner we may consider Peter so far forth
as man, or so far forth as animal, without framing the
forementioned abstract idea, either of man or of animal, in as
much as all that is perceived is not considered.

17. It were an endless, as well as an useless thing, to trace
the Schoolmen, those great masters of abstraction, through all
the manifold inextricable labyrinths of error and dispute,
which their doctrine of abstract natures and notions seems to
have led them into. What bickerings and controversies, and
what a learned dust have been raised about those matters, and
what mighty advantage hath been from thence derived to
mankind, are things at this day too clearly known to need
being insisted on. And it had been well if the ill effects of that
doctrine were confined to those only who make the most
avowed profession of it. When men consider the great pains,
industry and parts, that have for so many ages been laid out
on the cultivation and advancement of the sciences, and that
notwithstanding all this, the far greater part of them remain
full of darkness and uncertainty, and disputes that are like
never to have an end, and even those that are thought to be

supported by the most clear and cogent demonstrations, contain in them paradoxes which are perfectly irreconcilable to the understandings of men, and that taking all together, a small portion of them doth supply any real benefit to mankind, otherwise than by being an innocent diversion and amusement. I say, the consideration of all this is apt to throw them into a despondency, and perfect contempt of all study. But this may perhaps cease, upon a view of the false principles that have obtained in the world, amongst all which there is none, methinks, hath a more wide influence over the thoughts of speculative men, than this of abstract general ideas.

18. I come now to consider the source of this prevailing notion, and that seems to me to be language. And surely nothing of less extent than reason itself could have been the source of an opinion so universally received. The truth of this appears as from other reasons, so also from the plain confession of the ablest patrons of abstract ideas, who acknowledge that they are made in order to naming; from which it is a clear consequence, that if there had been no such thing as speech or universal signs, there never had been any thought of abstraction. See b. 3. c. 6. sect. 39 and elsewhere of *The Essay on Human Understanding*. Let us therefore examine the manner wherein words have contributed to the origin of that mistake. First then, 'tis thought that every name hath, or ought to have, one only precise and settled signification, which inclines men to think there are certain *abstract, determinate ideas*, which constitute the true and only immediate signification of each general name. And that it is by the mediation of these abstract ideas, that a general name comes to signify any particular thing. Whereas, in truth, there is no such thing as one precise and definite signification annexed to any general name, they all signifying indifferently a great number of particular ideas. All which doth evidently follow from what has been already said, and will clearly appear to anyone by a little reflexion. To this it will be objected, that every name that has a definition, is thereby restrained to one certain signification. For example, a *triangle* is defined to be a *plane surface comprehended by three right lines*; by which that name is limited to denote one certain idea and no other. To which I

answer, that in the definition it is not said whether the surface be great or small, black or white, nor whether the sides are long or short, equal or unequal, nor with what angles they are inclined to each other; in all which there may be great variety, and consequently there is no one settled idea which limits the signification of the word *triangle*. 'Tis one thing for to keep a name constantly to the same definition, and another to make it stand everywhere for the same idea: the one is necessary, the other useless and impracticable.*

19. But to give a farther account how words came to produce the doctrine of abstract ideas, it must be observed that it is a received opinion, that language has no other end but the communicating our ideas, and that every significant name stands for an idea. This being so, and it being withal certain, that names, which yet are not thought altogether insignificant, do not always mark out particular conceivable ideas, it is straightway concluded that they stand for abstract notions. That there are many names in use amongst speculative men, which do not always suggest to others determinate particular ideas, is what nobody will deny. And a little attention will discover, that it is not necessary (even in the strictest reasonings) significant names which stand for ideas should, every time they are used, excite in the understanding the ideas they are made to stand for: in reading and discoursing, names being for the most part used as letters are in *algebra*, in which though a particular quantity be marked by each letter, yet to proceed right it is not requisite that in every step each letter suggest to your thoughts, that particular quantity it was appointed to stand for.

20. Besides, the communicating of ideas marked by words is not the chief and only end of language,* as is commonly supposed. There are other ends, as the raising of some passion, the exciting to, or deterring from an action, the putting the mind in some particular disposition; to which the former is in many cases barely subservient, and sometimes entirely omitted, when these can be obtained without it, as I think doth not infrequently happen in the familiar use of language. I entreat the reader to reflect with himself, and see if it doth not often happen either in hearing or reading a

discourse, that the passions of fear, love, hatred, admiration, disdain, and the like arise, immediately in his mind upon the perception of certain words, without any ideas coming between. At first, indeed, the words might have occasioned ideas that were fit to produce those emotions; but, if I mistake not, it will be found that when language is once grown familiar, the hearing of the sounds or sight of the characters is oft immediately attended with those passions, which at first were wont to be produced by the intervention of ideas, that are now quite omitted. May we not, for example, be affected with the promise of a *good thing*, though we have not an idea of what it is? Or is not the being threatened with danger sufficient to excite a dread, though we think not of any particular evil likely to befall us, nor yet frame to ourselves an idea of danger in abstract? If anyone shall join ever so little reflection of his own to what has been said, I believe it will evidently appear to him, that general names are often used in the propriety of language without the speaker's designing them for marks of ideas in his own, which he would have them raise in the mind of the hearer. Even proper names themselves do not seem always spoken, with a design to bring into our view the ideas of those individuals that are supposed to be marked by them. For example, when a Schoolman tells me *Aristotle hath said it*, all I conceive he means by it, is to dispose me to embrace his opinion with the deference and submission which custom has annexed to that name. And this effect may be so instantly produced in the minds of those who are accustomed to resign their judgment to the authority of that philosopher, as it is impossible any idea either of his person, writings, or reputation should go before. Innumerable examples of this kind may be given, but why should I insist on those things, which everyone's experience will, I doubt not, plentifully suggest unto him?

21. We have, I think, shewn the impossibility of *abstract ideas*. We have considered what has been said for them by their ablest patrons; and endeavoured to shew they are of no use for those ends, to which they are thought necessary. And lastly, we have traced them to the source from whence they flow, which appears to be language. It cannot be denied that

words are of excellent use, in that by their means all that stock of knowledge which has been purchased by the joint labours of inquisitive men in all ages and nations, may be drawn into the view and made the possession of one single person. But at the same time it must be owned that most parts of knowledge have been strangely perplexed and darkened by the abuse of words, and general ways of speech wherein they are delivered. Since therefore words are so apt to impose on the understanding, whatever ideas I consider, I shall endeavour to take them bare and naked into my view, keeping out of my thoughts, so far as I am able, those names which long and constant use hath so strictly united with them; from which I may expect to derive the following advantages.

22. First, I shall be sure to get clear of all controversies purely verbal; the springing up of which weeds in almost all the sciences has been a main hindrance to the growth of true and sound knowledge. Secondly, this seems to be a sure way to extricate myself out of that fine and subtle net of *abstract ideas*, which has so miserably perplexed and entangled the minds of men, and that with this peculiar circumstance, that by how much the finer and more curious was the wit of any man, by so much the deeper was he like to be ensnared, and faster held therein. Thirdly, so long as I confine my thoughts to my own ideas divested of words, I do not see how I can easily be mistaken. The objects I consider, I clearly and adequately know. I cannot be deceived in thinking I have an idea which I have not. It is not possible for me to imagine, that any of my own ideas are alike or unlike, that are not truly so. To discern the agreements or disagreements there are between my ideas, to see what ideas are included in any compound idea, and what not, there is nothing more requisite, than an attentive perception of what passes in my own understanding.

23. But the attainment of all these advantages doth presuppose an entire deliverance from the deception of words, which I dare hardly promise myself; so difficult a thing it is to dissolve an union so early begun, and confirmed by so long a habit as that betwixt words and ideas. Which difficulty seems to have been very much increased by the doctrine of *abstrac-*

tion. For so long as men thought abstract ideas were annexed to their words, it doth not seem strange that they should use words for ideas: it being found an impracticable thing to lay aside the word, and retain the abstract idea in the mind, which in itself was perfectly inconceivable. This seems to me the principal cause, why those men who have so emphatically recommended to others, the laying aside all use of words in their meditations, and contemplating their bare ideas, have yet failed to perform it themselves. Of late many have been very sensible of the absurd opinions and insignificant disputes, which grow out of the abuse of words.* And in order to remedy these evils they advise well, that we attend to the ideas signified, and draw off our attention from the words which signify them. But how good soever this advice may be, they have given others, it is plain they could not have a due regard to it themselves, so long as they thought the only immediate use of words was to signify ideas, and that the immediate signification of every general name was a *determinate, abstract idea*.

24. But these being known to be mistakes, a man may with greater ease prevent his being imposed on by words. He that knows he has no other than particular ideas, will not puzzle himself in vain to find out and conceive the abstract idea, annexed to any name. And he that knows names do not always stand for ideas, will spare himself the labour of looking for ideas, where there are none to be had. It were therefore to be wished that everyone would use his utmost endeavours, to obtain a clear view of the ideas he would consider, separating from them all that dress and encumbrance of words which so much contribute to blind the judgment and divide the attention. In vain do we extend our view into the heavens, and pry into the entrails of the earth, in vain do we consult the writings of learned men, and trace the dark footsteps of antiquity; we need only draw the curtain of words, to behold the fairest tree of knowledge, whose fruit is excellent, and within the reach of our hand.

25. Unless we take care to clear the first principles of knowledge, from the embarras and delusion of words, we may make infinite reasonings upon them to no purpose; we may

draw consequences from consequences, and be never the wiser. The farther we go, we shall only lose ourselves the more irrecoverably, and be the deeper entangled in difficulties and mistakes. Whoever therefore designs to read the following sheets, I entreat him to make my words the occasion of his own thinking, and endeavour to attain the same train of thoughts in reading, that I had in writing them. By this means it will be easy for him to discover the truth or falsity of what I say. He will be out of all danger of being deceived by my words, and I do not see how he can be led into an error by considering his own naked, undisguised ideas.

OF THE PRINCIPLES OF
HUMAN KNOWLEDGE

PART I*

1. It is evident to anyone who takes a survey of the objects of human knowledge, that they are either ideas actually imprinted on the senses, or else such as are perceived by attending to the passions and operations of the mind,* or lastly ideas formed by help of memory and imagination, either compounding, dividing, or barely representing those originally perceived in the aforesaid ways. By sight I have the ideas of light and colours with their several degrees and variations. By touch I perceive, for example, hard and soft, heat and cold, motion and resistance, and of all these more and less either as to quantity or degree. Smelling furnishes me with odours; the palate with tastes, and hearing conveys sounds to the mind in all their variety of tone and composition. And as several of these are observed to accompany each other, they come to be marked by one name, and so to be reputed as one thing. Thus, for example, a certain colour, taste, smell, figure and consistence having been observed to go together, are accounted one distinct thing, signified by the name *apple*. Other collections of ideas constitute a stone, a tree, a book, and the like sensible things; which, as they are pleasing or disagreeable, excite the passions of love, hatred, joy, grief, and so forth.

2. But besides all that endless variety of ideas or objects of knowledge, there is likewise something which knows or perceives them, and exercises divers operations, as willing, imagining, remembering about them. This perceiving, active being is what I call *mind*, *spirit*, *soul* or *myself*. By which words I do not denote any one of my ideas, but a thing entirely distinct from them, wherein they exist, or, which is the same thing, whereby they are perceived; for the existence of an idea consists in being perceived.

3. That neither our thoughts, nor passions, nor ideas formed by the imagination, exist without the mind, is what everybody will allow. And it seems no less evident that the various sensations or ideas imprinted on the sense, however blended or combined together (that is, whatever objects they compose) cannot exist otherwise than in a mind perceiving them. I think an intuitive knowledge may be obtained of this, by anyone that shall attend to what is meant by the term *exist* when applied to sensible things. The table I write on, I say, exists, that is, I see and feel it; and if I were out of my study I should say it existed, meaning thereby that if I was in my study I might perceive it, or that some other spirit actually does perceive it. There was an odour, that is, it was smelled; there was a sound, that is to say, it was heard; a colour or figure, and it was perceived by sight or touch. This is all that I can understand by these and the like expressions. For as to what is said of the absolute existence of unthinking things without any relation to their being perceived, that seems perfectly unintelligible. Their *esse* is *percipi*, nor is it possible they should have any existence, out of the minds or thinking things which perceive them.

4. It is indeed an opinion strangely prevailing amongst men, that houses, mountains, rivers, and in a word all sensible objects have an existence natural or real, distinct from their being perceived by the understanding. But with how great an assurance and acquiescence soever this principle may be entertained in the world; yet whoever shall find in his heart to call it in question, may, if I mistake not, perceive it to involve a manifest contradiction. For what are the forementioned objects but the things we perceive by sense, and what do we perceive besides our own ideas or sensations; and is it not plainly repugnant that any one of these or any combination of them should exist unperceived?

5. If we throughly examine this tenet, it will, perhaps, be found at bottom to depend on the doctrine of *abstract ideas*. For can there be a nicer strain of abstraction than to distinguish the existence of sensible objects from their being perceived, so as to conceive them existing unperceived? Light and colours, heat and cold, extension and figures, in a word

the things we see and feel, what are they but so many sensations, notions, ideas or impressions on the sense; and is it possible to separate, even in thought, any of these from perception? For my part I might as easily divide a thing from itself. I may indeed divide in my thoughts or conceive apart from each other those things which, perhaps, I never perceived by sense so divided. Thus I imagine the trunk of a human body without the limbs, or conceive the smell of rose without thinking on the rose itself. So far I will not deny I can abstract, if that may properly be called *abstraction*, which extends only to the conceiving separately such objects, as it is possible may really exist or be actually perceived asunder. But my conceiving or imagining power does not extend beyond the possibility of real existence or perception. Hence as it is impossible for me to see or feel anything without an actual sensation of that thing, so is it impossible for me to conceive in my thoughts any sensible thing or object distinct from the sensation or perception of it.*

6. Some truths there are so near and obvious to the mind, that a man need only open his eyes to see them. Such I take this important one to be, to wit, that all the choir of heaven and furniture of the earth, in a word all those bodies which compose the mighty frame of the world, have not any subsistence without a mind, that their being is to be perceived or known; that consequently so long as they are not actually perceived by me, or do not exist in my mind or that of any other created spirit, they must either have no existence at all, or else subsist in the mind of some eternal spirit: it being perfectly unintelligible and involving all the absurdity of abstraction, to attribute to any single part of them an existence independent of a spirit. To be convinced of which, the reader need only reflect and try to separate in his own thoughts the being of a sensible thing from its being perceived.*

7. From what has been said, it follows, there is not any other substance than *spirit*, or that which perceives. But for the fuller proof of this point, let it be considered, the sensible qualities are colour, figure, motion, smell, taste, and such like, that is, the ideas perceived by sense. Now for an idea to exist in an unperceiving thing, is a manifest contradiction; for to

have an idea is all one as to perceive: that therefore wherein colour, figure, and the like qualities exist, must perceive them; hence it is clear there can be no unthinking substance or *substratum* of those ideas.*

8. But say you, though the ideas themselves do not exist without the mind, yet there may be things like them whereof they are copies or resemblances, which things exist without the mind, in an unthinking substance. I answer, an idea can be like nothing but an idea;* a colour or figure can be like nothing but another colour or figure. If we look but ever so little into our thoughts, we shall find it impossible for us to conceive a likeness except only between our ideas. Again, I ask whether those supposed originals or external things, of which our ideas are the pictures or representations, be themselves perceivable or no? If they are, then they are ideas, and we have gained our point; but if you say they are not, I appeal to anyone whether it be sense, to assert a colour is like something which is invisible; hard or soft, like something which is intangible; and so of the rest.

9. Some there are* who make a distinction betwixt *primary* and *secondary* qualities: by the former, they mean extension, figure motion, rest, solidity or impenetrability and number: by the latter they denote all other sensible qualities, as colours, sounds, tastes, and so forth. The ideas we have of these they acknowledge not to be the resemblances of anything existing without the mind or unperceived; but they will have our ideas of the primary qualities to be patterns or images of things which exist without the mind, in an unthinking substance which they call *matter*. By matter therefore we are to understand an inert, senseless substance, in which extension, figure, and motion, do actually subsist. But it is evident from what we have already shewn, that extension, figure and motion are only ideas existing in the mind, and that an idea can be like nothing but another idea, and that consequently neither they nor their archetypes can exist in an unperceiving substance. Hence it is plain, that the very notion of what is called *matter* or *corporeal substance*, involves a contradiction in it.

10. They who assert that figure, motion, and the rest of the primary or original qualities do exist without the mind, in

unthinking substances, do at the same time acknowledge that colours, sounds, heat, cold, and such like secondary qualities, do not, which they tell us are sensations existing in the mind alone, that depend on and are occasioned by the different size, texture and motion of the minute particles of matter. This they take for an undoubted truth, which they can demonstrate beyond all exception. Now if it be certain, that those original qualities are inseparably united with the other sensible qualities, and not, even in thought, capable of being abstracted from them, it plainly follows that they exist only in the mind. But I desire anyone to reflect and try, whether he can by any abstraction of thought, conceive the extension and motion of a body, without all other sensible qualities. For my own part, I see evidently that it is not in my power to frame an idea of a body extended and moved, but I must withal give it some colour or other sensible quality which is acknowledged to exist only in the mind. In short, extension, figure, and motion, abstracted from all other qualities, are inconceivable.* Where therefore the other sensible qualities are, there must these be also, to wit, in the mind and nowhere else.

11. Again, *great* and *small*, *swift* and *slow*,* are allowed to exist nowhere without the mind, being entirely relative, and changing as the frame or position of the organs of sense varies. The extension therefore which exists without the mind, is neither great nor small, the motion neither swift nor slow, that is, they are nothing at all. But say you, they are extension in general, and motion in general: thus we see how much the tenet of extended, moveable substances existing without the mind, depends on that strange doctrine of *abstract ideas*. And here I cannot but remark, how nearly the vague and indeterminate description of matter or corporeal substance, which the modern philosophers are run into by their own principles, resembles that antiquated and so much ridiculed notion of *materia prima*,* to be met with in Aristotle and his followers. Without extension solidity cannot be conceived; since therefore it has been shewn that extension exists not in an unthinking substance, the same must also be true of solidity.

12. That number is entirely the creature of the mind, even though the other qualities be allowed to exist without, will be evident to whoever considers, that the same thing bears a different denomination of number, as the mind views it with different respects.* Thus, the same extension is one or three or thirty six, according as the mind considers it with reference to a yard, a foot, or an inch. Number is so visibly relative, and dependent on men's understanding, that it is strange to think how anyone should give it an absolute existence without the mind. We say one book, one page, one line; all these are equally units, though some contain several of the others. And in each instance it is plain, the unit relates to some particular combination of ideas arbitrarily put together by the mind.

13. Unity I know some will have to be a simple or uncompounded idea, accompanying all other ideas into the mind.* That I have any such idea answering the word *unity*, I do not find; and if I had, methinks I could not miss finding it; on the contrary it should be the most familiar to my understanding, since it is said to accompany all other ideas, and to be perceived by all the ways of sensation and reflexion. To say no more, it is an *abstract idea*.

14. I shall farther add, that after the same manner, as modern philosophers prove certain sensible qualities to have no existence in matter, or without the mind, the same thing may be likewise proved of all other sensible qualities whatsoever. Thus, for instance, it is said that heat and cold are affections only of the mind, and not at all patterns of real beings, existing in the corporeal substances which excite them, for that the same body which appears cold to one hand, seems warm to another. Now why may we not as well argue that figure and extension are not patterns or resemblances of qualities existing in matter, because to the same eye at different stations, or eyes of a different texture at the same station, they appear various, and cannot therefore be the images of anything settled and determinate without the mind? Again, it is proved that sweetness is not really in the sapid thing, because the thing remaining unaltered the sweetness is changed into bitter, as in case of a fever or otherwise vitiated palate. Is it not

as reasonable to say, that motion is not without the mind, since if the succession of ideas in the mind become swifter, the motion, it is acknowledged, shall appear slower without any alteration in any external object.

15. In short, let anyone consider those arguments, which are thought manifestly to prove that colours and tastes exist only in the mind, and he shall find they may with equal force, be brought to prove the same thing of extension, figure, and motion. Though it must be confessed this method of arguing doth not so much prove that there is no extension or colour in an outward object, as that we do not know by sense which is the true extension or colour of the object.* But the arguments foregoing plainly shew it to be impossible that any colour or extension at all, or other sensible quality whatsoever, should exist in an unthinking subject without the mind, or in truth, that there should be any such thing as an outward object.

16. But let us examine a little the received opinion. It is said* extension is a mode or accident of matter, and that matter is the *substratum* that supports it. Now I desire that you would explain what is meant by matter's *supporting* extension: say you, I have no idea of matter, and therefore cannot explain it. I answer, though you have no positive, yet if you have any meaning at all, you must at least have a relative idea of matter; though you know not what it is, yet you must be supposed to know what relation it bears to accidents, and what is meant by its supporting them. It is evident *support* cannot here be taken in its usual or literal sense, as when we say that pillars support a building: in what sense therefore must it be taken?

17. If we inquire into what the most accurate philosophers declare themselves to mean by *material substance*; we shall find them acknowledge, they have no other meaning annexed to those sounds, but the idea of being in general, together with the relative notion of its supporting accidents. The general idea of being appeareth to me the most abstract and incomprehensible of all other; and as for its supporting accidents, this, as we have just now observed, cannot be understood in the common sense of those words; it must therefore be taken in some other sense, but what that is they do not

explain. So that when I consider the two parts or branches which make the signification of the words *material substance*, I am convinced there is no distinct meaning annexed to them. But why should we trouble ourselves any farther, in discussing this material *substratum* or support of figure and motion, and other sensible qualities? Does it not suppose they have an existence without the mind? And is not this a direct repugnancy, and altogether inconceivable?

18. But though it were possible that solid, figured, moveable substances may exist without the mind, corresponding to the ideas we have of bodies, yet how is it possible for us to know this?* Either we must know it by sense, or by reason. As for our senses, by them we have the knowledge only of our sensations, ideas, or those things that are immediately perceived by sense, call them what you will: but they do not inform us that things exist without the mind, or unperceived, like to those which are perceived. This the materialists themselves acknowledge. It remains therefore that if we have any knowledge at all of external things, it must be by reason, inferring their existence from what is immediately perceived by sense. But what reason can induce us to believe the existence of bodies without the mind, from what we perceive, since the very patrons of matter themselves do not pretend, there is any necessary connexion betwixt them and our ideas? I say it is granted on all hands (and what happens in dreams, phrensies, and the like, puts it beyond dispute) that it is possible we might be affected with all the ideas we have now, though no bodies existed without, resembling them. Hence it is evident the supposition of external bodies is not necessary for the producing our ideas: since it is granted they are produced sometimes, and might possibly be produced always in the same order we see them in at present, without their concurrence.

19. But though we might possibly have all our sensations without them, yet perhaps it may be thought easier to conceive and explain the manner of their production, by supposing external bodies in their likeness rather than otherwise; and so it might be at least probable there are such things as bodies that excite their ideas in our minds. But

neither can this be said; for though we give the materialists their external bodies, they by their own confession are never the nearer knowing how our ideas are produced: since they own themselves unable to comprehend in what manner body can act upon spirit, or how it is possible it should imprint any idea in the mind. Hence it is evident the production of ideas or sensations in our minds, can be no reason why we should suppose matter or corporeal substances, since that is acknowledged to remain equally inexplicable with, or without this supposition. If therefore it were possible for bodies to exist without the mind, yet to hold they do so, must needs be a very precarious opinion; since it is to suppose, without any reason at all, that God has created innumerable beings that are entirely useless, and serve to no manner of purpose.

20. In short, if there were external bodies, it is impossible we should ever come to know it; and if there were not, we might have the very same reasons to think there were that we have now. Suppose, what no one can deny possible, an intelligence, without the help of external bodies, to be affected with the same train of sensations or ideas that you are, imprinted in the same order and with like vividness in his mind. I ask whether that intelligence hath not all the reason to believe the existence of corporeal substances, represented by his ideas, and exciting them in his mind, that you can possibly have for believing the same thing? Of this there can be no question; which one consideration is enough to make any reasonable person suspect the strength of whatever arguments he may think himself to have, for the existence of bodies without the mind.

21. Were it necessary to add any farther proof against the existence of matter, after what has been said, I could instance several of those errors and difficulties (not to mention impieties) which have sprung from that tenet. It has occasioned numberless controversies and disputes in philosophy, and not a few of far greater moment in religion. But I shall not enter into the detail of them in this place, as well because I think, arguments a posteriori are unnecessary for confirming what has been, if I mistake not, sufficiently demonstrated a

priori, as because I shall hereafter find occasion to say some-what of them.*

22. I am afraid I have given cause to think me needlessly prolix in handling this subject. For to what purpose is it to dilate on that which may be demonstrated with the utmost evidence in a line or two, to anyone that is capable of the least reflexion? It is but looking into your own thoughts, and so trying whether you can conceive it possible for a sound, or figure, or motion, or colour, to exist without the mind, or unperceived. This easy trial may make you see, that what you contend for, is a downright contradiction. Insomuch that I am content to put the whole upon this issue; if you can but con-ceive it possible for one extended moveable substance, or in general, for any one idea or anything like an idea, to exist otherwise than in a mind perceiving it, I shall readily give up the cause: And as for all that *compages* of external bodies which you contend for, I shall grant you its existence, though you cannot either give me any reason why you believe it exists, or assign any use to it when it is supposed to exist. I say, the bare possibility of your opinion's being true, shall pass for an argument that it is so.

23. But say you, surely there is nothing easier than to im-agine trees, for instance, in a park, or books existing in a closet, and nobody by to perceive them.* I answer, you may so, there is no difficulty in it: but what is all this, I beseech you, more than framing in your mind certain ideas which you call *books* and *trees*, and at the same time omitting to frame the idea of anyone that may perceive them? But do not you yourself perceive or think of them all the while? This there-fore is nothing to the purpose: it only shows you have the power of imagining or forming ideas in your mind; but it doth not shew that you can conceive it possible, the objects of your thought may exist without the mind: to make out this, it is necessary that you conceive them existing unconceived or unthought of, which is a manifest repugnancy. When we do our utmost to conceive the existence of external bodies, we are all the while only contemplating our own ideas. But the mind taking no notice of itself, is deluded to think it can and doth conceive bodies existing unthought of or without the

mind; though at the same time they are apprehended by or exist in itself. A little attention will discover to anyone the truth and evidence of what is here said, and make it unnecessary to insist on any other proofs against the existence of material substance.

24. It is very obvious, upon the least inquiry into our own thoughts, to know whether it be possible for us to understand what is meant, by the *absolute existence of sensible objects in themselves, or without the mind*. To me it is evident those words mark out either a direct contradiction, or else nothing at all. And to convince others of this, I know no readier or fairer way, than to entreat they would calmly attend to their own thoughts: and if by this attention, the emptiness or repugnancy of those expressions does appear, surely nothing more is requisite for their conviction. It is on this therefore that I insist, to wit, that the absolute existence of unthinking things are words without a meaning, or which include a contradiction. This is what I repeat and inculcate, and earnestly recommend to the attentive thoughts of the reader.

25. All our ideas, sensations, or the things which we perceive, by whatsoever names they may be distinguished, are visibly inactive, there is nothing of power or agency included in them. So that one idea or object of thought cannot produce, or make any alteration in another. To be satisfied of the truth of this, there is nothing else requisite but a bare observation of our ideas. For since they and every part of them exist only in the mind, it follows that there is nothing in them but what is perceived. But whoever shall attend to his ideas, whether of sense or reflexion, will not perceive in them any power or activity; there is therefore no such thing contained in them.* A little attention will discover to us that the very being of an idea implies passiveness and inertness in it, insomuch that it is impossible for an idea to do anything, or, strictly speaking, to be the cause of anything: neither can it be the resemblance or pattern of any active being, as is evident from sect. 8. Whence it plainly follows that extension, figure and motion, cannot be the cause of our sensations. To say therefore, that these are the effects of powers resulting from the

configuration, number, motion, and size of corpuscles, must certainly be false.

26. We perceive a continual succession of ideas, some are anew excited, others are changed or totally disappear. There is therefore some cause of these ideas whereon they depend, and which produces and changes them. That this cause cannot be any quality or idea or combination of ideas, is clear from the preceding section. It must therefore be a substance; but it has been shewn that there is no corporeal or material substance: it remains therefore that the cause of ideas is an incorporeal active substance or spirit.

27. A spirit is one simple, undivided, active being: as it perceives ideas, it is called the *understanding*, and as it produces or otherwise operates about them, it is called the *will*. Hence there can be no idea formed of a soul or spirit: for all ideas whatever, being passive and inert, *vide* sect. 25, they cannot represent unto us, by way of image or likeness, that which acts. A little attention will make it plain to anyone, that to have an idea which shall be like that active principle of motion and change of ideas, is absolutely impossible. Such is the nature of *spirit* or that which acts, that it cannot be of itself perceived, but only by the effects which it produceth. If any man shall doubt of the truth of what is here delivered, let him but reflect and try if he can frame the idea of any power or active being; and whether he hath ideas of two principal powers, marked by the names *will* and *understanding*, distinct from each other as well as from a third idea of substance or being in general, with a relative notion of its supporting or being the subject of the aforesaid powers, which is signified by the name *soul* or *spirit*. This is what some hold; but so far as I can see, the words *will*, *soul*, *spirit*, do not stand for different ideas, or in truth, for any idea at all, but for something which is very different from ideas, and which being an agent cannot be like unto, or represented by, any idea whatsoever. Though it must be owned at the same time, that we have some notion of soul, spirit, and the operations of the mind, such as willing, loving, hating, in as much as we know or understand the meaning of those words.*

28. I find I can excite ideas in my mind at pleasure, and vary and shift the scene as oft as I think fit. It is no more than willing, and straightway this or that idea arises in my fancy: and by the same power it is obliterated, and makes way for another. This making and unmaking of ideas doth very properly denominate the mind active. Thus much is certain, and grounded on experience: but when we talk of unthinking agents, or of exciting ideas exclusive of volition, we only amuse ourselves with words.

29. But whatever power I may have over my own thoughts, I find the ideas actually perceived by sense have not a like dependence on my will. When in broad day-light I open my eyes, it is not in my power to choose whether I shall see or no, or to determine what particular objects shall present themselves to my view; and so likewise as to the hearing and other senses, the ideas imprinted on them are not creatures of my will. There is therefore some other will or spirit that produces them.

30. The ideas of sense are more strong, lively, and distinct than those of the imagination; they have likewise a steadiness, order, and coherence, and are not excited at random, as those which are the effects of human wills often are, but in a regular train or series, the admirable connexion whereof sufficiently testifies the wisdom and benevolence of its Author. Now the set rules or established methods, wherein the mind we depend on excites in us the ideas of sense, are called the *Laws of Nature*: and these we learn by experience, which teaches us that such and such ideas are attended with such and such other ideas, in the ordinary course of things.

31. This gives us a sort of foresight, which enables us to regulate our actions for the benefit of life.* And without this we should be eternally at a loss: we could not know how to act anything that might procure us the least pleasure, or remove the least pain of sense. That food nourishes, sleep refreshes, and fire warms us; that to sow in the seed-time is the way to reap in the harvest, and, in general, that to obtain such or such ends, such or such means are conducive, all this we know, not by discovering any necessary connexion between our ideas, but only by the observation of the settled laws of Nature,

without which we should be all in uncertainty and confusion, and a grown man no more know how to manage himself in the affairs of life, than an infant just born.

32. And yet this consistent uniform working, which so evidently displays the goodness and wisdom of that governing spirit whose will constitutes the Laws of Nature, is so far from leading our thoughts to him, that it rather sends them a wandering after second causes. For when we perceive certain ideas of sense constantly followed by other ideas, and we know this is not of our doing, we forthwith attribute power and agency to the ideas themselves, and make one the cause of another, than which nothing can be more absurd and unintelligible. Thus, for example, having observed that when we perceive by sight a certain round luminous figure, we at the same time perceive by touch the idea or sensation called *heat*, we do from thence conclude the sun to be the cause of heat. And in like manner perceiving the motion and collision of bodies to be attended with sound, we are inclined to think the latter an effect of the former.

33. The ideas imprinted on the senses by the Author of Nature are called *real things*: and those excited in the imagination being less regular, vivid and constant, are more properly termed *ideas*, or *images of things*, which they copy and represent. But then our sensations, be they never so vivid and distinct, are nevertheless *ideas*, that is, they exist in the mind, or are perceived by it, as truly as the ideas of its own framing. The ideas of sense are allowed to have more reality in them, that is, to be more strong, orderly, and coherent than the creatures of the mind; but this is no argument that they exist without the mind. They are also less dependent on the spirit, or thinking substance which perceives them, in that they are excited by the will of another and more powerful spirit: yet still they are *ideas*, and certainly no *idea*, whether faint or strong, can exist otherwise than in a mind perceiving it.

34. Before we proceed any farther, it is necessary to spend some time in answering objections which may probably be made against the principles hitherto laid down. In doing of which, if I seem too prolix to those of quick apprehensions, I hope it may be pardoned, since all men do not equally appre-

hend things of this nature; and I am willing to be understood by everyone. First then, it will be objected that by the foregoing principles, all that is real and substantial in Nature is banished out of the world: and instead thereof a chimerical scheme of ideas takes place. All things that exist, exist only in the mind, that is, they are purely notional. What therefore becomes of the sun, moon, and stars? What must we think of houses, rivers, mountains, trees, stones; nay, even of our own bodies? Are all these but so many chimeras and illusions on the fancy? To all which, and whatever else of the same sort may be objected, I answer, that by the principles premised, we are not deprived of any one thing in Nature. Whatever we see, feel, hear, or anywise conceive or understand, remains as secure as ever, and is as real as ever. There is a *rerum natura*, and the distinction between realities and chimeras retains its full force. This is evident from sects. 29, 30, and 33, where we have shewn what is meant by *real things* in opposition to *chimeras*, or ideas of our own framing; but then they both equally exist in the mind, and in that sense are alike *ideas*.

35. I do not argue against the existence of any one thing that we can apprehend, either by sense or reflexion. That the things I see with mine eyes and touch with my hands do exist, really exist, I make not the least question. The only thing whose existence we deny, is that which philosophers call matter or corporeal substance. And in doing of this, there is no damage done to the rest of mankind, who, I dare say, will never miss it. The atheist indeed will want the colour of an empty name to support his impiety; and the philosophers may possibly find, they have lost a great handle for trifling and disputation.

36. If any man thinks this detracts from the existence or reality of things, he is very far from understanding what hath been premised in the plainest terms I could think of. Take here an abstract of what has been said. There are spiritual substances, minds, or human souls, which will or excite ideas in themselves at pleasure: but these are faint, weak, and unsteady in respect of others they perceive by sense, which being impressed upon them according to certain rules or laws of Nature, speak themselves the effects of a mind more powerful

and wise than human spirits. These latter are said to have more *reality* in them than the former: by which is meant that they are more affecting, orderly, and distinct, and that they are not fictions of the mind perceiving them. And in this sense, the sun that I see by day is the real sun, and that which I imagine by night is the idea of the former. In the sense here given of *reality*, it is evident that every vegetable, star, mineral, and in general each part of the mundane system, is as much a *real being* by our principles as by any other. Whether others mean anything by the term *reality* different from what I do, I entreat them to look into their own thoughts and see.

37. It will be urged that thus much at least is true, to wit, that we take away all corporeal substances. To this my answer is, that if the word *substance* be taken in the vulgar sense, for a combination of sensible qualities, such as extension, solidity, weight, and the like; this we cannot be accused of taking away. But if it be taken in a philosophic sense, for the support of accidents or qualities without the mind: then indeed I acknowledge that we take it away, if one may be said to take away that which never had any existence, not even in the imagination.

38. But, say you, it sounds very harsh to say we eat and drink ideas, and are clothed with ideas. I acknowledge it does so, the word *idea* not being used in common discourse to signify the several combinations of sensible qualities, which are called *things*: and it is certain that any expression which varies from the familiar use of language, will seem harsh and ridiculous. But this doth not concern the truth of the proposition, which in other words is no more than to say, we are fed and clothed with those things which we perceive immediately by our senses. The hardness or softness, the colour, taste, warmth, figure, and such like qualities, which combined together constitute the several sorts of victuals and apparel, have been shewn to exist only in the mind that perceives them; and this is all that is meant by calling them *ideas*; which word, if it was as ordinarily used as *thing*, would sound no harsher nor more ridiculous than it. I am not for disputing about the propriety, but the truth of the expression. If therefore you agree with me that we eat and drink, and are clad

with the immediate objects of sense which cannot exist unperceived or without the mind: I shall readily grant it is more proper or conformable to custom, that they should be called things rather than ideas.*

39. If it be demanded why I make use of the word *idea*, and do not rather in compliance with custom call them things. I answer, I do it for two reasons: first, because the term *thing*, in contradistinction to *idea*, is generally supposed to denote somewhat existing without the mind: secondly, because *thing* hath a more comprehensive signification than *idea*, including spirits or thinking things as well as ideas. Since therefore the objects of sense exist only in the mind, and are withal thoughtless and inactive, I chose to mark them by the word *idea*, which implies those properties.

40. But say what we can, someone perhaps may be apt to reply, he will still believe his senses, and never suffer any arguments, how plausible soever, to prevail over the certainty of them. Be it so, assert the evidence of sense as high as you please, we are willing to do the same. That what I see, hear and feel doth exist, that is to say, is perceived by me, I no more doubt than I do of my own being. But I do not see how the testimony of sense can be alleged, as a proof for the existence of anything, which is not perceived by sense. We are not for having any man turn *sceptic*, and disbelieve his senses; on the contrary we give them all the stress and assurance imaginable; nor are there any principles more opposite to scepticism, than those we have laid down, as shall be hereafter clearly shewn.

41. Secondly, it will be objected that there is a great difference betwixt real fire, for instance, and the idea of fire, betwixt dreaming or imagining one's self burnt, and actually being so: this and the like may be urged in opposition to our tenets. To all which the answer is evident from what hath been already said, and I shall only add in this place, that if real fire be very different from the idea of fire, so also is the real pain that it occasions, very different from the idea of the same pain: and yet nobody will pretend that real pain either is, or can possibly be, in an unperceiving thing or without the mind, any more than its idea.

42. Thirdly, it will be objected that we see things actually without or at a distance from us, and which consequently do not exist in the mind, it being absurd that those things which are seen at the distance of several miles, should be as near to us as our own thoughts. In answer to this, I desire it may be considered, that in a dream we do oft perceive things as existing at a great distance off, and yet for all that, those things are acknowledged to have their existence only in the mind.

43. But for the fuller clearing of this point, it may be worth while to consider, how it is that we perceive distance and things placed at a distance by sight. For that we should in truth see external space, and bodies actually existing in it, some nearer, others farther off, seems to carry with it some opposition to what hath been said, of their existing nowhere without the mind. The consideration of this difficulty it was, that gave birth to my *Essay towards a new Theory of Vision*, which was published not long since. Wherein it is shewn that *distance* or outness is neither immediately of itself perceived by sight, nor yet apprehended or judged of by lines and angles, or anything that hath a necessary connexion with it: but that it is only suggested to our thoughts, by certain visible ideas and sensations attending vision, which in their own nature have no manner of similitude or relation, either with distance, or things placed at a distance. But by a connexion taught us by experience, they come to signify and suggest them to us, after the same manner that words of any language suggest the ideas they are made to stand for. Insomuch that a man born blind, and afterwards made to see, would not, at first sight, think the things he saw, to be without his mind, or at any distance from him. See sect. 41 of the forementioned treatise.

44. The ideas of sight and touch make two species, entirely distinct and heterogeneous. The former are marks and prognostics of the latter. That the proper objects of sight neither exist without the mind, nor are the images of external things, was shewn even in that treatise. Though throughout the same, the contrary be supposed true of tangible objects: not that to suppose that vulgar error, was necessary for establishing the notion therein laid down; but because it was beside

my purpose to examine and refute it in a discourse concerning *vision*. So that in strict truth the ideas of sight, when we apprehend by them distance and things placed at a distance, do not suggest or mark out to us things actually existing at a distance, but only admonish us what ideas of touch will be imprinted in our minds at such and such distances of time, and in consequence of such and such actions. It is, I say, evident from what has been said in the foregoing parts of this treatise, and in sect. 147, and elsewhere of the essay concerning vision, that visible ideas are the language whereby the governing spirit, on whom we depend, informs us what tangible ideas he is about to imprint upon us, in case we excite this or that motion in our own bodies. But for a fuller information in this point, I refer to the essay itself.

45. Fourthly, it will be objected that from the foregoing principles it follows, things are every moment annihilated and created anew. The objects of sense exist only when they are perceived: the trees therefore are in the garden, or the chairs in the parlour, no longer than while there is somebody by to perceive them. Upon shutting my eyes all the furniture in the room is reduced to nothing, and barely upon opening them it is again created. In answer to all which, I refer the reader to what has been said in sects. 3, 4, &c. and desire he will consider whether he means anything by the actual existence of an idea, distinct from its being perceived. For my part, after the nicest inquiry I could make, I am not able to discover that anything else is meant by those words. And I once more entreat the reader to sound his own thoughts, and not suffer himself to be imposed on by words. If he can conceive it possible either for his ideas or their archetypes to exist without being perceived, then I give up the cause: but if he cannot, he will acknowledge it is unreasonable for him to stand up in defence of he knows not what, and pretend to charge on me as an absurdity, the not assenting to those propositions which at bottom have no meaning in them.

46. It will not be amiss to observe, how far the received principles of philosophy are themselves chargeable with those pretended absurdities. It is thought strangely absurd that upon closing my eyelids, all the visible objects round me

should be reduced to nothing; and yet is not this what philosophers commonly acknowledge, when they agree on all hands, that light and colours, which alone are the proper and immediate objects of sight, are mere sensations that exist no longer than they are perceived? Again, it may to some perhaps seem very incredible, that things should be every moment creating, yet this very notion is commonly taught in the Schools. For the Schoolmen, though they acknowledge the existence of matter, and that the whole mundane fabrick is framed out of it, are nevertheless of opinion that it cannot subsist without the divine conservation, which by them is expounded to be a continual creation.*

47. Farther, a little thought will discover to us, that though we allow the existence of matter or corporeal substance, yet it will unavoidably follow from the principles which are now generally admitted, that the particular bodies of what kind soever, do none of them exist whilst they are not perceived. For it is evident from sect. 11 and the following sections, that the matter philosophers contend for, is an incomprehensible somewhat which hath none of those particular qualities, whereby the bodies falling under our senses are distinguished one from another. But to make this more plain, it must be remarked, that the infinite divisibility of matter is now universally allowed, at least by the most approved and considerable philosophers, who on the received principles demonstrate it beyond all exception. Hence it follows, that there is an infinite number of parts in each particle of matter, which are not perceived by sense. The reason therefore, that any particular body seems to be of a finite magnitude, or exhibits only a finite number of parts to sense, is not because it contains no more, since in itself it contains an infinite number of parts, but because the sense is not acute enough to discern them. In proportion therefore as the sense is rendered more acute, it perceives a greater number of parts in the object, that is, the object appears greater, and its figure varies, those parts in its extremities which were before unperceivable, appearing now to bound it in very different lines and angles from those perceived by an obtuser sense. And at length, after various changes of size and shape, when the sense becomes infinitely

acute, the body shall seem infinite. During all which there is no alteration in the body, but only in the sense. Each body therefore considered in itself, is infinitely extended, and consequently void of all shape or figure. From which it follows, that though we should grant the existence of matter to be ever so certain, yet it is withal as certain, the materialists themselves are by their own principles forced to acknowledge, that neither the particular bodies perceived by sense, nor anything like them exists without the mind. Matter, I say, and each particle thereof is according to them, infinite and shapeless,* and it is the mind that frames all that variety of bodies which compose the visible world, any one whereof does not exist longer than it is perceived.

48. If we consider it, the objection proposed in sect. 45 will not be found reasonably charged on the principles we have premised, so as in truth to make any objection at all against our notions. For though we hold indeed the objects of sense to be nothing else but ideas which cannot exist unperceived; yet we may not hence conclude they have no existence except only while they are perceived by us, since there may be some other spirit that perceives them, though we do not. Wherever bodies are said to have no existence without the mind, I would not be understood to mean this or that particular mind, but all minds whatsoever. It does not therefore follow from the foregoing principles, that bodies are annihilated and created every moment, or exist not at all during the intervals between our perception of them.

49. Fifthly, it may perhaps be objected, that if extension and figure exist only in the mind, it follows that the mind is extended and figured; since extension is a mode or attribute, which (to speak with the Schools) is predicated of the subject in which it exists. I answer, those qualities are in the mind only as they are perceived by it, that is, not by way of *mode* or *attribute*, but only by way of *idea*; and it no more follows, that the soul or mind is extended because extension exists in it alone, than it does that it is red or blue, because those colours are on all hands acknowledged to exist in it, and nowhere else. As to what philosophers say of subject and mode, that seems very groundless and unintelligible. For instance, in this

proposition, a die is hard, extended and square, they will have it that the word *die* denotes a subject or substance, distinct from the hardness, extension and figure, which are predicated of it, and in which they exist. This I cannot comprehend: to me a die seems to be nothing distinct from those things which are termed its modes or accidents. And to say a die is hard, extended and square, is not to attribute those qualities to a subject distinct from and supporting them, but only an explication of the meaning of the word *die*.

50. Sixthly, you will say there have been a great many things explained by matter and motion: take away these, and you destroy the whole corpuscular philosophy, and undermine those mechanical principles which have been applied with so much success to account for the phenomena. In short, whatever advances have been made, either by ancient or modern philosophers, in the study of Nature, do all proceed on the supposition, that corporeal substance or matter doth really exist. To this I answer, that there is not any one phenomenon explained on that supposition, which may not as well be explained without it, as might easily be made appear by an induction of particulars. To explain the phenomena, is all one as to shew, why upon such and such occasions we are affected with such and such ideas. But how matter should operate on a spirit, or produce any idea in it, is what no philosopher will pretend to explain. It is therefore evident, there can be no use of matter in natural philosophy. Besides, they who attempt to account for things, do it not by corporeal substance, but by figure, motion, and other qualities, which are in truth no more than mere ideas, and therefore cannot be the cause of anything, as hath been already shewn. See sect. 25.

51. Seventhly, it will upon this be demanded whether it does not seem absurd to take away natural causes, and ascribe everything to the immediate operation of spirits? We must no longer say upon these principles that fire heats, or water cools, but that a spirit heats, and so forth. Would not a man be deservedly laughed at, who should talk after this manner? I answer, he would so; in such things we ought to *think with the learned, and speak with the vulgar*.* They who to demonstration are convinced of the truth of the Copernican system,

do nevertheless say the sun rises, the sun sets, or comes to the meridian: and if they affected a contrary style in common talk, it would without doubt appear very ridiculous. A little reflexion on what is here said will make it manifest, that the common use of language would receive no manner of alteration or disturbance from the admission of our tenets.

52. In the ordinary affairs of life, any phrases may be retained, so long as they excite in us proper sentiments, or dispositions to act in such a manner as is necessary for our well-being, how false soever they may be, if taken in a strict and speculative sense. Nay this is unavoidable, since propriety being regulated by custom, language is suited to the received opinions, which are not always the truest. Hence it is impossible, even in the most rigid philosophic reasonings, so far to alter the bent and genius of the tongue we speak, as never to give a handle for cavillers to pretend difficulties and inconsistencies. But a fair and ingenuous reader will collect the sense, from the scope and tenor and connexion of a discourse, making allowances for those inaccurate modes of speech, which use has made inevitable.

53. As to the opinion that there are no corporeal causes, this has been heretofore maintained by some of the Schoolmen, as it is of late by others among the modern philosophers,* who though they allow matter to exist, yet will have God alone to be the immediate efficient cause of all things. These men saw, that amongst all the objects of sense, there was none which had any power or activity included in it, and that by consequence this was likewise true of whatever bodies they supposed to exist without the mind, like unto the immediate objects of sense. But then, that they should suppose an innumerable multitude of created beings, which they acknowledge are not capable of producing any one effect in Nature, and which therefore are made to no manner of purpose, since God might have done everything as well without them; this I say, though we should allow it possible, must yet be a very unaccountable and extravagant supposition.

54. In the eighth place, the universal concurrent assent of mankind may be thought by some, an invincible argument in behalf of matter, or the existence of external things. Must we

suppose the whole world to be mistaken? And if so, what cause can be assigned of so widespread and predominant an error? I answer, first, that upon a narrow inquiry, it will not perhaps be found, so many as is imagined do really believe the existence of matter or things without the mind. Strictly speaking, to believe that which involves a contradiction, or has no meaning in it, is impossible: and whether the foregoing expressions are not of that sort, I refer it to the impartial examination of the reader. In one sense indeed, men may be said to believe that matter exists, that is, they act as if the immediate cause of their sensations, which affects them every moment and is so nearly present to them, were some senseless unthinking being. But that they should clearly apprehend any meaning marked by those words, and form thereof a settled speculative opinion, is what I am not able to conceive. This is not the only instance wherein men impose upon themselves, by imagining they believe those propositions they have often heard, though at bottom they have no meaning in them.

55. But secondly, though we should grant a notion to be ever so universally and stedfastly adhered to, yet this is but a weak argument of its truth, to whoever considers what a vast number of prejudices and false opinions are everywhere embraced with the utmost tenaciousness, by the unreflecting (which are the far greater) part of mankind. There was a time when the Antipodes and motion of the earth were looked upon as monstrous absurdities, even by men of learning: and if it be considered what a small proportion they bear to the rest of mankind, we shall find that at this day, those notions have gained but a very inconsiderable footing in the world.

56. But it is demanded, that we assign a cause of this prejudice, and account for its obtaining in the world. To this I answer, that men knowing they perceived several ideas, whereof they themselves were not the authors, as not being excited from within, nor depending on the operation of their wills, this made them maintain, those ideas or objects of perception had an existence independent of, and without the mind, without ever dreaming that a contradiction was involved in those words. But philosophers having plainly seen, that the immediate objects of perception do not exist without

the mind, they in some degree corrected the mistake of the vulgar, but at the same time run into another which seems no less absurd, to wit, that there are certain objects really existing without the mind, or having a subsistence distinct from being perceived, of which our ideas are only images or resemblances, imprinted by those objects on the mind. And this notion of the philosophers owes its origin to the same cause with the former, namely, their being conscious that they were not the authors of their own sensations, which they evidently knew were imprinted from without, and which therefore must have some cause, distinct from the minds on which they are imprinted.

57. But why they should suppose the ideas of sense to be excited in us by things in their likeness, and not rather have recourse to *spirit* which alone can act, may be accounted for, first, because they were not aware of the repugnancy there is, as well in supposing things like unto our ideas existing without, as in attributing to them power or activity. Secondly, because the supreme spirit which excites those ideas in our minds, is not marked out and limited to our view by any particular finite collection of sensible ideas, as human agents are by their size, complexion, limbs, and motions. And thirdly, because his operations are regular and uniform. Whenever the course of Nature is interrupted by a miracle, men are ready to own the presence of a superior agent. But when we see things go on in the ordinary course, they do not excite in us any reflection; their order and concatenation, though it be an argument of the greatest wisdom, power, and goodness in their Creator, is yet so constant and familiar to us, that we do not think them the immediate effects of a *free spirit*: especially since inconstancy and mutability in acting, though it be an imperfection, is looked on as a mark of *freedom*.

58. Tenthly, it will be objected, that the notions we advance, are inconsistent with several sound truths in philosophy and mathematics. For example, the motion of the earth is now universally admitted by astronomers, as a truth grounded on the clearest and most convincing reasons; but on the foregoing principles, there can be no such thing. For motion being only an idea, it follows that if it be not

perceived, it exists not; but the motion of the earth is not perceived by sense. I answer, that tenet, if rightly understood, will be found to agree with the principles we have premised: for the question, whether the earth moves or no, amounts in reality to no more than this, to wit, whether we have reason to conclude from what hath been observed by astronomers, that if we were placed in such and such circumstances, and such or such a position and distance, both from the earth and sun, we should perceive the former to move among the choir of the planets, and appearing in all respects like one of them: and this, by the established rules of Nature, which we have no reason to mistrust, is reasonably collected from the phenomena.

59. We may, from the experience we have had of the train and succession of ideas in our minds, often make, I will not say uncertain conjectures, but sure and well-grounded predictions, concerning the ideas we shall be affected with, pursuant to a great train of actions, and be enabled to pass a right judgment of what would have appeared to us, in case we were placed in circumstances very different from those we are in at present. Herein consists the knowledge of Nature, which may preserve its use and certainty very consistently with what hath been said. It will be easy to apply this to whatever objections of the like sort may be drawn from the magnitude of the stars, or any other discoveries in astronomy or Nature.

60. In the eleventh place, it will be demanded to what purpose serves that curious organization of plants, and the admirable mechanism in the parts of animals; might not vegetables grow, and shoot forth leaves and blossoms, and animals perform all their motions, as well without as with all that variety of internal parts so elegantly contrived and put together, which being ideas have nothing powerful or operative in them, nor have any necessary connexion with the effects ascribed to them? If it be a spirit that immediately produces every effect by a *fiat*, or act of his will, we must think all that is fine and artificial in the works, whether of man or Nature, to be made in vain. By this doctrine, though an artist hath made the spring and wheels, and every movement of a watch, and adjusted them in such a manner as he knew

would produce the motions he designed; yet he must think all this done to no purpose, and that it is an intelligence which directs the index, and points to the hour of the day. If so, why may not the intelligence do it, without his being at the pains of making the movements, and putting them together? Why does not an empty case serve as well as another? And how comes it to pass, that whenever there is any fault in the going of a watch, there is some corresponding disorder to be found in the movements, which being mended by a skilful hand, all is right again? The like may be said of all the clockwork of Nature, great part whereof is so wonderfully fine and subtle, as scarce to be discerned by the best microscope. In short, it will be asked, how upon our principles any tolerable account can be given, or any final cause assigned of an innumerable multitude of bodies and machines framed with the most exquisite art, which in the common philosophy have very apposite uses assigned them, and serve to explain abundance of phenomena.

61. To all which I answer, first, that though there were some difficulties relating to the administration of providence, and the uses by it assigned to the several parts of Nature, which I could not solve by the foregoing principles, yet this objection could be of small weight against the truth and certainty of those things which may be proved a priori, with the utmost evidence. Secondly, but neither are the received principles free from the like difficulties; for it may still be demanded, to what end God should take those round-about methods of effecting things by instruments and machines, which no one can deny might have been effected by the mere command of his will, without all that *apparatus*: nay, if we narrowly consider it, we shall find the objection may be retorted with greater force on those who hold the existence of those machines without the mind; for it has been made evident, that solidity, bulk, figure, motion and the like, have no *activity* or *efficacy* in them, so as to be capable of producing any one effect in Nature. See sect. 25. Whoever therefore supposes them to exist (allowing the supposition possible) when they are not perceived, does it manifestly to no purpose; since the only use that is assigned to them, as they exist

unperceived, is that they produce those perceivable effects, which in truth cannot be ascribed to anything but spirit.

62. But to come nearer the difficulty, it must be observed, that though the fabrication of all those parts and organs be not absolutely necessary to the producing any effect, yet it is necessary to the producing of things in a constant, regular way, according to the Laws of Nature. There are certain general laws that run through the whole chain of natural effects: these are learned by the observation and study of Nature, and are by men applied as well to the framing artificial things for the use and ornament of life, as to the explaining the various phenomena: which explication consists only in shewing the conformity any particular phenomenon hath to the general Laws of Nature, or, which is the same thing, in discovering the *uniformity* there is in the production of natural effects; as will be evident to whoever shall attend to the several instances, wherein philosophers pretend to account for appearances. That there is a great and conspicuous use in these regular constant methods of working observed by the Supreme Agent, hath been shewn in sect. 31. And it is no less visible, that a particular size, figure, motion and disposition of parts are necessary, though not absolutely to the producing any effect, yet to the producing it according to the standing mechanical Laws of Nature. Thus, for instance, it cannot be denied that God, or the intelligence which sustains and rules the ordinary course of things might, if he were minded to produce a miracle, choose all the motions on the dial-plate of a watch, though nobody had ever made the movements, and put them in it: but yet if he will act agreeably to the rules of mechanism, by him for wise ends established and maintained in the Creation, it is necessary that those actions of the watchmaker, whereby he makes the movements and rightly adjusts them, precede the production of the aforesaid motions; as also that any disorder in them be attended with the perception of some corresponding disorder in the movements, which being once corrected all is right again.

63. It may indeed on some occasions be necessary, that the Author of Nature display his overruling power in producing some appearance out of the ordinary series of things. Such

exceptions from the general rules of Nature are proper to surprise and awe men into an acknowledgement of the Divine Being: but then they are to be used but seldom, otherwise there is a plain reason why they should fail of that effect. Besides, God seems to choose the convincing our reason of his attributes by the works of Nature, which discover so much harmony and contrivance in their make, and are such plain indications of wisdom and beneficence in their Author, rather than to astonish us into a belief of his being by anomalous and surprising events.

64. To set this matter in a yet clearer light, I shall observe that what has been objected in sect. 60 amounts in reality to no more than this: ideas are not anyhow and at random produced, there being a certain order and connexion between them, like to that of cause and effect: there are also several combinations of them, made in a very regular and artificial manner, which seem like so many instruments in the hand of Nature, that being hid as it were behind the scenes, have a secret operation in producing those appearances which are seen on the theatre of the world, being themselves discernible only to the curious eye of the philosopher. But since one idea cannot be the cause of another, to what purpose is that connexion? And since those instruments, being barely *ineffi-cacious perceptions* in the mind, are not subservient to the production of natural effects; it is demanded why they are made, or, in other words, what reason can be assigned why God should make us, upon a close inspection into his works, behold so great variety of ideas, so artfully laid together, and so much according to rule, it not being credible, that he would be at the expense (if one may so speak) of all that art and regularity to no purpose?

65. To all which my answer is, first, that the connexion of ideas does not imply the relation of *cause* and *effect*, but only of a mark or *sign* with the thing *signified*. The fire which I see is not the cause of the pain I suffer upon my approaching it, but the mark that forewarns me of it. In like manner, the noise that I hear is not the effect of this or that motion or collision of the ambient bodies, but the sign thereof. Secondly, the reason why ideas are formed into machines, that is, artificial

and regular combinations, is the same with that for combining letters into words. That a few original ideas may be made to signify a great number of effects and actions, it is necessary they be variously combined together: and to the end their use be permanent and universal, these combinations must be made by *rule*, and with *wise contrivance*. By this means abundance of information is conveyed unto us, concerning what we are to expect from such and such actions, and what methods are proper to be taken, for the exciting such and such ideas: which in effect is all that I conceive to be distinctly meant, when it is said that by discerning the figure, texture, and mechanism of the inward parts of bodies, whether natural or artificial, we may attain to know the several uses and properties depending thereon, or the nature of the thing.

66. Hence it is evident, that those things which under the notion of a cause co-operating or concurring to the production of effects, are altogether inexplicable, and run us into great absurdities, may be very naturally explained, and have a proper and obvious use assigned them, when they are considered only as marks or signs for our information. And it is the searching after, and endeavouring to understand those signs instituted by the Author of Nature, that ought to be the employment of the natural philosopher, and not the pretending to explain things by corporeal causes; which doctrine seems to have too much estranged the minds of men from that active principle, that supreme and wise spirit, *in whom we live, move, and have our being.**

67. In the twelfth place, it may perhaps be objected, that though it be clear from what has been said, that there can be no such thing as an inert, senseless, extended, solid, figured, moveable substance, existing without the mind, such as philosophers describe matter: yet if any man shall leave out of his idea of *matter*, the positive ideas of extension, figure, solidity and motion, and say that he means only by that word, an inert senseless substance, that exists without the mind, or unperceived, which is the occasion of our ideas, or at the presence whereof God is pleased to excite ideas in us: it doth not appear, but that matter taken in this sense may possibly exist. In answer to which I say, first, that it seems no

less absurd to suppose a substance without accidents, than it is to suppose accidents without a substance. But secondly, though we should grant this unknown substance may possibly exist, yet where can it be supposed to be? That it exists not in the mind is agreed, and that it exists not in place is no less certain; since all extension exists only in the mind, as hath been already proved. It remains therefore that it exists nowhere at all.

68. Let us examine a little the description that is here given us of *matter*. It neither acts, nor perceives, nor is perceived: for this is all that is meant by saying it is an inert, senseless, unknown substance; which is a definition entirely made up of negatives, excepting only the relative notion of its standing under or supporting: but then it must be observed, that it *supports* nothing at all; and how nearly this comes to the description of a *non-entity*, I desire may be considered. But, say you, it is the *unknown occasion*, at the presence of which, ideas are excited in us by the will of God.* Now I would fain know how anything can be present to us, which is neither perceivable by sense nor reflexion, nor capable of producing any idea in our minds, nor is at all extended, nor hath any form, nor exists in any place. The words *to be present*, when thus applied, must needs be taken in some abstract and strange meaning, and which I am not able to comprehend.

69. Again, let us examine what is meant by *occasion*: so far as I can gather from the common use of language, that word signifies, either the agent which produces any effect, or else something that is observed to accompany, or go before it, in the ordinary course of things. But when it is applied to matter as above described, it can be taken in neither of those senses. For matter is said to be passive and inert, and so cannot be an agent or efficient cause. It is also unperceivable, as being devoid of all sensible qualities, and so cannot be the occasion of our perceptions in the latter sense: as when the burning my finger is said to be the occasion of the pain that attends it. What therefore can be meant by calling matter an *occasion*? This term is either used in no sense at all, or else in some sense very distant from its received signification.

70. You will perhaps say that matter, though it be not perceived by us, is nevertheless perceived by God, to whom it is the occasion of exciting ideas in our minds. For, say you, since we observe our sensations to be imprinted in an orderly and constant manner, it is but reasonable to suppose there are certain constant and regular occasions of their being produced. That is to say, that there are certain permanent and distinct parcels of matter, corresponding to our ideas, which, though they do not excite them in our minds, or any ways immediately affect us, as being altogether passive and unperceivable to us, they are nevertheless to God, by whom they are perceived, as it were so many occasions to remind him when and what ideas to imprint on our minds: that so things may go on in a constant uniform manner.

71. In answer to this I observe, that as the notion of matter is here stated, the question is no longer concerning the existence of a thing distinct from *spirit* and *idea*, from perceiving and being perceived: but whether there are not certain ideas, of I know not what sort, in the mind of God, which are so many marks or notes that direct him how to produce sensations in our minds, in a constant and regular method: much after the same manner as a musician is directed by the notes of music to produce that harmonious train and composition of sound, which is called a *tune*; though they who hear the music do not perceive the notes, and may be entirely ignorant of them. But this notion of matter seems too extravagant to deserve a confutation. Besides, it is in effect no objection against what we have advanced, to wit, that there is no senseless, unperceived *substance*.

72. If we follow the light of reason, we shall, from the constant uniform method of our sensations, collect the goodness and wisdom of the *spirit* who excites them in our minds. But this is all that I can see reasonably concluded from thence. To me, I say, it is evident that the being of a *spirit infinitely wise, good, and powerful* is abundantly sufficient to explain all the appearances of Nature. But as for *inert senseless matter*, nothing that I perceive has any the least connexion with it, or leads to the thoughts of it. And I would fain see anyone

explain any the meanest phenomenon in Nature by it, or shew any manner of reason, though in the lowest rank of probability, that he can have for its existence; or even make any tolerable sense or meaning of that supposition. For as to its being an occasion, we have, I think, evidently shewn that with regard to us it is no occasion: it remains therefore that it must be, if at all, the occasion to God of exciting ideas in us; and what this amounts to, we have just now seen.

73. It is worth while to reflect a little on the motives which induced men to suppose the existence of material substance; that so having observed the gradual ceasing, and expiration of those motives or reasons, we may proportionably withdraw the assent that was grounded on them. First therefore, it was thought that colour, figure, motion, and the rest of the sensible qualities or accidents, did really exist without the mind; and for this reason, it seemed needful to suppose some unthinking *substratum* or *substance* wherein they did exist, since they could not be conceived to exist by themselves. Afterwards, in process of time, men being convinced that colours, sounds, and the rest of the sensible secondary qualities had no existence without the mind, they stripped this *substratum* or material substance of those qualities, leaving only the primary ones, figure, motion, and such like, which they still conceived to exist without the mind, and consequently to stand in need of a material support. But it having been shewn, that none, even of these, can possibly exist otherwise than in a spirit or mind which perceives them, it follows that we have no longer any reason to suppose the being of *matter*. Nay, that it is utterly impossible there should be any such thing, so long as that word is taken to denote an *unthinking substratum* of qualities or accidents, wherein they exist without the mind.

74. But though it be allowed by the *materialists* themselves, that matter was thought of only for the sake of supporting accidents; and the reason entirely ceasing, one might expect the mind should naturally, and without any reluctance at all, quit the belief of what was solely grounded thereon. Yet the prejudice is riveted so deeply in our thoughts, that we can scarce tell how to part with it, and are therefore inclined, since the *thing* itself is indefensible, at least to retain the *name*;

which we apply to I know not what abstracted and indefinite notions of *being*, or *occasion*, though without any shew or reason, at least so far as I can see. For what is there on our part, or what do we perceive amongst all the ideas, sensations, notions, which are imprinted on our minds, either by sense or reflexion, from whence may be inferred the existence of an inert, thoughtless, unperceived occasion? and on the other hand, on the part of an *all-sufficient spirit*, what can there be that should make us believe, or even suspect, he is *directed* by an inert occasion to excite ideas in our minds?

75. It is a very extraordinary instance of the force of prejudice, and much to be lamented, that the mind of man retains so great a fondness against all the evidence of reason, for a stupid thoughtless *somewhat*, by the interposition whereof it would, as it were, screen itself from the providence of God, and remove him farther off from the affairs of the world. But though we do the utmost we can, to secure the belief of *matter*, though when reason forsakes us, we endeavour to support our opinion on the bare possibility of the thing, and though we indulge ourselves in the full scope of an imagination not regulated by reason, to make out that poor *possibility*, yet the upshot of all is, that there are certain *unknown ideas* in the mind of God; for this, if anything, is all that I conceive to be meant by *occasion* with regard to God. And this, at the bottom, is no longer contending for the *thing*, but for the *name*.

76. Whether therefore there are such ideas in the mind of God, and whether they may be called by the name *matter*, I shall not dispute. But if you stick to the notion of an unthinking substance, or support of extension, motion, and other sensible qualities, then to me it is most evidently impossible there should be any such thing. Since it is a plain repugnancy, that those qualities should exist in or be supported by an unperceiving substance.

77. But say you, though it be granted that there is no thoughtless support of extension, and the other qualities or accidents which we perceive; yet there may, perhaps, be some inert unperceiving substance, or *substratum* of some other qualities, as incomprehensible to us as colours are to a man born blind, because we have not a sense adapted to them.

But if we had a new sense, we should possibly no more doubt of their existence, than a blind man made to see does of the existence of light and colours. I answer, first, if what you mean by the word *matter* be only the unknown support of unknown qualities, it is no matter whether there is such a thing or no, since it no way concerns us: and I do not see the advantage there is in disputing about we know not *what*, and we know not *why*.

78. But secondly, if we had a new sense, it could only furnish us with new ideas or sensations: and then we should have the same reason against their existing in an unperceiving substance, that has been already offered with relation to figure, motion, colour, and the like. Qualities, as hath been shewn, are nothing else but *sensations* or *ideas*, which exist only in a *mind* perceiving them; and this is true not only of the ideas we are acquainted with at present, but likewise of all possible ideas whatsoever.

79. But you will insist, what if I have no reason to believe the existence of matter, what if I cannot assign any use to it, or explain anything by it, or even conceive what is meant by that word? Yet still it is no contradiction to say that matter exists, and that this matter is *in general* a *substance*, or *occasion of ideas*; though, indeed, to go about to unfold the meaning, or adhere to any particular explication of those words, may be attended with great difficulties. I answer, when words are used without a meaning, you may put them together as you please, without danger of running into a contradiction. You may say, for example, that *twice two* is equal to *seven*, so long as you declare you do not take the words of that proposition in their usual acceptation, but for marks of you know not what. And by the same reason you may say, there is an inert thoughtless substance without accidents, which is the occasion of our ideas. And we shall understand just as much by one proposition, as the other.

80. In the last place, you will say, what if we give up the cause of material substance, and assert, that matter is an unknown *somewhat*, neither substance nor accident, spirit nor idea, inert, thoughtless, indivisible, immoveable, unextended, existing in no place? For, say you, whatever may be urged

against *substance* or *occasion*, or any other positive or relative notion of matter, hath no place at all, so long as this *negative* definition of matter is adhered to. I answer, you may, if so it shall seem good, use the word *matter* in the same sense, that other men use *nothing*, and so make those terms convertible in your style. For after all, this is what appears to me to be the result of that definition, the parts whereof when I consider with attention, either collectively, or separate from each other, I do not find that there is any kind of effect or impression made on my mind, different from what is excited by the term *nothing*.

81. You will reply perhaps, that in the foresaid definition is included, what doth sufficiently distinguish it from nothing, the positive, abstract idea of *quiddity*, *entity*, or *existence*. I own indeed, that those who pretend to the faculty of framing abstract general ideas, do talk as if they had such an idea, which is, say they, the most abstract and general notion of all, that is to me the most incomprehensible of all others. That there are a great variety of spirits of different orders and capacities, whose faculties, both in number and extent, are far exceeding those the Author of my being has bestowed on me, I see no reason to deny. And for me to pretend to determine by my own few, stinted, narrow inlets of perception, what ideas the inexhaustible power of the Supreme Spirit may imprint upon them, were certainly the utmost folly and presumption. Since there may be, for aught that I know, innumerable sorts of ideas or sensations, as different from one another, and from all that I have perceived, as colours are from sounds. But how ready soever I may be, to acknowledge the scantiness of my comprehension, with regard to the endless variety of spirits and ideas, that might possibly exist, yet for any one to pretend to a notion of entity or existence, *abstracted* from *spirit* and *idea*, from perceiving and being perceived, is, I suspect, a downright repugnancy and trifling with words. It remains that we consider the objections, which may possibly be made on the part of religion.

82. Some there are* who think, that though the arguments for the real existence of bodies, which are drawn from reason, be allowed not to amount to demonstration, yet the Holy

Scriptures are so clear in the point, as will sufficiently convince every good Christian, that bodies do really exist, and are something more that mere ideas; there being in Holy Writ innumerable facts related, which evidently suppose the reality of timber, and stone, mountains, and rivers, and cities, and human bodies. To which I answer, that no sort of writings whatever, sacred or profane, which use those and the like words in the vulgar acceptation, or so as to have a meaning in them, are in danger of having their truth called in question by our doctrine. That all those things do really exist, that there are bodies, even corporeal substances, when taken in the vulgar sense, has been shown to be agreeable to our principles: and the difference betwixt *things* and *ideas, realities* and *chimeras*, has been distinctly explained. And I do not think, that either what philosophers call *matter*, or the existence of objects without the mind, is anywhere mentioned in Scripture.

83. Again, whether there be, or be not external things, it is agreed on all hands, that the proper use of words, is the marking out conceptions, or things only as they are known and perceived by us; whence it plainly follows, that in the tenets we have laid down, there is nothing inconsistent with the right use and significancy of *language*, and that discourse of what kind soever, so far as it is intelligible, remains undisturbed. But all this seems so manifest, from what hath been set forth in the premises, that it is needless to insist any farther on it.

84. But it will be urged, that miracles do, at least, lose much of their stress and import by our principles. What must we think of Moses's rod, was it not *really* turned into a serpent, or was there only a change of *ideas* in the minds of the spectators? And can it be supposed, that our Saviour did no more at the marriage-feast in Cana, than impose on the sight, and smell, and taste of the guests, so as to create in them the appearance or idea only of wine? The same may be said of all other miracles: which, in consequence of the foregoing principles, must be looked upon only as so many cheats, or illusion of fancy. To this I reply, that the rod was changed into a real serpent, and the water into real wine. That this doth not, in

the least, contradict what I have elsewhere said, will be evident from sects. 34 and 35. But this business of *real* and *imaginary* hath been already so plainly and fully explained, and so often referred to, and the difficulties about it are so easily answered from what hath gone before, that it were an affront to the reader's understanding, to resume the explication of it in this place. I shall only observe, that if at table all who were present should see, and smell, and taste, and drink wine, and find the effects of it, with me there could be no doubt of its reality. So that, at bottom, the scruple concerning real miracles hath no place at all on ours, but only on the received principles, and consequently maketh rather *for*, than *against* what hath been said.

85. Having done with the objections, which I endeavoured to propose in the clearest light, and gave them all the force and weight I could, we proceed in the next place to take a view of our tenets in their consequences. Some of these appear at first sight, as that several difficult and obscure questions, on which abundance of speculation hath been thrown away, are entirely banished from philosophy. Whether corporeal substance can think? Whether matter be infinitely divisible? And how it operates on spirit? these and the like inquiries have given infinite amusement to philosophers in all ages. But depending on the existence of *matter*, they have no longer any place on our principles. Many other advantages there are, as well with regard to *religion* as the *sciences*, which it is easy for anyone to deduce from what hath been premised. But this will appear more plainly in the sequel.

86. From the principles we have laid down, it follows, human knowledge may naturally be reduced to two heads, that of *ideas*, and that of *spirits*. Of each of these I shall treat in order. And first as to ideas or unthinking things, our knowledge of these hath been very much obscured and confounded, and we have been led into very dangerous errors, by supposing a twofold existence of the objects of sense, the one *intelligible*, or in the mind, the other *real* and without the mind: whereby unthinking things are thought to have a natural subsistence of their own, distinct from being perceived by spirits. This which, if I mistake not, hath been shewn to be a

most groundless and absurd notion, is the very root of *scepticism*; for so long as men thought that real things subsisted without the mind, and that their knowledge was only so far forth *real* as it was conformable to *real things*, it follows, they could not be certain that they had any real knowledge at all. For how can it be known, that the things which are perceived, are conformable to those which are not perceived, or exist without the mind?

87. Colour, figure, motion, extension and the like, considered only as so many *sensations* in the mind, are perfectly known, there being nothing in them which is not perceived. But if they are looked on as notes or images, referred to *things* or *archetypes** existing without the mind, then are we involved all in *scepticism*. We see only the appearances, and not the real qualities of things. What may be the extension, figure, or motion of anything really and absolutely, or in itself, it is impossible for us to know, but only the proportion or the relation they bear to our senses. Things remaining the same, our ideas vary, and which of them, or even whether any of them at all represent the true quality really existing in the thing, it is out of our reach to determine. So that, for aught we know, all we see, hear, and feel, may be only phantom and vain chimera, and not at all agree with the real things, existing in *rerum natura*. All this scepticism follows, from our supposing a difference between *things* and *ideas*, and that the former have a subsistence without the mind, or unperceived. It were easy to dilate on this subject, and shew how the arguments urged by *sceptics* in all ages, depend on the supposition of external objects.

88. So long as we attribute a real existence to unthinking things, distinct from their being perceived, it is not only impossible for us to know with evidence the nature of any real unthinking being, but even that it exists. Hence it is, that we see philosophers distrust their senses, and doubt of the existence of heaven and earth, of everything they see or feel, even of their own bodies. And after all their labour and struggle of thought, they are forced to own, we cannot attain to any self-evident or demonstrative knowledge of the existence of sensible things. But all this doubtfulness, which so bewilders and

confounds the mind, and makes *philosophy* ridiculous in the eyes of the world, vanishes, if we annex a meaning to our words, and do not amuse ourselves with the terms *absolute, external, exist*, and such like, signifying we know not what. I can as well doubt of my own being, as of the being of those things which I actually perceive by sense: it being a manifest contradiction, that any sensible object should be immediately perceived by sight or touch, and at the same time have no existence in Nature, since the very existence of an unthinking being consists in *being perceived*.

89. Nothing seems of more importance, towards erecting a firm system of sound and real knowledge, which may be proof against the assaults of *scepticism*, than to lay the beginning in a distinct explication of what is meant by *thing, reality, existence*: for in vain shall we dispute concerning the real existence of things, or pretend to any knowledge thereof, so long as we have not fixed the meaning of those words. *Thing* or *being* is the most general name of all, it comprehends under it two kinds entirely distinct and heterogeneous, and which have nothing common but the name, to wit, *spirits* and *ideas*. The former are *active, indivisible substances*: the latter are *inert, fleeting, dependent beings*, which subsist not by themselves, but are supported by, or exist in minds or spiritual substances. We comprehend our own existence by inward feeling or reflexion, and that of other spirits by reason.* We may be said to have some knowledge or notion of our own minds, of spirits and active beings, whereof in a strict sense we have not ideas. In like manner we know and have a notion of relations between things or ideas, which relations are distinct from the ideas or things related, inasmuch as the latter may be perceived by us without our perceiving the former. To me it seems that ideas, spirits and relations are all in their respective kinds, the object of human knowledge and subject of discourse: and that the term *idea* would be improperly extended to signify everything we know or have any notion of.

90. Ideas imprinted on the senses are real things, or do really exist; this we do not deny, but we deny they can subsist without the minds which perceive them, or that they are resemblances of any archetypes existing without the mind: since

the very being of a sensation or idea consists in being perceived, and an idea can be like nothing but an idea. Again, the things perceived by sense may be termed *external*, with regard to their origin, in that they are not generated from within, by the mind itself, but imprinted by a spirit distinct from that which perceives them. Sensible objects may likewise be said to be without the mind, in another sense, namely when they exist in some other mind. Thus when I shut my eyes, the things I saw may still exist, but it must be in another mind.*

91. It were a mistake to think, that what is here said derogates in the least from the reality of things. It is acknowledged on the received principles, that extension, motion, and in a word all sensible qualities, have need of a support, as not being able to subsist by themselves. But the objects perceived by sense, are allowed to be nothing but combinations of those qualities, and consequently cannot subsist by themselves. Thus far it is agreed on all hands. So that in denying the things perceived by sense, an existence independent of a substance, or support wherein they may exist, we detract nothing from the received opinion of their *reality*, and are guilty of no innovation in that respect. All the difference is, that according to us the unthinking beings perceived by sense, have no existence distinct from being perceived, and cannot therefore exist in any other substance, than those unextended, indivisible substances, or *spirits*, which act, and think, and perceive them: whereas philosophers vulgarly hold, that the sensible qualities exist in an inert, extended, unperceiving substance, which they call *matter*, to which they attribute a natural subsistence, exterior to all thinking beings, or distinct from being perceived by any mind whatsoever, even the eternal mind of the Creator, wherein they suppose only ideas of the corporeal substances created by him: if indeed they allow them to be at all created.

92. For as we have shewn the doctrine of matter or corporeal substance, to have been the main pillar and support of *scepticism*, so likewise upon the same foundation have been raised all the impious schemes of *atheism* and irreligion. Nay so great a difficulty hath it been thought, to conceive matter produced out of nothing, that the most celebrated among the

ancient philosophers, even of these who maintained the being of a God, have thought matter to be uncreated and coeternal* with him. How great a friend material substance hath been to *atheists* in all ages, were needless to relate. All their monstrous systems have so visible and necessary a dependence on it, that when this corner-stone is once removed, the whole fabric cannot choose but fall to the ground; insomuch that it is no longer worthwhile, to bestow a particular consideration on the absurdities of every wretched sect of *atheists*.

93. That impious and profane persons should readily fall in with those systems which favour their inclinations, by deriding immaterial substance, and supposing the soul to be divisible and subject to corruption as the body; which exclude all freedom, intelligence, and design from the formation of things, and instead thereof make a self-existent, stupid, unthinking substance the root and origin of all beings. That they should hearken to those who deny a providence, or inspection of a superior mind over the affairs of the world, attributing the whole series of events either to blind chance or fatal necessity, arising from the impulse of one body on another. All this is very natural. And on the other hand, when men of better principles observe the enemies of religion lay so great a stress on *unthinking matter*, and all of them use so much industry and artifice to reduce everything to it; methinks they should rejoice to see them deprived of their grand support, and driven from that only fortress, without which your Epicureans, Hobbists, and the like, have not even the shadow of a pretence, but become the most cheap and easy triumph in the world.

94. The existence of matter, or bodies unperceived, has not only been the main support of *atheists* and *fatalists*, but on the same principle doth *idolatry* likewise in all its various forms depend. Did men but consider that the sun, moon, and stars, and every other object of the senses, are only so many sensations in their minds, which have no other existence but barely being perceived, doubtless they would never fall down, and worship their own *ideas*; but rather address their homage to that eternal invisible Mind which produces and sustains all things.*

95. The same absurd principle, by mingling itself with the articles of our faith, hath occasioned no small difficulties to Christians. For example, about the *resurrection*, how many scruples and objections have been raised by Socinians* and others? But do not the most plausible of them depend on the supposition, that a body is denominated the *same*, with regard not to the form or that which is perceived by sense, but the material substance which remains the same under several forms? Take away this *material substance*, about the identity whereof all the dispute is, and mean by *body* what every plain ordinary person means by that word, to wit, that which is immediately seen and felt, which is only a combination of sensible qualities, or ideas: and then their most unanswerable objections come to nothing.

96. Matter being once expelled out of Nature, drags with it so many sceptical and impious notions, such an incredible number of disputes and puzzling questions, which have been thorns in the sides of divines, as well as philosophers, and made so much fruitless work for mankind; that if the arguments we have produced against it, are not found equal to demonstration (as to me they evidently seem) yet I am sure all friends to knowledge, peace, and religion, have reason to wish they were.

97. Beside the external existence of the objects of perception, another great source of errors and difficulties, with regard to ideal knowledge, is the doctrine of *abstract ideas*, such as it hath been set forth in the Introduction. The plainest things in the world, those we are most intimately acquainted with, and perfectly know, when they are considered in an abstract way, appear strangely difficult and incomprehensible. Time, place, and motion, taken in particular or concrete, are what everybody knows; but having passed through the hands of a metaphysician, they become too abstract and fine, to be apprehended by men of ordinary sense. Bid your servant meet you at such a *time*, in such a *place*, and he shall never stay to deliberate on the meaning of those words: in conceiving that particular time and place, or the motion by which he is to get thither, he finds not the least difficulty. But if *time* be

taken, exclusive of all those particular actions and ideas that diversify the day, merely for the continuation of existence, or duration in abstract, then it will perhaps gravel even a philosopher to comprehend it.

98. Whenever I attempt to frame a simple idea of *time*, abstracted from the succession of ideas in my mind, which flows uniformly, and is participated by all beings, I am lost and embrangled in inextricable difficulties. I have no notion of it at all, only I hear others say, it is infinitely divisible, and speak of it in such a manner as leads me to entertain odd thoughts of my existence: since that doctrine lays one under an absolute necessity of thinking, either that he passes away innumerable ages without a thought, or else that he is annihilated every moment of his life: both which seem equally absurd. Time therefore being nothing, abstracted from the succession of ideas in our minds,* it follows that the duration of any finite spirit must be estimated by the number of ideas or actions succeeding each other in that same spirit or mind. Hence it is a plain consequence that the soul always thinks:* and in truth whoever shall go about to divide in his thoughts, or abstract the *existence* of a spirit from its *cogitation*, will, I believe, find it no easy task.

99. So likewise, when we attempt to abstract extension and motion from all other qualities, and consider them by themselves, we presently lose sight of them, and run into great extravagancies. All which depend on a two-fold abstraction: first, it is supposed that extension, for example, may be abstracted from all other sensible qualities; and secondly, that the entity of extension may be abstracted from its being perceived. But whoever shall reflect, and take care to understand what he says, will, if I mistake not, acknowledge that all sensible qualities are alike *sensations*, and alike *real*; that where the extension is, there is the colour too, to wit, in his mind, and that their archetypes can exist only in some other *mind*: and that the objects of sense are nothing but those sensations combined, blended, or (if one may so speak) concreted together: none of all which can be supposed to exist unperceived.

100. What it is for a man to be happy, or an object good,* everyone may think he knows. But to frame an abstract idea of *happiness*, prescinded from all particular pleasure, or of *goodness*, from everything that is good, this is what few can pretend to. So likewise, a man may be just and virtuous, without having precise ideas of *justice* and *virtue*. The opinion that those and the like words stand for general notions abstracted from all particular persons and actions, seems to have rendered morality difficult, and the study thereof of less use to mankind. And in effect, the doctrine of *abstraction* has not a little contributed towards spoiling the most useful parts of knowledge.

101. The two great provinces of speculative science, conversant about ideas received from sense and their relations, are *natural philosophy* and *mathematics*; with regard to each of these I shall make some observations. And first, I shall say somewhat of natural philosophy. On this subject it is, that the *sceptics* triumph: all that stock of arguments they produce to depreciate our faculties, and make mankind appear ignorant and low, are drawn principally from this head, to wit, that we are under an invincible blindness as to the *true* and *real* nature of things. This they exaggerate, and love to enlarge on. We are miserably bantered, say they, by our senses, and amused only with the outside and shew of things. The real essence, the internal qualities, and constitution of every the meanest object, is hid from our view; something there is in every drop of water, every grain of sand, which it is beyond the power of human understanding to fathom or comprehend. But it is evident from what has been shewn, that all this complaint is groundless, and that we are influenced by false principles to that degree as to mistrust our senses, and think we know nothing of those things which we perfectly comprehend.

102. One great inducement to our pronouncing ourselves ignorant of the nature of things, is the current opinion that everything includes within itself the cause of its properties: or that there is in each object an inward essence, which is the source whence its discernible qualities flow, and whereon they depend. Some have pretended to account for appearances by occult qualities, but of late they are mostly resolved into

mechanical causes, to wit, the figure, motion, weight, and such like qualities of insensible particles:* whereas in truth, there is no other agent or efficient cause than *spirit*, it being evident that motion, as well as all other *ideas*, is perfectly inert. See sect. 25. Hence, to endeavour to explain the production of colours or sounds, by figure, motion, magnitude and the like, must needs be labour in vain. And accordingly, we see the attempts of that kind are not at all satisfactory. Which may be said, in general, of those instances, wherein one idea or quality is assigned for the cause of another. I need not say, how many *hypotheses* and speculations are left out, and how much the study of Nature is abridged by this doctrine.

103. The great mechanical principle now in vogue is *attraction*. That a stone falls to the earth, or the sea swells towards the moon, may to some appear sufficiently explained thereby. But how are we enlightened by being told this is done by attraction? Is it that that word signifies the manner of the tendency, and that it is by the mutual drawing of bodies, instead of their being impelled or protruded towards each other? But nothing is determined of the manner or action, and it may as truly (for aught we know) be termed *impulse* or *protrusion* as *attraction*. Again, the parts of steel we see cohere firmly together, and this also is accounted for by attraction; but in this, as in the other instances, I do not perceive that anything is signified besides the effect itself; for as to the manner of the action whereby it is produced, or the cause which produces it, these are not so much as aimed at.

104. Indeed, if we take a view of the several phenomena, and compare them together, we may observe some likeness and conformity between them. For example, in the falling of a stone to the ground, in the rising of the sea towards the moon, in cohesion and crystallization, there is something alike, namely an union or mutual approach of bodies. So that any one of these or the like phenomena, may not seem strange or surprising to a man who hath nicely observed and compared the effects of Nature. For that only is thought so which is uncommon, or a thing by itself, and out of the ordinary course of our observation. That bodies should tend towards the centre of the earth, is not thought strange, because it is

what we perceive every moment of our lives. But that they should have a like gravitation towards the centre of the moon, may seem odd and unaccountable to most men, because it is discerned only in the tides. But a philosopher, whose thoughts take in a larger compass of Nature, having observed a certain similitude of appearances, as well in the heavens as the earth, that argue innumerable bodies to have a mutual tendency towards each other, which he denotes by the general name *attraction*, whatever can be reduced to that, he thinks justly accounted for. Thus he explains the tides by the attraction of the terraqueous globe towards the moon, which to him doth not appear odd or anomalous, but only a particular example of a general rule or law of Nature.

105. If therefore we consider the difference there is betwixt natural philosophers and other men, with regard to their knowledge of the phenomena, we shall find it consists, not in an exacter knowledge of the efficient cause that produces them, for that can be no other than the *will of a spirit*, but only in a greater largeness of comprehension, whereby analogies, harmonies, and agreements are discovered in the works of Nature, and the particular effects explained, that is, reduced to general rules, see sect. 62, which rules grounded on the analogy, and uniformness observed in the production of natural effects, are most agreeable, and sought after by the mind; for that they extend our prospect beyond what is present, and near to us, and enable us to make very probable conjectures, touching things that may have happened at very great distances of time and place, as well as to predict things to come; which sort of endeavour towards omniscience, is much affected by the mind.

106. But we should proceed warily in such things: for we are apt to lay too great a stress on analogies, and to the prejudice of truth, humour that eagerness of the mind, whereby it is carried to extend its knowledge into general theorems. For example, gravitation, or mutual attraction, because it appears in many instances, some are straightway for pronouncing *universal*;* and that to *attract, and be attracted by every other body, is an essential quality inherent in all bodies whatsoever*. Whereas it appears the fixed stars have no such

tendency towards each other: and so far is that gravitation, from being *essential* to bodies, that, in some instances a quite contrary principle seems to shew itself: as in the perpendicular growth of plants, and the elasticity of the air. There is nothing necessary or essential in the case, but it depends entirely on the will of the *governing spirit*, who causes certain bodies to cleave together, or tend towards each other, according to various laws, whilst he keeps others at a fixed distance; and to some he gives a quite contrary tendency to fly asunder, just as he sees convenient.

107. After what has been premised, I think we may lay down the following conclusions. First, it is plain philosophers amuse themselves in vain, when they inquire for any natural efficient cause, distinct from a *mind* or *spirit*. Secondly, considering the whole creation is the workmanship of a *wise and good agent*, it should seem to become philosophers, to employ their thoughts (contrary to what some hold) about the final causes of things: and I must confess, I see no reason, why pointing out the various ends, to which natural things are adapted, and for which they were originally with unspeakable wisdom contrived, should not be thought one good way of accounting for them, and altogether worthy a philosopher. Thirdly, from what hath been premised no reason can be drawn, why the history of Nature should not still be studied, and observations and experiments made, which, that they are of use to mankind, and enable us to draw any general conclusions, is not the result of any immutable habitudes, or relations between things themselves, but only of God's goodness and kindness to men in the administration of the world. See sects. 30 and 31. Fourthly, by a diligent observation of the phenomena within our view, we may discover the general laws of Nature, and from them deduce the other phenomena, I do not say *demonstrate*; for all deductions of that kind depend on a supposition that the Author of Nature always operates uniformly, and in a constant observance of those rules we take for principles: which we cannot evidently know.

108. Those men* who frame general rules from the phenomena, and afterwards derive the phenomena from those rules, seem to consider signs rather than causes. A man

may well understand natural signs without knowing their analogy, or being able to say by what rule a thing is so or so. And as it is very possible to write improperly, through too strict an observance of general grammar-rules: so in arguing from general rules of Nature, it is not impossible we may extend the analogy too far, and by that means run into mistakes.

109. As in reading other books, a wise man will choose to fix his thoughts on the sense and apply it to use, rather than lay them out in grammatical remarks on the language; so in perusing the volume of Nature, it seems beneath the dignity of the mind to affect an exactness in reducing each particular phenomenon to general rules, or shewing how it follows from them. We should propose to ourselves nobler views, such as to recreate and exalt the mind, with a prospect of the beauty, order, extent, and variety of natural things: hence, by proper inferences, to enlarge our notions of the grandeur, wisdom, and beneficence of the Creator: and lastly, to make the several parts of the Creation, so far as in us lies, subservient to the ends they were designed for, God's glory, and the sustentation and comfort of ourselves and fellow-creatures.

110. The best key for the aforesaid analogy, or natural science, will be easily acknowledged to be a certain celebrated treatise of *mechanics*: in the entrance of which justly admired treatise,* time, space and motion, are distinguished into *absolute* and *relative*, *true* and *apparent*, *mathematical* and *vulgar*: which distinction, as it is at large explained by the author, doth suppose those quantities to have an existence without the mind; and that they are ordinarily conceived with relation to sensible things, to which nevertheless in their own nature, they bear no relation at all.

111. As for *time*, as it is there taken in an absolute or abstracted sense, for the duration or perseverance of the existence of things, I have nothing more to add concerning it, after what hath been already said on that subject, sects. 97 and 98. For the rest, this celebrated author holds there is an *absolute space*, which, being unperceivable to sense, remains in itself similar and immoveable: and relative space to be the measure

thereof, which being moveable, and defined by its situation in respect of sensible bodies, is vulgarly taken for immoveable space. *Place* he defines to be that part of space which is occupied by any body. And according as the space is absolute or relative, so also is the place. *Absolute motion* is said to be the translation of a body from absolute place to absolute place, as relative motion is from one relative place to another. And because the parts of absolute space, do not fall under our senses, instead of them we are obliged to use their sensible measures: and so define both place and motion with respect to bodies, which we regard as immoveable. But it is said, in philosophical matters we must abstract from our senses, since it may be, that none of those bodies which seem to be quiescent, are truly so: and the same thing which is moved relatively, may be really at rest. As likewise one and the same body may be in relative rest and motion, or even moved with contrary relative motions at the same time, according as its place is variously defined. All which ambiguity is to be found in the apparent motions, but not at all in the true or absolute, which should therefore be alone regarded in philosophy. And the true, we are told, are distinguished from apparent or relative motions by the following properties. First, in true or absolute motion, all parts which preserve the same position with respect to the whole, partake of the motions of the whole, Secondly, the place being moved, that which is placed therein is also moved: so that a body moving in a place which is in motion, doth participate the motion of its place. Thirdly, true motion is never generated or changed, otherwise than by force impressed on the body itself. Fourthly, true motion is always changed by force impressed on the body moved. Fifthly, in circular motion barely relative, there is no centrifugal force, which nevertheless in that which is true or absolute, is proportional to the quantity of motion.

112. But notwithstanding what hath been said, it doth not appear to me, that there can be any motion other than *relative*: so that to conceive motion, there must be at least conceived two bodies, whereof the distance or position in regard to each other is varied. Hence if there was one only body

in being, it could not possibly be moved. This seems evident, in that the idea I have of motion doth necessarily include relation.

113. But though in every motion it be necessary to conceive more bodies than one, yet it may be that one only is moved, namely that on which the force causing the change of distance is impressed, or in other words, that to which the action is applied. For however some may define relative motion, so as to term that body *moved*, which changes its distance from some other body, whether the force or action causing that change were applied to it, or no: yet as relative motion is that which is perceived by sense, and regarded in the ordinary affairs of life, it should seem that every man of common sense knows what it is, as well as the best philosopher: now I ask anyone, whether in his sense of motion as he walks along the streets, the stones he passes over may be said to *move*, because they change distance with his feet? To me it seems, that though motion includes a relation of one thing to another, yet it is not necessary that each term of the relation be denominated from it. As a man may think of somewhat which doth not think, so a body may be moved to or from another body, which is not therefore itself in motion.

114. As the place happens to be variously defined, the motion which is related to it varies. A man in a ship may be said to be quiescent, with relation to the sides of the vessel, and yet move with relation to the land. Or he may move eastward in respect of the one, and westward in respect of the other. In the common affairs of life, men never go beyond the earth to define the place of any body: and what is quiescent in respect of that, is accounted *absolutely* to be so. But philosophers who have a greater extent of thought, and juster notions of the system of things, discover even the earth itself to be moved. In order therefore to fix their notions, they seem to conceive the corporeal world as finite, and the utmost unmoved walls or shell thereof to be the place, whereby they estimate true motions. If we sound our own conceptions, I believe we may find all the absolute motion we can frame an idea of, to be at bottom no other than relative motion thus defined. For as hath been already observed, absolute motion

exclusive of all external relation is incomprehensible: and to this kind of relative motion, all the above-mentioned properties, causes, and effects ascribed to absolute motion, will, if I mistake not, be found to agree. As to what is said of the centrifugal force, that it doth not at all belong to circular relative motion: I do not see how this follows from the experiment* which is brought to prove it. See *Philosophiae Naturalis Principia Mathematica, in Schol. Def.* VIII. For the water in the vessel, at that time wherein it is said to have the greatest relative circular motion, hath, I think, no motion at all: as is plain from the foregoing section.

115. For to denominate a body *moved*, it is requisite, first, that it change its distance or situation with regard to some other body: and secondly, that the force or action occasioning that change be applied to it. If either of these be wanting, I do not think that agreeably to the sense of mankind, or the propriety of language, a body can be said to be in motion. I grant indeed, that it is possible for us to think a body, which we see change its distance from some other, to be moved, though it have no force applied to it (in which sense there may be apparent motion), but then it is, because the force causing the change of distance, is imagined by us to be applied or impressed on that body thought to move. Which indeed shews we are capable of mistaking a thing to be in motion which is not, and that is all.

116. From what hath been said, it follows that the philosophic consideration of motion doth not imply the being of an *absolute space*, distinct from that which is perceived by sense, and related to bodies: which that it cannot exist without the mind, is clear upon the same principles, that demonstrate the like of all other objects of sense. And perhaps, if we inquire narrowly, we shall find we cannot even frame an idea of *pure space*, exclusive of all body. This I must confess seems impossible, as being a most abstract idea. When I excite a motion in some part of my body, if it be free or without resistance, I say there is *space:* but if I find a resistance, then I say there is *body:* and in proportion as the resistance to motion is lesser or greater, I say the *space* is more or less *pure.* So that when I speak of pure or empty space, it is not to be

supposed, that the word *space* stands for an idea distinct from, or conceivable without body and motion. Though indeed we are apt to think every noun substantive stands for a distinct idea, that may be separated from all others: which hath occasioned infinite mistakes. When therefore supposing all the world to be annihilated besides my own body, I say there still remains *pure space*: thereby nothing else is meant, but only that I conceive it possible, for the limbs of my body to be moved on all sides without the least resistance: but if that too were annihilated, then there could be no motion, and consequently no space. Some perhaps may think the sense of seeing doth furnish them with the idea of pure space; but it is plain from what we have elsewhere shewn, that the ideas of space and distance are not obtained by that sense. See the *Essay concerning Vision*.

117. What is here laid down, seems to put an end to all those disputes and difficulties, which have sprung up amongst the learned concerning the nature of *pure space*. But the chief advantage arising from it, is, that we are freed from that dangerous *dilemma*, to which several who have employed their thoughts* on this subject, imagine themselves reduced, to wit, of thinking either that real space is God, or else that there is something beside God which is eternal, uncreated, infinite, indivisible, immutable. Both which may justly be thought pernicious and absurd notions. It is certain that not a few divines, as well as philosophers of great note, have, from the difficulty they found in conceiving either limits or annihilation of space, concluded it must be *divine*. And some of late have set themselves particularly to shew, that the incommunicable attributes of God agree to it. Which doctrine, how unworthy soever it may seem of the Divine Nature, yet I do not see how we can get clear of it, so long as we adhere to the received opinions.

118. Hitherto of natural philosophy: we come now to make some inquiry concerning that other great branch of speculative knowledge, to wit, *mathematics*. These, how celebrated soever they may be, for their clearness and certainty of demonstration, which is hardly anywhere else to be found, cannot nevertheless be supposed altogether free from mistakes; if in

their principles there lurks some secret error, which is common to the professors of those sciences with the rest of mankind. Mathematicians, though they deduce their theorems from a great height of evidence, yet their first principles are limited by the consideration of quantity: and they do not ascend into any inquiry concerning those transcendental maxims, which influence all the particular sciences, each part whereof, mathematics not excepted, doth consequently participate of the errors involved in them. That the principles laid down by mathematicians are true, and their way of deduction from those principles clear and incontestable, we do not deny. But we hold, there may be certain erroneous maxims of greater extent than the object of mathematics, and for that reason not expressly mentioned, though tacitly supposed throughout the whole progress of that science; and that the ill effects of those secret unexamined errors are diffused through all the branches thereof. To be plain, we suspect the mathematicians are, as well as other men, concerned in the errors arising from the doctrine of abstract general ideas, and the existence of objects without the mind.

119. *Arithmetic* hath been thought to have for its object abstract ideas of *number*. Of which to understand the properties and mutual habitudes is supposed no mean part of speculative knowledge. The opinion of the pure and intellectual nature of numbers in abstract, hath made them in esteem with those philosophers, who seem to have affected an uncommon fineness and elevation of thought. It hath set a price on the most trifling numerical speculations which in practice are of no use, but serve only for amusement: and hath therefore so far infected the minds of some, that they have dreamt of mighty *mysteries* involved in numbers, and attempted the explication of natural things by them. But if we inquire into our own thoughts, and consider what hath been premised, we may perhaps entertain a low opinion of those high flights and abstractions, and look on all inquiries about numbers, only as so many *difficiles nugae*,* so far as they are not subservient to practice, and promote the benefit of life.

120. Unity in abstract we have before considered in sect. 13, from which and what hath been said in the Introduction,

it plainly follows there is not any such idea. But number being defined a *collection of units*, we may conclude that, if there be no such thing as unity or unit in abstract, there are no ideas of number in abstract denoted by the numerical names and figures. The theories therefore in arithmetic, if they are abstracted from the names and figures, as likewise from all use and practice, as well as from the particular things numbered, can be supposed to have nothing at all for their object. Hence we may see, how entirely the science of numbers is subordinate to practice, and how jejune and trifling it becomes, when considered as a matter of mere speculation.

121. However since there may be some, who, deluded by the specious shew of discovering abstracted verities, waste their time in arithmetical theorems and problems which have not any use: it will not be amiss, if we more fully consider, and expose the vanity of that pretence; and this will plainly appear, by taking a view of arithmetic in its infancy, and observing what it was that originally put men on the study of that science, and to what scope they directed it. It is natural to think that at first, men, for ease of memory and help of computation, made use of counters, or in writing of single strokes, points or the like, each whereof was made to signify an unit, that is, some one thing of whatever kind they had occasion to reckon. Afterwards they found out the more compendious ways, of making one character stand in place of several strokes, or points. And lastly, the notation of the Arabians or Indians came into use, wherein by the repetition of a few characters or figures, and varying the signification of each figure according to the place it obtains, all numbers may be most aptly expressed: which seems to have been done in imitation of language, so that an exact analogy is observed betwixt the notation by figures and names, the nine simple figures answering the nine first numeral names and places in the former, corresponding to denominations in the latter. And agreeably to those conditions of the simple and local value of figures, were contrived methods of finding from the given figures or marks of the parts, what figures and how placed, are proper to denote the whole or *vice versa*. And having found the sought figures, the same rule or analogy

being observed throughout, it is easy to read them into words; and so the number becomes perfectly known. For then the number of any particular things is said to be known, when we know the name or figures (with their due arrangement) that according to the standing analogy belong to them. For these signs being known, we can by the operations of arithmetic, know the signs of any part of the particular sums signified by them; and thus computing in signs (because of the connexion established betwixt them and the distinct multitudes of things, whereof one is taken for an unit), we may be able rightly to sum up, divide, and proportion the things themselves that we intend to number.

122. In *arithmetic* therefore we regard not the *things* but the *signs*, which nevertheless are not regarded for their own sake, but because they direct us how to act with relation to things, and dispose rightly of them. Now agreeably to what we have before observed, of words in general (sect. 19. Introd.) it happens here likewise, that abstract ideas are thought to be signified by numeral names or characters, while they do not suggest ideas of particular things to our minds. I shall not at present enter into a more particular dissertation on this subject; but only observe that it is evident from what hath been said, those things which pass for abstract truths and theorems concerning numbers, are, in reality, conversant about no object distinct from particular numerable things, except only names and characters; which originally came to be considered, on no other account but their being *signs*, or capable to represent aptly, whatever particular things men had need to compute. Whence it follows, that to study them for their own sake* would be just as wise, and to as good purpose, as if a man, neglecting the true use or original intention and subserviency of language, should spend his time in impertinent criticisms upon words, or reasonings and controversies purely verbal.

123. From numbers we proceed to speak of *extension*, which considered as relative, is the object of geometry. The *infinite* divisibility of *finite* extension, though it is not expressly laid down, either as an axiom or theorem in the elements of that science, yet is throughout the same everywhere

supposed, and thought to have so inseparable and essential a connexion with the principles and demonstrations in geometry, that mathematicians never admit it into doubt, or make the least question of it. And as this notion is the source from whence do spring all those amusing geometrical paradoxes, which have such a direct repugnancy to the plain common sense of mankind, and are admitted with so much reluctance into a mind not yet debauched by learning: so is it the principal occasion of all that nice and extreme subtlety, which renders the study of *mathematics* so difficult and tedious. Hence if we can make it appear, that no finite extension contains innumerable parts, or is infinitely divisible, it follows that we shall at once clear the science of geometry from a great number of difficulties and contradictions, which have ever been esteemed a reproach to human reason, and withal make the attainment thereof a business of much less time and pains, than it hitherto hath been.

124. Every particular finite extension, which may possibly be the object of our thought, is an *idea* existing only in the mind, and consequently each part thereof must be perceived. If therefore I cannot perceive innumerable parts in any finite extension that I consider, it is certain they are not contained in it: but it is evident, that I cannot distinguish innumerable parts in any particular line, surface, or solid, which I either perceive by sense, or figure to myself in my mind: wherefore I conclude they are not contained in it. Nothing can be plainer to me, than that the extensions I have in view are no other than my own ideas, and it is no less plain, that I cannot resolve any one of my ideas into an infinite number of other ideas, that is, that they are not infinitely divisible. If by *finite extension* be meant something distinct from a finite idea, I declare I do not know what that is, and so cannot affirm or deny anything of it. But if the terms *extension, parts*, and the like, are taken in any sense conceivable, that is, for ideas; then to say a finite quantity or extension consists of parts infinite in number, is so manifest a contradiction, that everyone at first sight acknowledges it to be so. And it is impossible it should ever gain the assent of any reasonable creature, who is not brought to it by gentle and slow degrees, as a converted Gentile to the belief

of *transubstantiation*. Ancient and rooted prejudices do often pass into principles: and those propositions which once obtain the force and credit of a *principle*, are not only themselves, but likewise whatever is deducible from them, thought privileged from all examination. And there is no absurdity so gross, which by this means the mind of man may not be prepared to swallow.

125. He whose understanding is prepossessed with the doctrine of abstract general ideas, may be persuaded, that (whatever be thought of the ideas of sense), extension in *abstract* is infinitely divisible. And one who thinks the objects of sense exist without the mind, will perhaps in virtue thereof be brought to admit, that a line but an inch long may contain innumerable parts really existing, though too small to be discerned. These errors are grafted as well in the minds of *geometricians*, as of other men, and have a like influence on their reasonings; and it were no difficult thing, to shew how the arguments from geometry made use of to support the infinite divisibility of extension, are bottomed on them. At present we shall only observe in general, whence it is that the mathematicians are all so fond and tenacious of this doctrine.

126. It hath been observed in another place, that the theorems and demonstrations in geometry are conversant about universal ideas (sect. 15. Introd.). Where it is explained in what sense this ought to be understood, to wit, that the particular lines and figures included in the diagram, are supposed to stand for innumerable others of different sizes: or in other words, the geometer considers them abstracting from their magnitude: which doth not imply that he forms an abstract idea, but only that he cares not what the particular magnitude is, whether great or small, but looks on that as a thing indifferent to the demonstration: hence it follows, that a line in the scheme, but an inch long, must be spoken of, as though it contained ten thousand parts, since it is regarded not in itself, but as it is universal; and it is universal only in its signification, whereby it represents innumerable lines greater than itself, in which may be distinguished ten thousand parts or more, though there may not be above an inch in it. After this manner the properties of the lines signified are (by a very usual

figure) transferred to the sign, and thence through mistake thought to appertain to it considered in its own nature.

127. Because there is no number of parts so great, but it is possible there may be a line containing more, the inch-line is said to contain parts more than any assignable number; which is true, not of the inch taken absolutely, but only for the things signified by it. But men not retaining that distinction in their thoughts, slide into a belief that the small particular line described on paper contains in itself parts innumerable. There is no such thing as the ten-thousandth part of an *inch*;* but there is of a *mile* or *diameter of the earth*, which may be signified by that inch. When therefore I delineate a triangle on paper, and take one side not above an inch, for example, in length to be the *radius*: this I consider as divided into ten thousand or an hundred thousand parts, or more. For though the ten-thousandth part of that line considered in itself, is nothing at all, and consequently may be neglected without any error or inconveniency; yet these described lines being only marks standing for greater quantities, whereof it may be the ten-thousandth part is very considerable, it follows, that to prevent notable errors in practice, the *radius* must be taken of ten thousand parts, or more.

128. From what hath been said the reason is plain why, to the end any theorem may become universal in its use, it is necessary we speak of the lines described on paper, as though they contained parts which really they do not. In doing of which, if we examine the matter throughly, we shall perhaps discover that we cannot conceive an inch itself as consisting of, or being divisible into a thousand parts, but only some other line which is far greater than an inch, and represented by it. And that when we say a line is *infinitely divisible*, we must mean a line which is *infinitely great*. What we have here observed seems to be the chief cause, why to suppose the infinite divisibility of finite extension hath been thought necessary in geometry.

129. The several absurdities and contradictions which flowed from this false principle might, one would think, have been esteemed so many demonstrations against it. But by I know not what *logic*, it is held that proofs a posteriori are not

to be admitted against propositions relating to infinity. As though it were not impossible even for an infinite mind to reconcile contradictions. Or as if anything absurd and repugnant could have a necessary connexion with truth, or flow from it. But whoever considers the weakness of this pretence, will think it was contrived on purpose to humour the laziness of the mind, which had rather acquiesce in an indolent scepticism, than be at the pains to go through with a severe examination of those principles it hath ever embraced for true.

130. Of late the speculations about infinites have run so high, and grown to such strange notions, as have occasioned no small scruples and disputes among the geometers of the present age. Some there are of great note, who not content with holding that finite lines may be divided into an infinite number of parts, do yet farther maintain, that each of those infinitesimals is itself subdivisible into an infinity of other parts, or infinitesimals of a second order, and so on *ad infinitum*. These, I say, assert there are infinitesimals of infinitesimals of infinitesimals, without ever coming to an end. So that according to them an inch doth not barely contain an infinite number of parts, but an infinity of an infinity of an infinity *ad infinitum* of parts. Others there be who hold all orders of infinitesimals below the first to be nothing at all, thinking it with good reason absurd, to imagine there is any positive quantity or part of extension, which though multiplied infinitely, can ever equal the smallest given extension. And yet on the other hand it seems no less absurd, to think the square, cube, or other power of a positive real root, should itself be nothing at all; which they who hold infinitesimals of the first order denying all of the subsequent orders, are obliged to maintain.

131. Have we not therefore reason to conclude, that they are *both* in the wrong, and that there is in effect no such thing as parts infinitely small, or an infinite number of parts contained in any finite quantity? But you will say, that if this doctrine obtains, it will follow the very foundations of geometry are destroyed: and those great men who have raised that science to so astonishing an height, have been all the while building a castle in the air. To this it may be replied, that

whatever is useful in geometry and promotes the benefit of human life, doth still remain firm and unshaken on our principles. That science considered as practical, will rather receive advantage than any prejudice from what hath been said. But to set this in a due light, may be the subject of a distinct inquiry. For the rest, though it should follow that some of the more intricate and subtle parts of *speculative mathematics* may be pared off without any prejudice to truth; yet I do not see what damage will be thence derived to mankind. On the contrary, it were highly to be wished, that men of great abilities and obstinate application would draw off their thoughts from those amusements, and employ them in the study of such things as lie nearer the concerns of life, or have a more direct influence on the manners.

132. If it be said that several theorems undoubtedly true, are discovered by methods in which infinitesimals are made use of, which could never have been, if their existence included a contradiction in it. I answer, that upon a thorough examination it will not be found, that in any instance it is necessary to make use of or conceive infinitesimal parts of finite lines, or even quantities less than the *minimum sensibile*: nay, it will be evident this is never done, it being impossible.*

133. By what we have premised, it is plain that very numerous and important errors have taken their rise from those false principles, which were impugned in the foregoing parts of this treatise. And the opposites of those erroneous tenets at the same time appear to be most fruitful principles, from whence do flow innumerable consequences highly advantageous to true philosophy as well as to religion. Particularly, *matter* or *the absolute existence of corporeal objects*, hath been shewn to be that wherein the most avowed and pernicious enemies of all knowledge, whether human or divine, have ever placed their chief strength and confidence. And surely, if by distinguishing the real existence of unthinking things from their being perceived, and allowing them a subsistence of their own out of the minds of spirits, no one thing is explained in Nature; but on the contrary a great many inexplicable difficulties arise: if the supposition of matter is barely precarious, as not being grounded on so much as one single reason: if its consequences cannot endure the light of examination

and free inquiry, but screen themselves under the dark and general pretence of *infinites being incomprehensible*: if withal the removal of this *matter* be not attended with the least evil consequence, if it be not even missed in the world, but everything as well, nay much easier conceived without it: if lastly, both *sceptics* and *atheists* are for ever silenced upon supposing only spirits and ideas, and this scheme of things is perfectly agreeable both to *reason* and *religion*: methinks we may expect it should be admitted and firmly embraced, though it were proposed only as an *hypothesis*, and the existence of matter had been allowed possible, which yet I think we have evidently demonstrated that it is not.

134. True it is, that in consequence of the foregoing principles, several disputes and speculations, which are esteemed no mean parts of learning, are rejected as useless. But how great a prejudice soever against our notions, this may give to those who have already been deeply engaged, and made large advances in studies of that nature: yet by others, we hope it will not be thought any just ground of dislike to the principles and tenets herein laid down, that they abridge the labour of study, and make human sciences more clear, compendious, and attainable, than they were before.

135. Having dispatched what we intended to say concerning the knowledge of *ideas*, the method we proposed leads us, in the next place, to treat of *spirits*: with regard to which, perhaps human knowledge is not so deficient as is vulgarly imagined. The great reason that is assigned for our being thought ignorant of the nature of spirits, is, our not having an idea of it. But surely it ought not to be looked on as a defect in a human understanding, that it does not perceive the idea of *spirit*, if it is manifestly impossible there should be any such *idea*. And this, if I mistake not, has been demonstrated in sect. 27: to which I shall here add that a spirit has been shown to be the only substance or support, wherein the unthinking beings or ideas can exist: but that this *substance* which supports or perceives ideas should itself be an *idea* or like an *idea*, is evidently absurd.

136. It will perhaps be said, that we want a sense (as some have imagined) proper to know substances withal, which if we had, we might know our own soul, as we do a triangle. To this

I answer, that in case we had a new sense bestowed upon us, we could only receive thereby some new sensations of ideas of sense. But I believe nobody will say, that what he means by the terms *soul* and *substance*, is only some particular sort of idea or sensation. We may therefore infer, that all things duly considered, it is not more reasonable to think our faculties defective, in that they do not furnish us with an idea of spirit or active thinking substance, than it would be if we should blame them for not being able to comprehend a *round square*.

137. From the opinion that spirits are to be known after the manner of an idea or sensation, have risen many absurd and heterodox tenets, and much scepticism about the nature of the soul. It is even probable, that this opinion may have produced a doubt in some, whether they had any soul at all distinct from their body, since upon inquiry they could not find they had an idea of it. That an *idea* which is inactive, and the existence whereof consists in being perceived, should be the image or likeness of an agent subsisting by itself, seems to need no other refutation, than barely attending to what is meant by those words. But perhaps you will say, that though an *idea* cannot resemble a *spirit*, in its thinking, acting, or subsisting by itself, yet it may in some other respects: and it is not necessary that an idea or image be in all respects like the original.

138. I answer, if it does not in those mentioned, it is impossible it should represent it in any other thing. Do but leave out the power of willing, thinking, and perceiving ideas, and there remains nothing else wherein the idea can be like a spirit. For by the word *spirit* we mean only that which thinks, wills, and perceives; this, and this alone, constitutes the signification of that term. If therefore it is impossible that any degree of those powers should be represented in an idea, it is evident there can be no idea of a spirit.

139. But it will be objected, that if there is no idea signified by the terms *soul*, *spirit*, and *substance*, they are wholly insignificant, or have no meaning in them. I answer, those words do mean or signify a real thing, which is neither an idea nor like an idea, but that which perceives ideas, and wills, and reasons about them. What I am myself, that which I denote by

the term I, is the same with what is meant by *soul* or *spiritual substance*. If it be said that this is only quarrelling at a word, and that since the immediate significations of other names are by common consent called *ideas*, no reason can be assigned, why that which is signified by the name *spirit* or *soul* may not partake in the same appellation. I answer, all the unthinking objects of the mind agree, in that they are entirely passive, and their existence consists only in being perceived: whereas a soul or spirit is an active being, whose existence consists not in being perceived, but in perceiving ideas and thinking. It is therefore necessary, in order to prevent equivocation and confounding natures perfectly disagreeing and unlike, that we distinguish between *spirit* and *idea*. See sect. 27.

140. In a large sense indeed, we may be said to have an idea, or rather a notion of *spirit*, that is, we understand the meaning of the word,* otherwise we could not affirm or deny anything of it. Moreover, as we conceive the ideas that are in the minds of other spirits by means of our own, which we suppose to be resemblances of them: so we know other spirits by means of our own soul, which in that sense is the image or idea of them, it having a like respect to other spirits, that blueness or heat by me perceived hath to those ideas perceived by another.

141. It must not* be supposed, that they who assert the natural immortality of the soul are of opinion, that it is absolutely incapable of annihilation even by the infinite power of the Creator who first gave it being: but only that it is not liable to be broken or dissolved by the ordinary Laws of Nature or motion. They indeed, who hold the soul of man to be only a thin vital flame, or system of animal spirits, make it perishing and corruptible as the body, since there is nothing more easily dissipated than such a being, which it is naturally impossible should survive the ruin of the tabernacle, wherein it is enclosed. And this notion hath been greedily embraced and cherished by the worst part of mankind, as the most effectual antidote against all impressions of virtue and religion. But it hath been made evident, that bodies of what frame or texture soever, are barely passive ideas in the mind, which is more distant and heterogeneous from them, than light is from dark-

ness. We have shewn that the soul is indivisible, incorporeal, unextended, and it is consequently incorruptible. Nothing can be plainer, than that the motions, changes, decays, and dissolutions which we hourly see befall natural bodies (and which is what we mean by the *course of Nature*) cannot possibly affect an active, simple, uncompounded substance: such a being therefore is indissoluble by the force of Nature, that is to say, *the soul of man is naturally immortal*.

142. After what hath been said, it is I suppose plain, that our souls are not to be known in the same manner as senseless inactive objects, or by way of *idea*. *Spirits* and *ideas* are things so wholly different, that when we say, *they exist, they are known*, or the like, these words must not be thought to signify anything common to both natures. There is nothing alike or common in them: and to expect that by any multiplication or enlargement of our faculties, we may be enabled to know a spirit as we do a triangle, seems as absurd as if we should hope to *see a sound*. This is inculcated because I imagine it may be of moment towards clearing several important questions, and preventing some very dangerous errors concerning the nature of the soul. We may not I think strictly be said to have an idea of an active being, or of an action, although we may be said to have a notion of them. I have some knowledge or notion of my mind, and its acts about ideas, inasmuch as I know or understand what is meant by those words. What I know, that I have some notion of. I will not say, that the terms *idea* and *notion* may not be used convertibly, if the world will have it so. But yet it conduceth to clearness and propriety, that we distinguish things very different by different names. It is also to be remarked, that all relations including an act of the mind, we cannot so properly be said to have an idea, but rather a notion of the relations or habitudes between things. But if in the modern way the word *idea* is extended to spirits, and relations and acts; this is after all an affair of verbal concern.*

143. It will not be amiss to add, that the doctrine of *abstract ideas* hath had no small share in rendering those sciences intricate and obscure, which are particularly conversant about spiritual things. Men have imagined they could frame abstract notions of the powers and acts of the mind, and consider them

prescinded, as well from the mind or spirit itself, as from their respective objects and effects. Hence a great number of dark and ambiguous terms presumed to stand for abstract notions, have been introduced into metaphysics and morality, and from these have grown infinite distractions and disputes amongst the learned.

144. But nothing seems more to have contributed towards engaging men in controversies and mistakes, with regard to the nature and operations of the mind, than the being used to speak of those things, in terms borrowed from sensible ideas. For example, the will is termed the *motion* of the soul: this infuses a belief, that the mind of man is as a ball in motion, impelled and determined by the objects of sense, as necessarily as that is by the stroke of a racket. Hence arise endless scruples and errors of dangerous consequence in morality. All which I doubt not may be cleared, and truth appear plain, uniform, and consistent, could but philosophers be prevailed on to retire into themselves, and attentively consider their own meaning.*

145. From what hath been said, it is plain that we cannot know the existence of other spirits, otherwise than by their operations, or the ideas by them excited in us. I perceive several motions, changes, and combinations of ideas, that inform me there are certain particular agents like myself, which accompany them, and concur in their production. Hence the knowledge I have of other spirits is not immediate, as is the knowledge of my ideas; but depending on the intervention of ideas, by me referred to agents or spirits distinct from myself, as effects or concomitant signs.

146. But though there be some things which convince us, human agents are concerned in producing them; yet it is evident to everyone, that those things which are called the works of Nature, that is, the far greater part of the ideas or sensations perceived by us, are not produced by, or dependent on the wills of men. There is therefore some other spirit that causes them, since it is repugnant that they should subsist by themselves. See sect. 29. But if we attentively consider the constant regularity, order, and concatenation of natural things, the surprising magnificence, beauty, and perfection

of the larger, and the exquisite contrivance of the smaller parts of the creation, together with the exact harmony and correspondence of the whole, but above all, the never enough admired laws of pain and pleasure, and the instincts or natural inclinations, appetites, and passions of animals; I say if we consider all these things, and at the same time attend to the meaning and import of the attributes, one, eternal, infinitely wise, good, and perfect, we shall clearly perceive that they belong to the aforesaid spirit, *who works all in all*,* and *by whom all things consist*.*

147. Hence it is evident, that God is known as certainly and immediately as any other mind or spirit whatsoever, distinct from ourselves. We may even assert, that the existence of God is far more evidently perceived than the existence of men; because the effects of Nature are infinitely more numerous and considerable, than those ascribed to human agents. There is not any one mark that denotes a man, or effect produced by him, which doth not more strongly evince the being of that spirit who is the *Author of Nature*. For it is evident that in affecting other persons,* the will of man hath no other object, than barely the motion of the limbs of his body; but that such a motion should be attended by, or excite any idea in the mind of another, depends wholly on the will of the Creator. He alone it is who *upholding all things by the Word of his Power*,* maintains that intercourse between spirits, whereby they are able to perceive the existence of each other. And yet this pure and clear light which enlightens everyone, is itself invisible.

148. It seems to be a general pretence of the unthinking herd, that they cannot see God. Could we but see him, say they, as we see a man, we should believe that he is, and believing obey his commands. But alas we need only open our eyes to see the sovereign Lord of all things with a more full and clear view, than we do any one of our fellow-creatures. Not that I imagine we see God (as some will have it) by a direct and immediate view, or see corporeal things, not by themselves, but by seeing that which represents them in the essence of God, which doctrine is I must confess to me incomprehensible. But I shall explain my meaning. A human spirit or person is not perceived by sense, as not being an idea;

when therefore we see the colour, size, figure, and motions of a man, we perceive only certain sensations or ideas excited in our own minds: and these being exhibited to our view in sundry distinct collections, serve to mark out unto us the existence of finite and created spirits like ourselves. Hence it is plain, we do not see a man, if by *man* is meant that which lives, moves, perceives, and thinks as we do: but only such a certain collection of ideas, as directs us to think there is a distinct principle of thought and motion like to ourselves, accompanying and represented by it. And after the same manner we see God; all the difference is, that whereas some one finite and narrow assemblage of ideas denotes a particular human mind, whithersoever we direct our view, we do at all times and in all places perceive manifest tokens of the divinity: everything we see, hear, feel, or anywise perceive by sense, being a sign or effect of the Power of God; as is our perception of those very motions, which are produced by men.

149. It is therefore plain, that nothing can be more evident to anyone that is capable of the least reflexion, than the existence of God, or a spirit who is intimately present to our minds, producing in them all that variety of ideas or sensations, which continually affect us, on whom we have an absolute and entire dependence, in short, *in whom we live, and move, and have our being*. That the discovery of this great truth which lies so near and obvious to the mind, should be attained to by the reason of so very few, is a sad instance of the stupidity and inattention of men, who, though they are surrounded with such clear manifestations of the Deity, are yet so little affected by them, that they seem as it were blinded with excess of light.

150. But you will say, hath Nature no share in the production of natural things, and must they be all ascribed to the immediate and sole operation of God? I answer, if by *Nature* is meant only the visible *series* of effects, or sensations imprinted on our minds according to certain fixed and general laws: then it is plain, that Nature taken in this sense cannot produce anything at all. But if by *Nature* is meant some being distinct from God, as well as from the Laws of Nature, and things perceived by sense, I must confess that word is to me an

empty sound, without any intelligible meaning annexed to it. Nature in this acceptation is a vain *chimera* introduced by those heathens, who had not just notions of the omnipresence and infinite perfection of God. But it is more unaccountable, that it should be received among Christians professing belief in the Holy Scriptures, which constantly ascribe those effects to the immediate hand of God, that heathen philosophers are wont to impute to *Nature. The Lord, he causeth the vapours to ascend; he maketh lightnings with rain; he bringeth forth the wind out of his treasures,* Jerem., chap. 10. ver. 13. *He turneth the shadow of death into the morning, and maketh the day dark with night,* Amos, chap. 5. ver. 8. *He visiteth the earth, and maketh it soft with showers: he blesseth the springing thereof, and crowneth the year with his goodness; so that the pastures are clothed with flocks, and the valleys are covered over with corn.* See Psalm 65. But notwithstanding that this is the constant language of Scripture; yet we have I know not what aversion from believing, that God concerns himself so nearly in our affairs. Fain would we suppose him at a great distance off, and substitute some blind unthinking deputy in his stead, though (if we may believe Saint Paul) *he be not far from every one of us.*

151. It will I doubt not be objected, that the slow and gradual methods observed in the production of natural things, do not seem to have for their cause the immediate hand of an *almighty Agent.* Besides, monsters, untimely births, fruits blasted in the blossom, rains falling in desert places, miseries incident to human life, are so many arguments that the whole frame of Nature is not immediately actuated and superintended by a spirit of infinite wisdom and goodness. But the answer to this objection is in a good measure plain from sect. 62, it being visible, that the aforesaid methods of Nature are absolutely necessary, in order to working by the most simple and general rules, and after a steady and consistent manner; which argues both the *wisdom* and *goodness* of God. Such is the artificial contrivance of this mighty machine of Nature, that whilst its motions and various phenomena strike on our senses, the hand which actuates the whole is itself unperceivable to men of flesh and blood. *Verily* (saith the

prophet) *thou art a God that hidest thyself*, Isaiah, chap. 45.
ver. 15. But though God conceal himself from the eyes of the
sensual and *lazy*, who will not be at the least expence of
thought; yet to an unbiassed and attentive mind, nothing can
be more plainly legible, than the intimate presence of an *all-
wise Spirit*, who fashions, regulates, and sustains the whole
system of being. It is clear from what we have elsewhere
observed, that the operating according to general and stated
laws, is so necessary for our guidance in the affairs of life, and
letting us into the secret of Nature, that without it, all reach
and compass of thought, all human sagacity and design could
serve to no manner of purpose: it were even impossible there
should be any such faculties or powers in the mind. See sect.
31. Which one consideration abundantly out-balances whatever particular inconveniences may thence arise.

152. We should further consider, that the very blemishes
and defects of Nature are not without their use, in that they
make an agreeable fort of variety, and augment the beauty of
the rest of the creation, as shades in a picture serve to set off
the brighter and more enlightened parts. We would likewise
do well to examine, whether our taxing the waste of seeds and
embryos, and accidental destruction of plants and animals,
before they come to full maturity, as an imprudence in the
Author of Nature, be not the effect of prejudice contracted by
our familiarity with impotent and saving mortals. In *man*
indeed a thrifty management of those things, which he cannot
procure without much pains and industry, may be esteemed
wisdom. But we must not imagine, that the inexplicably fine
machine of an animal or vegetable, costs the great Creator
any more pains or trouble in its production than a pebble
doth: nothing being more evident, than that an omnipotent
spirit can indifferently produce everything by a mere *fiat* or
act of his will. Hence it is plain, that the splendid profusion of
natural things should not be interpreted, weakness or prodi-
gality in the agent who produces them, but rather be looked
on as an argument of the riches of his power.

153. As for the mixture of pain or uneasiness which is in the
world, pursuant to the general laws of Nature, and the actions
of finite imperfect spirits: this, in the state we are in at present

is indispensably necessary to our well-being. But our prospects are too narrow: we take, for instance, the idea of some one particular pain into our thoughts, and account it *evil*; whereas if we enlarge our view, so as to comprehend the various ends, connexions, and dependencies of things, on what occasions and in what proportions we are affected with pain and pleasure, the nature of human freedom, and the design with which we are put into the world; we shall be forced to acknowledge that those particular things, which considered in themselves appear to be *evil*, have the nature of *good*, when considered as linked with the whole system of beings.

154. From what hath been said it will be manifest to any considering person, that it is merely for want of attention and comprehensiveness of mind, that there are any favourers of *atheism* or the *Manichean heresy** to be found. Little and unreflecting souls may indeed burlesque the works of Providence, the beauty and order whereof they have not capacity, or will not be at the pains to comprehend. But those who are masters of any justness and extent of thought, and are withal used to reflect, can never sufficiently admire the divine traces of wisdom and goodness that shine throughout the economy of Nature. But what truth is there which shineth so strongly on the mind, that by an aversion of thought, a wilful shutting of the eyes, we may not escape seeing it? Is it therefore to be wondered at, if the generality of men, who are ever intent on business or pleasure, and little used to fix or open the eye of their mind, should not have all that conviction and evidence of the being of God, which might be expected in reasonable creatures?

155. We should rather wonder, that men can be found so stupid as to neglect, than that neglecting they should be unconvinced of such an evident and momentous truth. And yet it is to be feared that too many of parts and leisure, who live in Christian countries, are merely through a supine and dreadful negligence sunk into a sort of *atheism*. Since it is downright impossible, that a soul pierced and enlightened with a thorough sense of the omnipresence, holiness, and justice of that *Almighty Spirit*, should persist in a remorseless violation of his

laws. We ought therefore earnestly to meditate and dwell on those important points; that so we may attain conviction without all scruple, *that the eyes of the Lord are in every place beholding the evil and the good*; *that he is with us and keepeth us in all places whither we go, and giveth us bread to eat, and raiment to put on*; that he is present and conscious to our innermost thoughts; and that we have a most absolute and immediate dependence on him. A clear view of which great truths cannot choose but fill our hearts with an awful circumspection and holy fear, which is the stongest incentive to *virtue*, and the best guard against *vice*.

156. For after all, what deserves the first place in our studies, is the consideration of *God*, and our *duty*; which to promote, as it was the main drift and design of my labours, so shall I esteem them altogether useless and ineffectual, if by what I have said I cannot inspire my readers with a pious sense of the presence of God: and having shewn the falseness or vanity of those barren speculations, which make the chief employment of learned men, the better dispose them to reverence and embrace the salutary truths of the Gospel, which to know and to practise is the highest perfection of human nature.

THREE DIALOGUES

ANALYTICAL CONTENTS

(by page numbers)

First Dialogue

Concerns the basic arguments for the non-existence of the physical world and of material substance.

107–10   Introductory passages: the danger of scepticism; clarification of the concept by moving from classical to modern conception of scepticism.

111–12   Raises question of whether sensible things exist external to the mind.

112–25   Discussion of the objectivity of secondary qualities:

    112–16: Heat and cold; using *assimilation argument* and *argument from illusion*;

    116–18: Tastes; using same;

    118–19: Smells; using same;

    118–20: Sounds; using *causal argument*;

    120–6: Colours; using *illusion* in form of colour of sky and microscopic vision: Hylas supplements with *causal argument*.

126–33   Discussion of objectivity of primary qualities:

    126–8: Extension and shape; using *illusion* in form of difference in size perception between mites and men;

    128–9: Motion; using *illusion*;

    129–30: Solidity; using *illusion* and claim that resistance is feeling, not property of body;

    130–2: Absolute, non-specific extension;

    132–3: Pure intellect and abstracting ideas.

133–6   Distinction between sensations and their objects.

136–8   Matter as substratum.

139–40   Conceiving the unperceived.

140–2   Why visual depth is not externality.

142–7   Discussion of Lockean representationalism:

    Berkeley's three responses:

    143–5: (1) No way of knowing such an external world exists;

    145–6: (2) Diverse appearances could not represent a stable object;

    146–7: (3) Sensations and ideas could only be like sensations and ideas.

Second Dialogue

Consists of an introduction re-examining the 'modern philosophy', then two major parts: first he tries to show that his conclusions are not sceptical, and the role of God in this; second, various etiolated conceptions of matter, according to which it transcends sensible qualities, are discussed.

148–50   Introductory remarks on the 'modern philosophy'.

        148–9: Hylas cannot see how to avoid the causal explanation of the generation of ideas;

        149–50: Philonous' two replies: (1) inconsistent with previous proof that bodies are ideas; (2) that there could be no connection between the motion of nerves and sensations.

150–6   The role of God in making idealism non-sceptical:

        150–2: Philonous' eulogy on the beauty of the world; Hylas' response that this is inconsistent with previous sceptical conclusions;

        152–3: Not sceptical, because the world is mind-dependent, yet independent of my mind, so depends on divine mind;

        153–6: Berkeley's objection to Malebranche's view that we see all things in God.

156–68   Attenuated conceptions of matter:

        156–7: Matter as whatever causes ideas; *Reply*: could not, because inert;

        157–60: Matter as instrument for God's action; *Reply*: only use instrument if cannot act without;

        160–2: Matter as occasion for divine action; *Reply*: God does not need to be prompted;

        163–4: Matter as necessary idea with no empirical content; *Reply*: Challenge to form—i.e. produce image of—this idea;

        165–8: Hylas still feels matter needed for bare reality of things.

Third Dialogue

The major theme of this dialogue is Hylas' insistence that idealism is shocking even if true: it is disingenuous to present it as a version of common sense or as compatible with Christian doctrine.

169–73   Hylas accepts Philonous' conclusions, which he takes to be sceptical: they dispute whether the real object is identical with the appearances or with what lies behind them, and whether we can know what, if anything, lies behind them. Philonous says appearances are the real things.

173   Hylas raises question of ability of objects to exist when one is dead. Philonous replies they can, given the existence of God to perceive them.

173–7   How can we have idea of active being, such as God, and, if we can, why not of matter? *Reply*: we have a conscious intuition of ourselves and God is similar, with the limitations removed. We have no conscious contact with matter.

177   Is idealism not contrary to common sense? *Reply*: physical existence is equivalent to perceivability, only ideas are perceivable and ideas are actually perceived.

177–8   The differences between chimeras and reality: (1) vividness; (2) connectedness.

178–9   Is it not strange to say that only spirits and ideas exist? *Reply*: only verbally; Locke's theory is really stranger.

179–80 Idealism makes God responsible for evil; *Reply*: (1) it is neither better nor worse to act through an instrument; (2) it is the intent not the physical action that counts; (3) God is not the only spiritual agent.

181–2   How are illusions possible? *Reply*: ideas are never false, but inferences based on them can be.

182–3   Is the dispute not purely verbal? *Reply*: no, because it would not be correct to call an active, unextended being 'material'.

183–4   Would God not suffer pain and other imperfections? *Reply*: God knows ideas but does not suffer them by sense.

184–6   The laws of motion are proportional to the quantity of matter and so require its existence; *Reply*: the laws depend on qualities of matter, not substance.

186–8   Is God not deceiving us? At least the theory is a great 'novelty'; *Reply*: material substance is required neither by reason nor revelation. 'I am not for changing things into ideas but ideas into things.'

188–92 Can we perceive the same things when we have different ideas? *Reply*: not in a strict sense of 'same' but in a looser one.

192   'Same' requires an external archetype; *Reply*: there is one in God's mind.

193–5   If extended ideas are in the mind, then minds are extended;

Reply: ideas are 'in the mind' only in the sense of being perceived by it.

195–202 Idealism and creation:

195–7: If creation consists simply in things in God's mind being made available to us, then creation is conditional upon human existence; *Replies*: (1) there could be other finite spirits; (2) conditional existence will do, as for things unperceived in the desert;

197–9: If things are eternally in God's mind then they are never created; *Replies*: (1) they are created only relative to finite spirits; (2) and a similar problem must arise for any changeless God;

199–200: Ideas must exist in an ectypal and in an archetypal form;

200–202: The natural sense of scripture is idealist.

202–4 Advantages of idealism: (1) it makes science clear and non-metaphysical; (2) scepticism rests on the metaphysical belief in matter.

205–6 Certain mistakes in argument that Philonous thinks can be used against idealism.

206–8 It is possible to retain the term 'matter' only if one uses it with care.

208 Idealism comes from combining the vulgar truth that the things immediately perceived are real with the modern philosophical insight that the things we are aware of are ideas in the mind.

THE PREFACE*

Though it seems the general opinion of the world, no less than the design of Nature and Providence, that the end of speculation be practice, or the improvement and regulation of our lives and actions; yet those, who are most addicted to speculative studies, seem as generally of another mind. And, indeed, if we consider the pains that have been taken, to perplex the plainest things, that distrust of the senses, those doubts and scruples, those abstractions and refinements that occur in the very entrance of the sciences; it will not seem strange, that men of leisure and curiosity should lay themselves out in fruitless disquisitions, without descending to the practical parts of life, or informing themselves in the more necessary and important parts of knowledge.

Upon the common principles of philosophers, we are not assured of the existence of things from their being perceived. And we are taught to distinguish their real nature from that which falls under our senses. Hence arise scepticism *and* paradoxes. *It is not enough, that we see and feel, that we taste and smell a thing. Its true nature, its absolute external entity, is still concealed. For, though it be the fiction of our own brain, we have made it inaccessible to all our faculties. Sense is fallacious, reason defective. We spend our lives in doubting of those things which other men evidently know, and believing those things which they laugh at, and despise.*

In order, therefore, to divert the busy mind of man from vain researches, it seemed necessary to inquire into the source of its perplexities; and, if possible, to lay down such principles, as, by an easy solution of them, together with their own native evidence, may, at once, recommend themselves for genuine to the mind, and rescue it from those endless pursuits it is engaged in. Which, with a plain demonstration of the immediate Providence of an all-seeing God, and the natural immortality of the soul, should seem the readiest preparation, as well as the strongest motive, to the study and practice of virtue.

This design I proposed, in the First Part of a Treatise con-

cerning the Principles of Human Knowledge, *published in the year 1710. But, before I proceed to publish the Second Part, I thought it requisite to treat more clearly and fully of certain principles laid down in the First, and to place them in a new light. Which is the business of the following* Dialogues.

In this treatise, which does not presuppose in the reader, any knowledge of what was contained in the former, it has been my aim to introduce the notions I advance, into the mind, in the most easy and familiar manner; especially, because they carry with them a great opposition to the prejudices of philosophers, which have so far prevailed against the common sense and natural notions of mankind.

If the principles, which I here endeavour to propagate, are admitted for true; the consequences which, I think, evidently flow from thence, are, that atheism *and* scepticism *will be utterly destroyed, many intricate points made plain, great difficulties solved, several useless parts of science retrenched, speculation referred to practice, and men reduced from paradoxes to common sense.*

And although it may, perhaps, seem an uneasy reflexion to some, that when they have taken a circuit through so many refined and unvulgar notions, they should at last come to think like other men: yet, methinks, this return to the simple dictates of Nature, after having wandered through the wild mazes of philosophy, is not unpleasant. It is like coming home from a long voyage: a man reflects with pleasure on the many difficulties and perplexities he has passed through, sets his heart at ease, and enjoys himself with more satisfaction for the future.

As it was my intention to convince sceptics *and* infidels *by reason, so it has been my endeavour strictly to observe the most rigid laws of reasoning. And, to an impartial reader, I hope, it will be manifest, that the sublime notion of a God, and the comfortable expectation of immortality, do naturally arise from a close and methodical application of thought: whatever may be the result of that loose, rambling way, not altogether improperly termed* free-thinking, *by certain libertines in thought, who can no more endure the restraints of* logic, *than those of* religion, *or* government.

It will, perhaps, be objected to my design, that so far as it tends to ease the mind of difficult and useless inquiries, it can affect only a few speculative persons; but, if by their speculations rightly placed, the study of morality and the Law of Nature were brought more into fashion among men of parts and genius, the discouragements that draw to scepticism removed, the measures of right and wrong accurately defined, and the principles of natural religion reduced into regular systems, as artfully disposed and clearly connected as those of some other sciences: there are grounds to think, these effects would not only have a gradual influence in repairing the too much defaced sense of virtue in the world; but also, by shewing, that such parts of revelation, as lie within the reach of human inquiry, are most agreeable to right reason, would dispose all prudent, unprejudiced persons, to a modest and wary treatment of those sacred mysteries, which are above the comprehension of our faculties.

It remains, that I desire the reader to withhold his censure of these Dialogues, till he has read them through. Otherwise, he may lay them aside in a mistake of their design, or on account of difficulties or objections which he would find answered in the sequel. A treatise of this nature would require to be once read over coherently, in order to comprehend its design, the proofs, solution of difficulties, and the connexion and disposition of its parts. If it be thought to deserve a second reading; this, I imagine, will make the entire scheme very plain: especially, if recourse be had to an Essay I wrote, some years since, upon vision, and the Treatise concerning the Principles of Human Knowledge. Wherein divers notions advanced in these Dialogues, are farther pursued, or placed in different lights, and other points handled, which naturally tend to confirm and illustrate them.

THREE DIALOGUES BETWEEN
HYLAS AND PHILONOUS

THE FIRST DIALOGUE

PHILONOUS.* Good morrow, Hylas: I did not expect to find you abroad so early.

HYLAS.* It is indeed something unusual; but my thoughts were so taken up with a subject I was discoursing of last night, that finding I could not sleep, I resolved to rise and take a turn in the garden.

PHILONOUS. It happened well, to let you see what innocent and agreeable pleasures you lose every morning. Can there be a pleasanter time of the day, or a more delightful season of the year? That purple sky, these wild but sweet notes of birds, the fragrant bloom upon the trees and flowers, the gentle influence of the rising sun, these and a thousand nameless beauties of nature inspire the soul with secret transports; its faculties too being at this time fresh and lively, are fit for those meditations, which the solitude of a garden and tranquillity of the morning naturally dispose us to. But I am afraid I interrupt your thoughts: for you seemed very intent on something.

HYLAS. It is true, I was, and shall be obliged to you if you will permit me to go on in the same vein; not that I would by any means deprive myself of your company, for my thoughts always flow more easily in conversation with a friend, than when I am alone: but my request is, that you would suffer me to impart my reflexions to you.

PHILONOUS. With all my heart, it is what I should have requested myself, if you had not prevented me.

HYLAS. I was considering the odd fate of those men who have in all ages, through an affectation of being distinguished from the vulgar, or some unaccountable turn of thought, pretended either to believe nothing at all, or to believe the most extravagant things in the world. This however might be borne, if their paradoxes and scepticism did not draw after them some consequences of general disadvantage to mankind. But the mischief lieth here; that when men of less leisure see them who are supposed to have spent their whole time in the pursuits of knowledge, professing an entire ignorance of all things, or advancing such notions as are repugnant to plain and commonly received principles, they will be tempted to entertain suspicions concerning the most important truths, which they had hitherto held sacred and unquestionable.

PHILONOUS. I entirely agree with you, as to the ill tendency of the affected doubts of some philosophers, and fantastical conceits of others. I am even so far gone of late in this way of thinking, that I have quitted several of the sublime notions I had got in their schools for vulgar opinions. And I give it you on my word, since this revolt from metaphysical notions to the plain dictates of Nature and common sense, I find my understanding strangely enlightened, so that I can now easily comprehend a great many things which before were all mystery and riddle.

HYLAS. I am glad to find there was nothing in the accounts I heard of you.

PHILONOUS. Pray, what were those?

HYLAS. You were represented in last night's conversation, as one who maintained the most extravagant opinion that ever entered into the mind of man, to wit, that there is no such thing as *material substance* in the world.

PHILONOUS. That there is no such thing as what philosophers call *material substance*, I am seriously persuaded: but if I were made to see anything absurd or sceptical in this, I should then have the same reason to renounce this, that I imagine I have now to reject the contrary opinion.

HYLAS. What! can anything be more fantastical, more repugnant to common sense, or a more manifest piece of scepticism, than to believe there is no such thing as *matter*?

PHILONOUS. Softly, good Hylas. What if it should prove, that you, who hold there is, are by virtue of that opinion a greater *sceptic*, and maintain more paradoxes and repugnancies to common sense, than I who believe no such thing?

HYLAS. You may as soon persuade me, the part is greater than the whole, as that, in order to avoid absurdity and scepticism, I should ever be obliged to give up my opinion in this point.

PHILONOUS. Well then, are you content to admit that opinion for true, which upon examination shall appear most agreeable to common sense, and remote from scepticism?

HYLAS. With all my heart. Since you are for raising disputes about the plainest things in Nature, I am content for once to hear what you have to say.

PHILONOUS. Pray, Hylas, what do you mean by a *sceptic*?

HYLAS. I mean what all men mean, one that doubts of everything.

PHILONOUS. He then who entertains no doubt concerning some particular point, with regard to that point cannot be thought a *sceptic*.

HYLAS. I agree with you.

PHILONOUS. Whether doth doubting consist in embracing the affirmative or negative side of a question?

HYLAS. In neither; for whoever understands English, cannot but know that *doubting* signifies a suspense between both.

PHILONOUS. He then that denieth any point, can no more be said to doubt of it, than he who affirmeth it with the same degree of assurance.

HYLAS. True.

PHILONOUS. And consequently, for such his denial is no more to be esteemed a *sceptic* than the other.

HYLAS. I acknowledge it.

PHILONOUS. How cometh it to pass then, Hylas, that you pronounce me a *sceptic*, because I deny what you affirm, to wit, the existence of matter? Since, for ought you can tell, I am as peremptory in my denial, as you in your affirmation.*

HYLAS. Hold, Philonous, I have been a little out in my definition; but every false step a man makes in discourse is not to be insisted on. I said indeed, that a *sceptic* was one who doubted of everything; but I should have added, or who denies the reality and truth of things.

PHILONOUS. What things? Do you mean the principles and theorems of sciences? But these you know are universal intellectual notions, and consequently independent of

matter; the denial therefore of this doth not imply the denying them.

HYLAS. I grant it. But are there no other things? What think
you of distrusting the senses, of denying the real existence
of sensible things, or pretending to know nothing of them.
Is not this sufficient to denominate a man a *sceptic*?

PHILONOUS. Shall we therefore examine which of us it is
that denies the reality of sensible things, or professes the
greatest ignorance of them; since, if I take you rightly, he is
to be esteemed the greatest *sceptic*?

HYLAS. That is what I desire.

PHILONOUS. What mean you by sensible things?

HYLAS. Those things which are perceived by the senses. Can
you imagine that I mean anything else?

PHILONOUS. Pardon me, Hylas, if I am desirous clearly to
apprehend your notions, since this may much shorten our
inquiry. Suffer me then to ask you this farther question. Are
those things only perceived by the senses which are perceived immediately? Or may those things properly be said
to be *sensible*, which are perceived mediately, or not without the intervention of others?

HYLAS. I do not sufficiently understand you.

PHILONOUS. In reading a book, what I immediately perceive are the letters, but mediately, or by means of these,
are suggested to my mind the notions of God, virtue, truth,
&c. Now, that the letters are truly sensible things, or perceived by sense, there is no doubt: but I would know
whether you take the things suggested by them to be so too.

HYLAS. No certainly, it were absurd to think *God* or *Virtue*
sensible things, though they may be signified and suggested
to the mind by sensible marks, with which they have an
arbitrary connexion.

PHILONOUS. It seems then, that by *sensible things* you mean
those only which can be perceived immediately by sense.

HYLAS. Right.

PHILONOUS. Doth it not follow from this, that though I see
one part of the sky red, and another blue, and that my
reason doth thence evidently conclude there must be some
cause of that diversity of colours, yet that cause cannot be

said to be a sensible thing, or perceived by the sense of seeing?

HYLAS. It doth.

PHILONOUS. In like manner, though I hear variety of sounds, yet I cannot be said to hear the cause of those sounds.

HYLAS. You cannot.

PHILONOUS. And when by my touch I perceive a thing to be hot and heavy, I cannot say with any truth or propriety, that I feel the cause of its heat or weight.

HYLAS. To prevent any more questions of this kind, I tell you once for all, that by *sensible things* I mean those only which are perceived by sense, and that in truth the senses perceive nothing which they do not perceive immediately: for they make no inferences. The deducing therefore of causes or occasions from effects and appearances, which alone are perceived by sense, entirely relates to reason.

PHILONOUS. This point then is agreed between us, that *sensible things are those only which are immediately perceived by sense*. You will farther inform me, whether we immediately perceive by sight anything beside light, and colours, and figures: or by hearing, anything but sounds: by the palate, anything beside tastes: by the smell, beside odours: or by the touch, more than tangible qualities.

HYLAS. We do not.

PHILONOUS. It seems therefore, that if you take away all sensible qualities, there remains nothing sensible.

HYLAS. I grant it.

PHILONOUS. Sensible things therefore are nothing else but so many sensible qualities, or combinations of sensible qualities.

HYLAS. Nothing else.

PHILONOUS. Heat then is a sensible thing.

HYLAS. Certainly.

PHILONOUS. Doth the reality of sensible things consist in being perceived? or, is it something distinct from their being perceived, and that bears no relation to the mind?

HYLAS. To *exist* is one thing, and to be *perceived* is another.

PHILONOUS. I speak with regard to sensible things only: and

of these I ask, whether by their real existence you mean a subsistence exterior to the mind, and distinct from their being perceived?

HYLAS. I mean a real absolute being, distinct from, and without any relation to their being perceived.

PHILONOUS. Heat therefore, if it be allowed a real being, must exist without the mind.

HYLAS. It must.

PHILONOUS. Tell me, Hylas, is this real existence equally compatible to all degrees of heat, which we perceive: or is there any reason why we should attribute it to some, and deny it others? And if there be, pray let me know that reason.

HYLAS. Whatever degree of heat we perceive by sense, we may be sure the same exists in the object that occasions it.

PHILONOUS. What, the greatest as well as the least?

HYLAS. I tell you, the reason is plainly the same in respect of both: they are both perceived by sense; nay, the greater degree of heat is more sensibly perceived; and consequently, if there is any difference, we are more certain of its real existence than we can be of the reality of a lesser degree.

PHILONOUS. But is not the most vehement and intense degree of heat a very great pain?*

HYLAS. No one can deny it.

PHILONOUS. And is any unperceiving thing capable of pain or pleasure?

HYLAS. No certainly.

PHILONOUS. Is your material substance a senseless being, or a being endowed with sense and perception?

HYLAS. It is senseless, without doubt.

PHILONOUS. It cannot therefore be the subject of pain.

HYLAS. By no means.

PHILONOUS. Nor consequently of the greatest heat perceived by sense, since you acknowledge this to be no small pain.

HYLAS. I grant it.

PHILONOUS. What shall we say then of your external object; is it a material substance, or no?

HYLAS. It is a material substance with the sensible qualities inhering in it.

PHILONOUS. How then can a great heat exist in it, since you own it cannot in a material substance? I desire you would clear this point.

HYLAS. Hold, Philonous, I fear I was out in yielding intense heat to be a pain. It should seem rather, that pain is something distinct from heat, and the consequence or effect of it.

PHILONOUS. Upon putting your hand near the fire, do you perceive one simple uniform sensation, or two distinct sensations?

HYLAS. But one simple sensation.

PHILONOUS. Is not the heat immediately perceived?

HYLAS. It is.

PHILONOUS. And the pain?

HYLAS. True.

PHILONOUS. Seeing therefore they are both immediately perceived at the same time, and the fire affects you only with one simple, or uncompounded idea, it follows that this same simple idea is both the intense heat immediately perceived, and the pain; and consequently, that the intense heat immediately perceived, is nothing distinct from a particular sort of pain.

HYLAS. It seems so.

PHILONOUS. Again, try in your thoughts, Hylas, if you can conceive a vehement sensation to be without pain, or pleasure.

HYLAS. I cannot.

PHILONOUS. Or can you frame to yourself an idea of sensible pain or pleasure in general, abstracted from every particular idea of heat, cold, tastes, smells? &c.

HYLAS. I do not find that I can.

PHILONOUS. Doth it not therefore follow, that sensible pain is nothing distinct from those sensations or ideas, in an intense degree?

HYLAS. It is undeniable; and to speak the truth, I begin to suspect a very great heat cannot exist but in a mind perceiving it.

PHILONOUS. What! are you then in that *sceptical* state of suspense, between affirming and denying?

HYLAS. I think I may be positive in the point. A very violent and painful heat cannot exist without the mind.

PHILONOUS. It hath not therefore, according to you, any real being.

HYLAS. I own it.

PHILONOUS. Is it therefore certain, that there is no body in nature really hot?

HYLAS. I have not denied there is any real heat in bodies. I only say, there is no such thing as an intense real heat.

PHILONOUS. But did you not say before, that all degrees of heat were equally real: or if there was any difference, that the greater were more undoubtedly real than the lesser?

HYLAS. True: but it was, because I did not then consider the ground there is for distinguishing between them, which I now plainly see. And it is this: because intense heat is nothing else but a particular kind of painful sensation; and pain cannot exist but in a perceiving being; it follows that no intense heat can really exist in an unperceiving corporeal substance. But this is no reason why we should deny heat in an inferior degree to exist in such a substance.

PHILONOUS. But how shall we be able to discern those degrees of heat which exist only in the mind, from those which exist without it?

HYLAS. That is no difficult matter. You know, the least pain cannot exist unperceived; whatever therefore degree of heat is a pain, exists only in the mind. But as for all other degrees of heat, nothing obliges us to think the same of them.

PHILONOUS. I think you granted before, that no unperceiving being was capable of pleasure, any more than of pain.

HYLAS. I did.

PHILONOUS. And is not warmth, or a more gentle degree of heat than what causes uneasiness, a pleasure?

HYLAS. What then?

PHILONOUS. Consequently it cannot exist without the mind in any unperceiving substance, or body.

HYLAS. So it seems.

PHILONOUS. Since therefore, as well those degrees of heat that are not painful, as those that are, can exist only in a thinking substance; may we not conclude that external bodies are absolutely incapable of any degree of heat whatsoever?

HYLAS. On second thoughts, I do not think it so evident that warmth is a pleasure, as that a great degree of heat is a pain.

PHILONOUS. I do not pretend that warmth is as great a pleasure as heat is a pain. But if you grant it to be even a small pleasure, it serves to make good my conclusion.

HYLAS. I could rather call it an *indolence*. It seems to be nothing more than a privation of both pain and pleasure. And that such a quality or state as this may agree to an unthinking substance, I hope you will not deny.

PHILONOUS. If you are resolved to maintain that warmth, or a gentle degree of heat, is no pleasure, I know not how to convince you otherwise, than by appealing to your own sense. But what think you of cold?

HYLAS. The same that I do of heat. An intense degree of cold is a pain; for to feel a very great cold, is to perceive a great uneasiness: it cannot therefore exist without the mind; but a lesser degree of cold may, as well as a lesser degree of heat.

PHILONOUS. Those bodies therefore, upon whose application to our own, we perceive a moderate degree of heat, must be concluded to have a moderate degree of heat or warmth in them: and those, upon whose application we feel a like degree of cold, must be thought to have cold in them.

HYLAS. They must.

PHILONOUS. Can any doctrine be true that necessarily leads a man into an absurdity?

HYLAS. Without doubt it cannot.

PHILONOUS. Is it not an absurdity to think that the same thing should be at the same time both cold and warm?

HYLAS. It is.

PHILONOUS. Suppose now one of your hands hot, and the other cold, and that they are both at once put into the same vessel of water, in an intermediate state; will not the water seem cold to one hand, and warm to the other?

HYLAS. It will.

PHILONOUS. Ought we not therefore by your principles to conclude, it is really both cold and warm at the same time, that is, according to your own concession, to believe an absurdity.

HYLAS. I confess it seems so.

PHILONOUS. Consequently, the principles themselves are false, since you have granted that no true principle leads to an absurdity.

HYLAS. But after all, can anything be more absurd than to say, *there is no heat in the fire?*

PHILONOUS. To make the point still clearer; tell me, whether in two cases exactly alike, we ought not to make the same judgment?

HYLAS. We ought.

PHILONOUS. When a pin pricks your finger, doth it not rend and divide the fibres of your flesh?

HYLAS. It doth.

PHILONOUS. And when a coal burns your finger, doth it any more?

HYLAS. It doth not.

PHILONOUS. Since therefore you neither judge the sensation itself occasioned by the pin, nor anything like it to be in the pin; you should not, conformably to what you have now granted, judge the sensation occasioned by the fire, or anything like it, to be in the fire.

HYLAS. Well, since it must be so, I am content to yield this point, and acknowledge, that heat and cold are only sensations existing in our minds: but there still remain qualities enough to secure the reality of external things.

PHILONOUS. But what will you say, Hylas, if it shall appear that the case is the same with regard to all other sensible qualities, and that they can no more be supposed to exist without the mind, than heat and cold?

HYLAS. Then indeed you will have done something to the purpose; but that is what I despair of seeing proved.

PHILONOUS. Let us examine them in order. What think you of tastes, do they exist without the mind, or no?

HYLAS. Can any man in his senses doubt whether sugar is sweet, or wormwood bitter?

PHILONOUS. Inform me, Hylas. Is a sweet taste a particular kind of pleasure or pleasant sensation, or is it not?

HYLAS. It is.

PHILONOUS. And is not bitterness some kind of uneasiness or pain?

HYLAS. I grant it.

PHILONOUS. If therefore sugar and wormwood are unthinking corporeal substances existing without the mind, how can sweetness and bitterness, that is, pleasure and pain, agree to them?

HYLAS. Hold, Philonous, I now see what it was deluded me all this time. You asked whether heat and cold, sweetness and bitterness, were not particular sorts of pleasure and pain; to which I answered simply, that they were. Whereas I should have thus distinguished: those qualities, as perceived by us, are pleasures or pains, but not as existing in the external objects. We must not therefore conclude absolutely, that there is no heat in the fire, or sweetness in the sugar, but only that heat or sweetness, as perceived by us, are not in the fire or sugar. What say you to this?

PHILONOUS. I say it is nothing to the purpose. Our discourse proceeded altogether concerning sensible things, which you defined to be the things we *immediately perceive by our senses*. Whatever other qualities therefore you speak of, as distinct from these, I know nothing of them, neither do they at all belong to the point in dispute. You may indeed pretend to have discovered certain qualities which you do not perceive, and assert those insensible qualities exist in fire and sugar. But what use can be made of this to your present purpose, I am at a loss to conceive. Tell me then once more, do you acknowledge that heat and cold, sweetness and bitterness (meaning those qualities which are perceived by the senses) do not exist without the mind?

HYLAS. I see it is to no purpose to hold out, so I give up the cause as to those mentioned qualities. Though I profess it sounds oddly, to say that sugar is not sweet.

PHILONOUS. But for your farther satisfaction, take this along with you: that which at other times seems sweet, shall to a distempered palate appear bitter. And nothing can be plainer, than that divers persons perceive different tastes in the same food, since that which one man delights in, another abhors. And how could this be, if the taste was something really inherent in the food?

HYLAS. I acknowledge I know not how.

PHILONOUS. In the next place, odours are to be considered. And with regard to these, I would fain know, whether what hath been said of tastes doth not exactly agree to them? Are they not so many pleasing or displeasing sensations?

HYLAS. They are.

PHILONOUS. Can you then conceive it possible that they should exist in an unperceiving thing?

HYLAS. I cannot.

PHILONOUS. Or can you imagine, that filth and ordure affect those brute animals that feed on them out of choice, with the same smells which we perceive in them?

HYLAS. By no means.

PHILONOUS. May we not therefore conclude of smells, as of the other forementioned qualities, that they cannot exist in any but a perceiving substance or mind?

HYLAS. I think so.

PHILONOUS. Then as to sounds,* what must we think of them: are they accidents really inherent in external bodies, or not?

HYLAS. That they inhere not in the sonorous bodies, is plain from hence; because a bell struck in the exhausted receiver of an air-pump, sends forth no sound. The air therefore must be thought the subject of sound.

PHILONOUS. What reason is there for that, Hylas?

HYLAS. Because when any motion is raised in the air, we perceive a sound greater or lesser, in proportion to the air's motion; but without some motion in the air, we never hear any sound at all.

PHILONOUS. And granting that we never hear a sound but when some motion is produced in the air, yet I do not see how you can infer from thence, that the sound itself is in the air.

HYLAS. It is this very motion in the external air, that produces in the mind the sensation of *sound*. For, striking on the drum of the ear, it causeth a vibration, which by the auditory nerves being communicated to the brain, the soul is thereupon affected with the sensation called *sound*.

PHILONOUS. What! is sound then a sensation?

HYLAS. I tell you, as perceived by us, it is a particular sensation in the mind.

PHILONOUS. And can any sensation exist without the mind?

HYLAS. No certainly.

PHILONOUS. How then can sound, being a sensation exist in the air, if by the *air* you mean a senseless substance existing without the mind?

HYLAS. You must distinguish, Philonous, between sound as it is perceived by us, and as it is in itself; or (which is the same thing) between the sound we immediately perceive, and that which exists without us. The former indeed is a particular kind of sensation, but the latter is merely a vibrative or undulatory motion in the air.

PHILONOUS. I thought I had already obviated that distinction by the answer I gave when you were applying it in a like case before. But to say no more of that; are you sure then that sound is really nothing but motion?

HYLAS. I am.

PHILONOUS. Whatever therefore agrees to real sound, may with truth be attributed to motion.

HYLAS. It may.

PHILONOUS. It is then good sense to speak of *motion*, as of a thing that is *loud*, *sweet*, *acute*, or *grave*.

HYLAS. I see you are resolved not to understand me. Is it not evident, those accidents or modes belong only to sensible sound, or *sound* in the common acceptation of the word, but not to *sound* in the real and philosophic sense, which, as I just now told you, is nothing but a certain motion of the air?

PHILONOUS. It seems then there are two sorts of sound, the one vulgar, or that which is heard, the other philosophical and real.

HYLAS. Even so.

PHILONOUS. And the latter consists in motion.

HYLAS. I told you so before.

PHILONOUS. Tell me, Hylas, to which of the senses think you, the idea of motion belongs: to the hearing?

HYLAS. No certainly, but to the sight and touch.

PHILONOUS. It should follow then, that according to you, real sounds may possibly be *seen* or *felt*, but never *heard*.

HYLAS. Look you, Philonous, you may if you please make a jest of my opinion, but that will not alter the truth of things. I own indeed, the inferences you draw me into, sound something oddly; but common language, you know, is framed by, and for the use of the vulgar: we must not therefore wonder, if expressions adapted to exact philosophic notions, seem uncouth and out of the way.

PHILONOUS. Is it come to that? I assure you, I imagine myself to have gained no small point, since you make so light of departing from common phrases and opinions; it being a main part of our inquiry, to examine whose notions are widest of the common road, and most repugnant to the general sense of the world. But can you think it no more than a philosophical paradox, to say that *real sounds are never heard*, and that the idea of them is obtained by some other sense. And is there nothing in this contrary to nature and the truth of things?

HYLAS. To deal ingenuously, I do not like it. And after the concessions already made, I had as well grant that sounds too have no real being without the mind.

PHILONOUS. And I hope you will make no difficulty to acknowledge the same of colours.

HYLAS. Pardon me: the case of colours* is very different. Can anything be plainer, than that we see them on the objects?

PHILONOUS. The objects you speak of are, I suppose, corporeal substances existing without the mind.

HYLAS. They are.

PHILONOUS. And have true and real colours inhering in them?

HYLAS. Each visible object hath that colour which we see in it.

PHILONOUS. How! Is there anything visible but what we perceive by sight?

HYLAS. There is not.

PHILONOUS. And do we perceive anything by sense, which we do not perceive immediately?

HYLAS. How often must I be obliged to repeat the same thing? I tell you, we do not.

PHILONOUS. Have patience, good Hylas; and tell me once more, whether there is anything immediately perceived by the senses, except sensible qualities. I know you asserted there was not: but I would now be informed, whether you still persist in the same opinion.

HYLAS. I do.

PHILONOUS. Pray, is your corporeal substance either a sensible quality, or made up of sensible qualities?

HYLAS. What a question that is! who ever thought it was?

PHILONOUS. My reason for asking was, because in saying, *each visible object hath that colour which we see in it*, you make visible objects to be corporeal substances; which implies either that corporeal substances are sensible qualities, or else that there is something beside sensible qualities perceived by sight: but as this point was formerly agreed between us, and is still maintained by you, it is a clear consequence, that your corporeal substance is nothing distinct from sensible qualities.

HYLAS. You may draw as many absurd consequences as you please, and endeavour to perplex the plainest things; but you shall never persuade me out of my senses. I clearly understand my own meaning.

PHILONOUS. I wish you would make me understand it too. But since you are unwilling to have your notion of corporeal substance examined, I shall urge that point no farther. Only be pleased to let me know, whether the same colours which we see, exist in external bodies, or some other.

HYLAS. The very same.

PHILONOUS. What! are then the beautiful red and purple we see on yonder clouds, really in them? Or do you imagine they have in themselves any other form, than that of a dark mist or vapour?

HYLAS. I must own, Philonous, those colours are not really

in the clouds as they seem to be at this distance. They are only apparent colours.

PHILONOUS. *Apparent* call you them? how shall we distinguish these apparent colours from real?

HYLAS. Very easily. Those are to be thought apparent, which appearing only at a distance, vanish upon a nearer approach.

PHILONOUS. And those I suppose are to be thought real, which are discovered by the most near and exact survey.

HYLAS. Right.

PHILONOUS. Is the nearest and exactest survey made by the help of a microscope, or by the naked eye?

HYLAS. By a microscope, doubtless.

PHILONOUS. But a microscope often discovers colours in an object different from those perceived by the unassisted sight. And in case we had microscopes magnifying to any assigned degree; it is certain, that no object whatsoever viewed through them, would appear in the same colour which it exhibits to the naked eye.

HYLAS. And what will you conclude from all this? You cannot argue that there are really and naturally no colours on objects: because by artificial managements they may be altered, or made to vanish.

PHILONOUS. I think it may evidently be concluded from your own concessions, that all the colours we see with our naked eyes, are only apparent as those on the clouds, since they vanish upon a more close and accurate inspection, which is afforded us by a microscope. Then as to what you say by way of prevention: I ask you, whether the real and natural state of an object is better discovered by a very sharp and piercing sight, or by one which is less sharp?

HYLAS. By the former without doubt.

PHILONOUS. Is it not plain from *dioptrics*, that microscopes make the sight more penetrating, and represent objects as they would appear to the eye, in case it were naturally endowed with a most exquisite sharpness?

HYLAS. It is.

PHILONOUS. Consequently the microscopical representation is to be thought that which best sets forth the real nature of the thing, or what it is in itself. The colours therefore by it perceived, are more genuine and real, than those perceived otherwise.

HYLAS. I confess there is something in what you say.

PHILONOUS. Besides, it is not only possible but manifest, that there actually are animals, whose eyes are by Nature framed to perceive those things, which by reason of their minuteness escape our sight. What think you of those inconceivably small animals perceived by glasses? Must we suppose they are all stark blind? Or, in case they see, can it be imagined their sight hath not the same use in preserving their bodies from injuries, which appears in that of all other animals? And if it hath, is it not evident, they must see particles less than their own bodies, which will present them with a far different view in each object, from that which strikes our senses? Even our own eyes do not always represent objects to us after the same manner. In the *jaundice*, everyone knows that all things seem yellow. Is it not therefore highly probable, those animals in whose eyes we discern a very different texture from that of ours, and whose bodies abound with different humours, do not see the same colours in every object that we do? From all which, should it not seem to follow, that all colours are equally apparent, and that none of those which we perceive are really inherent in any outward object?

HYLAS. It should.

PHILONOUS. The point will be past all doubt, if you consider, that in case colours were real properties or affections inherent in external bodies, they could admit of no alteration, without some change wrought in the very bodies themselves: but is it not evident from what hath been said, that upon the use of microscopes, upon a change happening in the humours of the eye, or a variation of distance, without any manner of real alteration in the thing itself, the colours of any object are either changed, or totally disappear? Nay all other circumstances remaining the same, change but the situation of some objects, and they shall present different colours to the eye. The same thing happens upon viewing an object in various degrees of light.

And what is more known, than that the same bodies appear differently coloured by candle-light, from what they do in the open day? Add to these the experiment of a prism, which separating the heterogeneous rays of light, alters the colour of any object; and will cause the whitest to appear of a deep blue or red to the naked eye. And now tell me, whether you are still of opinion, that every body hath its true real colour inhering in it; and if you think it hath, I would fain know farther from you, what certain distance and position of the object, what peculiar texture and formation of the eye, what degree or kind of light is necessary for ascertaining that true colour, and distinguishing it from apparent ones.

HYLAS. I own myself entirely satisfied, that they are all equally apparent; and that there is no such thing as colour really inhering in external bodies, but that it is altogether in the light. And what confirms me in this opinion is, that in proportion to the light, colours are still more or less vivid; and if there be no light, then are there no colours perceived. Besides, allowing there are colours on external objects, yet how is it possible for us to perceive them? For no external body affects the mind, unless it act first on our organs of sense. But the only action of bodies is motion; and motion cannot be communicated otherwise than by impulse. A distant object therefore cannot act on the eye, nor consequently make itself or its properties perceivable to the soul. Whence it plainly follows, that it is immediately some contiguous substance, which operating on the eye occasions a perception of colours: and such is light.

PHILONOUS. How! is light then a substance?

HYLAS. I tell you, Philonous, external light is nothing but a thin fluid substance, whose minute particles being agitated with a brisk motion, and in various manners reflected from the different surfaces of outward objects to the eyes, communicate different motions to the optic nerves; which being propagated to the brain, cause therein various impressions: and these are attended with the sensations of red, blue, yellow, &c.

PHILONOUS. It seems then, the light doth no more than shake the optic nerves.

HYLAS. Nothing else.

PHILONOUS. And consequent to each particular motion of the nerves the mind is affected with a sensation, which is some particular colour.

HYLAS. Right.

PHILONOUS. And these sensations have no existence without the mind.

HYLAS. They have not.

PHILONOUS. How then do you affirm that colours are in the light, since by *light* you understand a corporeal substance external to the mind?

HYLAS. Light and colours, as immediately perceived by us, I grant cannot exist without the mind. But in themselves they are only the motions and configurations of certain insensible particles of matter.

PHILONOUS. Colours then in the vulgar sense, or taken for the immediate objects of sight, cannot agree to any but a perceiving substance.

HYLAS. That is what I say.

PHILONOUS. Well then, since you give up the point as to those sensible qualities, which are alone thought colours by all mankind beside, you may hold what you please with regard to those invisible ones of the philosophers. It is not my business to dispute about them; only I would advise you to bethink yourself, whether considering the inquiry we are upon, it be prudent for you to affirm, *the red and blue which we see are not real colours, but certain unknown motions and figures which no man ever did or can see, are truly so*. Are not these shocking notions, and are not they subject to as many ridiculous inferences, as those you were obliged to renounce before in the case of sounds?

HYLAS. I frankly own, Philonous, that it is in vain to stand out any longer. Colours, sounds, tastes, in a word, all those termed *secondary qualities*, have certainly no existence without the mind. But by this acknowledgment I must not be supposed to derogate anything from the reality of matter or external objects, seeing it is no more than several philosophers maintain, who nevertheless are the farthest imaginable from denying matter. For the clearer understanding of this, you must know sensible qualities are by philosophers divided into *primary* and *secondary*. The former are extension, figure, solidity, gravity, motion, and rest. And these they hold exist really in bodies. The latter are those above enumerated; or briefly, all sensible qualities beside the primary, which they assert are only so many sensations or ideas existing nowhere but in the mind. But all this, I doubt not, you are already apprised of. For my part, I have been a long time sensible there was such an opinion current among philosophers, but was never thoroughly convinced of its truth till now.

PHILONOUS. You are still then of opinion, that extension and figures are inherent in external unthinking substances.

HYLAS. I am.

PHILONOUS. But what if the same arguments which are brought against secondary qualities, will hold good against these also?

HYLAS. Why then I shall be obliged to think, they too exist only in the mind.

PHILONOUS. Is it your opinion, the very figure and extension which you perceive by sense, exist in the outward object or material substance?

HYLAS. It is.*

PHILONOUS. Have all other animals as good grounds to think the same of the figure and extension which they see and feel?

HYLAS. Without doubt, if they have any thought at all.

PHILONOUS. Answer me, Hylas. Think you the senses were bestowed upon all animals for their preservation and well-being in life? or were they given to men alone for this end?

HYLAS. I make no question but they have the same use in all other animals.

PHILONOUS. If so, is it not necessary they should be enabled by them to perceive their own limbs, and those bodies which are capable of harming them?

HYLAS. Certainly.

PHILONOUS. A mite* therefore must be supposed to see his own foot, and things equal or even less than it, as bodies of some considerable dimension; though at the same time they appear to you scarce discernible, or at best as so many visible points.

HYLAS. I cannot deny it.

PHILONOUS. And to creatures less than the mite they will seem yet larger.

HYLAS. They will.

PHILONOUS. Insomuch that what you can hardly discern, will to another extremely minute animal appear as some huge mountain.

HYLAS. All this I grant.

PHILONOUS. Can one and the same thing be at the same time in itself of different dimensions?

HYLAS. That were absurd to imagine.

PHILONOUS. But from what you have laid down it follows, that both the extension by you perceived, and that perceived by the mite itself, as likewise all those perceived by lesser animals, are each of them the true extension of the mite's foot, that is to say, by your own principles you are led into an absurdity.

HYLAS. There seems to be some difficulty in the point.

PHILONOUS. Again, have you not acknowledged that no real inherent property of any object can be changed, without some change in the thing itself?

HYLAS. I have.

PHILONOUS. But as we approach to or recede from an object, the visible extension varies, being at one distance ten or an hundred times greater than at another. Doth it not therefore follow from hence likewise, that it is not really inherent in the object?

HYLAS. I own I am at a loss what to think.

PHILONOUS. Your judgment will soon be determined, if you will venture to think as freely concerning this quality, as you have done concerning the rest. Was it not admitted as a good argument, that neither heat nor cold was in the water, because it seemed warm to one hand, and cold to the other?

HYLAS. It was.

PHILONOUS. Is it not the very same reasoning to conclude, there is no extension or figure in an object, because to one eye it shall seem little, smooth, and round, when at the same time it appears to the other, great, uneven, and angular?

HYLAS. The very same. But doth this latter fact ever happen?

PHILONOUS. You may at any time make the experiment, by looking with one eye bare, and with the other through a microscope.

HYLAS. I know not how to maintain it, and yet I am loth to give up *extension*, I see so many odd consequences following upon such a concession.

PHILONOUS. Odd, say you? After the concessions already made, I hope you will stick at nothing for its oddness.* But on the other hand should it not seem very odd, if the general reasoning which includes all other sensible qualities did not also include extension? If it be allowed that no idea nor anything like an idea can exist in an unperceiving substance, then surely it follows, that no figure or mode of extension, which we can either perceive or imagine, or have any idea of, can be really inherent in matter; not to mention the peculiar difficulty there must be, in conceiving a material substance, prior to and distinct from extension, to be the *substratum* of extension. Be the sensible quality what it will, figure, or sound, or colour; it seems alike impossible it should subsist in that which doth not perceive it.

HYLAS. I give up the point for the present, reserving still a right to retract my opinion, in case I shall hereafter discover any false step in my progress to it.

PHILONOUS. That is a right you cannot be denied. Figures and extension being dispatched, we proceed next to *motion*. Can a real motion in any external body be at the same time both very swift and very slow?

HYLAS. It cannot.

PHILONOUS. Is not the motion of a body swift in a reciprocal proportion to the time it takes up in describing any given space? Thus a body that describes a mile in an hour, moves three times faster than it would in case it described only a mile in three hours.

HYLAS. I agree with you.

PHILONOUS. And is not time measured by the succession of ideas in our minds?*

HYLAS. It is.

PHILONOUS. And is it not possible ideas should succeed one another twice as fast in your mind, as they do in mine, or in that of some spirit of another kind.

HYLAS. I own it.

PHILONOUS. Consequently the same body may to another seem to perform its motion over any space in half the time that it doth to you. And the same reasoning will hold as to any other proportion: that is to say, according to your principles (since the motions perceived are both really in the object) it is possible one and the same body shall be really moved the same way at once, both very swift and very slow. How is this consistent either with common sense, or with what you just now granted?

HYLAS. I have nothing to say to it.

PHILONOUS. Then as for *solidity*; either you do not mean any sensible quality by that word, and so it is beside our inquiry: or if you do, it must be either hardness or resistance. But both the one and the other are plainly relative to our sense: it being evident, that what seems hard to one animal, may appear soft to another, who hath greater force and firmness of limbs. Nor is it less plain, that the resistance I feel is not in the body.

HYLAS. I own the very sensation of resistance, which is all you immediately perceive, is not in the *body*, but the cause of that sensation is.

PHILONOUS. But the causes of our sensations are not things immediately perceived, and therefore not sensible. This point I thought had been already determined.

HYLAS. I own it was; but you will pardon me if I seem a little embarrassed: I know not how to quit my old notions.

PHILONOUS. To help you out, do but consider, that if extension be once acknowledged to have no existence without the mind, the same must necessarily be granted of motion, solidity, and gravity, since they all evidently suppose extension. It is therefore superfluous to inquire particularly concerning each of them. In denying extension, you have denied them all.to have any real existence.

HYLAS. I wonder, Philonous, if what you say be true, why those philosophers who deny the secondary qualities any real existence, should yet attribute it to the primary. If there is no difference between them, how can this be accounted for?

PHILONOUS. It is not my business to account for every opinion of the philosophers. But among other reasons which may be assigned for this, it seems probable, that pleasure and pain being rather annexed to the former than the latter, may be one. Heat and cold, tastes and smells, have something more vividly pleasing or disagreeable than the ideas of extension, figure, and motion, affect us with. And it being too visibly absurd to hold, that pain or pleasure can be in an unperceiving substance, men are more easily weaned from believing the external existence of the secondary, than the primary qualities. You will be satisfied there is something in this, if you recollect the difference you made between an intense and more moderate degree of heat, allowing the one a real existence, while you denied it to the other. But after all, there is no rational ground for that distinction; for surely an indifferent sensation is as truly *a sensation*, as one more pleasing or painful; and consequently should not any more than they be supposed to exist in an unthinking subject.

HYLAS. It is just come into my head, Philonous, that I have somewhere heard of a distinction between absolute and sensible extension. Now though it be acknowledged that *great* and *small*, consisting merely in the relation which other extended beings have to the parts of our own bodies, do not really inhere in the substances themselves; yet nothing obliges us to hold the same with regard to *absolute extension*, which is something abstracted from *great* and *small*, from this or that particular magnitude or figure. So likewise as to motion, *swift* and *slow* are altogether relative to the succession of ideas in our own minds. But it doth not follow, because those modifications of motion exist not without the mind, that therefore absolute motion abstracted from them doth not.

PHILONOUS. Pray what is it that distinguishes one motion, or one part of extension from another? Is it not something sensible, as some degree of swiftness or slowness, some certain magnitude or figure peculiar to each?

HYLAS. I think so.

PHILONOUS. These qualities therefore stripped of all sensible properties, are without all specific and numerical differences, as the Schools call them.

HYLAS. They are.

PHILONOUS. That is to say, they are extension in general, and motion in general.

HYLAS. Let it be so.

PHILONOUS. But it is an universally received maxim, that *everything which exists, is particular*. How then can motion in general, or extension in general exist in any corporeal substance?

HYLAS. I will take time to solve your difficulty.

PHILONOUS. But I think the point may be speedily decided. Without doubt you can tell, whether you are able to frame this or that idea. Now I am content to put our dispute on this issue. If you can frame in your thoughts a distinct abstract idea of motion or extension, divested of all those sensible modes, as swift and slow, great and small, round and square, and the like, which are acknowledged to exist only in the mind, I will then yield the point you contend for. But if you cannot, it will be unreasonable on your side to insist any longer upon what you have no notion of.

HYLAS. To confess ingenuously, I cannot.

PHILONOUS. Can you even separate the ideas of extension and motion, from the ideas of all those qualities which they who make the distinction, term *secondary*.

HYLAS. What! is it not an easy matter, to consider extension and motion by themselves, abstracted from all other sensible qualities? Pray how do the mathematicians treat of them?

PHILONOUS. I acknowledge, Hylas, it is not difficult to form general propositions and reasonings about those qualities, without mentioning any other; and in this sense to consider or treat of them abstractedly. But how doth it follow that because I can pronounce the word *motion* by itself, I can form the idea of it in my mind exclusive of body? Or because theorems may be made of extension and figures, without any mention of *great* or *small*, or any other sensible mode or quality; that therefore it is possible such an abstract idea of extension, without any particular size or figure, or sensible quality, should be distinctly formed, and apprehended by the mind? Mathematicians treat of quantity, without regarding what other sensible qualities it is attended with, as being altogether indifferent to their demonstrations. But when laying aside the words, they contemplate the bare ideas, I believe you will find, they are not the pure abstracted ideas of extension.

HYLAS. But what say you to *pure intellect*? May not abstracted ideas be framed by that faculty?

PHILONOUS. Since I cannot frame abstract ideas at all, it is plain, I cannot frame them by the help of *pure intellect*, whatsoever faculty you understand by those words. Besides, not to inquire into the nature of pure intellect and its spiritual objects, as *virtue*, *reason*, *God*, or the like; thus much seems manifest, that sensible things are only to be perceived by sense, or represented by the imagination. Figures therefore and extension being originally perceived by sense, do not belong to pure intellect. But for your farther satisfaction, try if you can frame the idea of any figure, abstracted from all particularities of size, or even from other sensible qualities.

HYLAS. Let me think a little—I do not find that I can.*

PHILONOUS. And can you think it possible, that should really exist in Nature, which implies a repugnancy in its conception?

HYLAS. By no means.

PHILONOUS. Since therefore it is impossible even for the mind to disunite the ideas of extension and motion from all other sensible qualities, doth it not follow, that where the one exist, there necessarily the other exist likewise?

HYLAS. It should seem so.

PHILONOUS. Consequently the very same arguments which

you admitted, as conclusive against the secondary qualities, are without any farther application of force against the primary too. Besides, if you will trust your senses, is it not plain all sensible qualities coexist, or to them, appear as being in the same place? Do they ever represent a motion, or figure, as being divested of all other visible and tangible qualities?

HYLAS. You need say no more on this head. I am free to own, if there be no secret error or oversight in our proceedings hitherto, that all sensible qualities are alike to be denied existence without the mind. But my fear is, that I have been too liberal in my former concessions, or overlooked some fallacy or other. In short, I did not take time to think.

PHILONOUS. For that matter, Hylas, you may take what time you please in reviewing the progress of our inquiry. You are at liberty to recover any slips you might have made, or offer whatever you have omitted, which makes for your first opinion.

HYLAS. One great oversight I take to be this: that I did not sufficiently distinguish the *object* from the *sensation*.* Now though this latter may not exist without the mind, yet it will not thence follow that the former cannot.

PHILONOUS. What object do you mean? the object of the senses?

HYLAS. The same.

PHILONOUS. It is then immediately perceived.

HYLAS. Right.

PHILONOUS. Make me to understand the difference between what is immediately perceived, and a sensation.

HYLAS. The sensation I take to be an act of the mind perceiving; beside which, there is something perceived; and this I call the *object*. For example, there is red and yellow on that tulip. But then the act of perceiving those colours is in me only, and not in the tulip.

PHILONOUS. What tulip do you speak of? is it that which you see?

HYLAS. The same.

PHILONOUS. And what do you see beside colour, figure, and extension?

HYLAS. Nothing.

PHILONOUS. What you would say then is, that the red and yellow are coexistent with the extension; is it not?

HYLAS. That is not all; I would say, they have a real existence without the mind, in some unthinking substance.

PHILONOUS. That the colours are really in the tulip which I see, is manifest. Neither can it be denied, that this tulip may exist independent of your mind or mine; but that any immediate object of the senses, that is, any idea, or combination of ideas, should exist in an unthinking substance, or exterior to all minds, is in itself an evident contradiction. Nor can I imagine how this follows from what you said just now, to wit that the red and yellow were on the tulip *you saw*, since you do not pretend to *see* that unthinking substance.

HYLAS. You have an artful way, Philonous, of diverting our inquiry from the subject.

PHILONOUS. I see you have no mind to be pressed that way. To return then to your distinction between *sensation* and *object*; if I take you right, you distinguish in every perception two things, the one an action of the mind, the other not.

HYLAS. True.

PHILONOUS. And this action cannot exist in, or belong to any unthinking thing; but whatever beside is implied in a perception, may.

HYLAS. That is my meaning.

PHILONOUS. So that if there was a perception without any act of the mind, it were possible such a perception should exist in an unthinking substance.

HYLAS. I grant it. But it is impossible there should be such a perception.

PHILONOUS. When is the mind said to be active?

HYLAS. When it produces, puts an end to, or changes anything.

PHILONOUS. Can the mind produce, discontinue, or change anything but by an act of the will?

HYLAS. It cannot.

PHILONOUS. The mind therefore is to be accounted active in its perceptions, so far forth as volition is included in them.

HYLAS. It is.

PHILONOUS. In plucking this flower, I am active, because I do it by the motion of my hand, which was consequent upon my volition; so likewise in applying it to my nose. But is either of these smelling?

HYLAS. No.

PHILONOUS. I act too in drawing the air through my nose; because my breathing so rather than otherwise, is the effect of my volition. But neither can this be called *smelling*: for if it were, I should smell every time I breathed in that manner.

HYLAS. True.

PHILONOUS. Smelling then is somewhat consequent to all this.

HYLAS. It is.

PHILONOUS. But I do not find my will concerned any farther. Whatever more there is, as that I perceive such a particular smell or any smell at all, this is independent of my will, and therein I am altogether passive. Do you find it otherwise with you, Hylas?

HYLAS. No, the very same.

PHILONOUS. Then as to seeing, is it not in your power to open your eyes, or keep them shut; to turn them this or that way?

HYLAS. Without doubt.

PHILONOUS. But doth it in like manner depend on your will, that in looking on this flower, you perceive *white* rather than any other colour? Or directing your open eyes toward yonder part of the heaven, can you avoid seeing the sun? Or is light or darkness the effect of your volition?

HYLAS. No certainly.

PHILONOUS. You are then in these respects altogether passive.

HYLAS. I am.

PHILONOUS. Tell me now, whether *seeing* consists in perceiving light and colours, or in opening and turning the eyes?

HYLAS. Without doubt, in the former.

PHILONOUS. Since therefore you are in the very perception

of light and colours altogether passive, what is become of that action you were speaking of, as an ingredient in every sensation? And doth it not follow from your own concessions, that the perception of light and colours, including no action in it, may exist in an unperceiving substance? And is not this a plain contradiction?

HYLAS. I know not what to think of it.

PHILONOUS. Besides, since you distinguish the *active* and *passive* in every perception, you must do it in that of pain. But how is it possible that pain, be it as little active as you please, should exist in an unperceiving substance? In short, do but consider the point, and then confess ingenuously, whether light and colours, tastes, sounds, &c. are not all equally passions or sensations in the soul. You may indeed call them *external objects*, and give them in words what subsistence you please. But examine your own thoughts, and then tell me whether it be not as I say?

HYLAS. I acknowledge, Philonous, that upon a fair observation of what passes in my mind, I can discover nothing else, but that I am a thinking being, affected with variety of sensations; neither is it possible to conceive how a sensation should exist in an unperceiving substance. But then on the other hand, when I look on sensible things in a different view, considering them as so many modes and qualities, I find it necessary to suppose a material *substratum*, without which they cannot be conceived to exist.

PHILONOUS. *Material substratum* call you it? Pray, by which of your senses came you acquainted with that being?

HYLAS. It is not itself sensible; its modes and qualities only being perceived by the senses.

PHILONOUS. I presume then, it was by reflexion and reason you obtained the idea of it.

HYLAS. I do not pretend to any proper positive idea of it. However I conclude it exists, because qualities cannot be conceived to exist without a support.

PHILONOUS. It seems then you have only a relative notion of it, or that you conceive it not otherwise than by conceiving the relation it bears to sensible qualities.

HYLAS. Right.

PHILONOUS. Be pleased therefore to let me know wherein that relation consists.

HYLAS. Is it not sufficiently expressed in the term *substratum*, or *substance*?

PHILONOUS. If so, the word *substratum* should import, that it is spread under the sensible qualities or accidents.

HYLAS. True.

PHILONOUS. And consequently under extension.

HYLAS. I own it.

PHILONOUS. It is therefore somewhat in its own nature entirely distinct from extension.

HYLAS. I tell you, extension is only a mode, and matter is something that supports modes. And is it not evident the thing supported is different from the thing supporting?

PHILONOUS. So that something distinct from, and exclusive of extension, is supposed to be the *substratum* of extension.

HYLAS. Just so.

PHILONOUS. Answer me, Hylas. Can a thing be spread without extension? or is not the idea of extension necessarily included in *spreading*?

HYLAS. It is.

PHILONOUS. Whatsoever therefore you suppose spread under anything, must have in itself an extension distinct from the extension of that thing under which it is spread.

HYLAS. It must.

PHILONOUS. Consequently every corporeal substance being the *substratum* of extension, must have in itself another extension by which it is qualified to be a *substratum*: and so on to infinity. And I ask whether this be not absurd in itself, and repugnant to what you granted just now, to wit, that the *substratum* was something distinct from, and exclusive of extension.

HYLAS. Ay but, Philonous, you take me wrong. I do not mean that matter is *spread* in a gross literal sense under extension. The word *substratum* is used only to express in general the same thing with *substance*.

PHILONOUS. Well then, let us examine the relation implied in the term *substance*. Is it not that it stands under accidents?

HYLAS. The very same.

PHILONOUS. But that one thing may stand under or support another, must it not be extended?

HYLAS. It must.

PHILONOUS. Is not therefore this supposition liable to the same absurdity with the former?

HYLAS. You still take things in a strict literal sense: that is not fair, Philonous.

PHILONOUS. I am not for imposing any sense on your words: you are at liberty to explain them as you please. Only I beseech you, make me understand something by them. You tell me, matter supports or stands under accidents. How! is it as your legs support your body?

HYLAS. No; that is the literal sense.

PHILONOUS. Pray let me know any sense, literal or not literal, that you understand it in.—— How long must I wait for an answer, Hylas?

HYLAS. I declare I know not what to say. I once thought I understood well enough what was meant by matter's supporting accidents. But now the more I think on it, the less can I comprehend it; in short, I find that I know nothing of it.

PHILONOUS. It seems then you have no idea at all, neither relative nor positive of matter; you know neither what it is in itself, nor what relation it bears to accidents.

HYLAS. I acknowledge it.

PHILONOUS. And yet you asserted, that you could not conceive how qualities or accidents should really exist, without conceiving at the same time a material support of them.

HYLAS. I did.

PHILONOUS. That is to say, when you conceive the real existence of qualities, you do withal conceive something which you cannot conceive.

HYLAS. It was wrong I own. But still I fear there is some fallacy or other. Pray what think you of this? It is just come into my head, that the ground of all our mistakes lies in your treating of each quality by itself. Now, I grant that each quality cannot singly subsist without the mind. Colour cannot without extension, neither can figure without some other sensible quality. But as the several qualities united or blended together form entire sensible things, nothing hinders why such things may not be supposed to exist without the mind.

PHILONOUS. Either, Hylas, you are jesting, or have a very bad memory. Though indeed we went through all the qualities by name one after another; yet my arguments, or rather your concessions nowhere tended to prove, that the secondary qualities did not subsist each alone by itself; but that they were not *at all* without the mind. Indeed in treating of figure and motion, we concluded they could not exist without the mind, because it was impossible even in thought to separate them from all secondary qualities, so as to conceive them existing by themselves. But then this was not the only argument made use of upon that occasion. But (to pass by all that hath been hitherto said, and reckon it for nothing, if you will have it so) I am content to put the whole upon this issue. If you can conceive it possible for any mixture or combination of qualities, or any sensible object whatever, to exist without the mind, then I will grant it actually to be so.

HYLAS. If it comes to that, the point will soon be decided. What more easy than to conceive a tree or house existing by itself, independent of, and unperceived by any mind whatsoever? I do at this present time conceive them existing after that manner.

PHILONOUS. How say you, Hylas, can you see a thing which is at the same time unseen?

HYLAS. No, that were a contradiction.

PHILONOUS. Is it not as great a contradiction to talk of *conceiving* a thing which is *unconceived*?*

HYLAS. It is.

PHILONOUS. The tree or house therefore which you think of, is conceived by you.

HYLAS. How should it be otherwise?

PHILONOUS. And what is conceived, is surely in the mind.

HYLAS. Without question, that which is conceived is in the mind.

PHILONOUS. How then came you to say, you conceived a

house or tree existing independent and out of all minds whatsoever?

HYLAS. That was I own an oversight; but stay, let me consider what led me into it.—It is a pleasant mistake enough. As I was thinking of a tree in a solitary place, where no one was present to see it, methought that was to conceive a tree as existing unperceived or unthought of, not considering that I myself conceived it all the while. But now I plainly see, that all I can do is to frame ideas in my own mind. I may indeed conceive in my own thoughts the idea of a tree, or a house, or a mountain, but that is all. And this is far from proving, that I can conceive them *existing out of the minds of all spirits*.

PHILONOUS. You acknowledge then that you cannot possibly conceive, how any one corporeal sensible thing should exist otherwise than in a mind.

HYLAS. I do.

PHILONOUS. And yet you will earnestly contend for the truth of that which you cannot so much as conceive.

HYLAS. I profess I know not what to think, but still there are some scruples remain with me. Is it not certain I see things at a distance? Do we not perceive the stars and moon, for example, to be a great way off? Is not this, I say, manifest to the senses?

PHILONOUS. Do you not in a dream too perceive those or the like objects?

HYLAS. I do.

PHILONOUS. And have they not then the same appearance of being distant?

HYLAS. They have.

PHILONOUS. But you do not thence conclude the apparitions in a dream to be without the mind?

HYLAS. By no means.

PHILONOUS. You ought not therefore to conclude that sensible objects are without the mind, from their appearance or manner wherein they are perceived.

HYLAS. I acknowledge it. But doth not my sense deceive me in those cases?

PHILONOUS. By no means. The idea or thing which you immediately perceive, neither sense nor reason inform you that it actually exists without the mind. By sense you only know that you are affected with such certain sensations of light and colours, &c. And these you will not say are without the mind.

HYLAS. True: but beside all that, do you not think the sight suggests something of *outness* or *distance*?

PHILONOUS. Upon approaching a distant object, do the visible size and figure change perpetually, or do they appear the same at all distances?

HYLAS. They are in a continual change.

PHILONOUS. Sight therefore doth not suggest or any way inform you, that the visible object you immediately perceive, exists at a distance,* or will be perceived when you advance farther onward, there being a continued series of visible objects succeeding each other, during the whole time of your approach.

HYLAS. It doth not; but still I know, upon seeing an object, what object I shall perceive after having passed over a certain distance: no matter whether it be exactly the same or no: there is still something of distance suggested in the case.

PHILONOUS. Good Hylas, do but reflect a little on the point, and then tell me whether there be any more in it than this. From the ideas you actually perceive by sight, you have by experience learned to collect what other ideas you will (according to the standing order of Nature) be affected with, after such a certain succession of time and motion.

HYLAS. Upon the whole, I take it to be nothing else.

PHILONOUS. Now is it not plain, that if we suppose a man born blind was on a sudden made to see, he could at first have no experience of what may be suggested by sight.

HYLAS. It is.

PHILONOUS. He would not then according to you have any notion of distance annexed to the things he saw; but would take them for a new set of sensations existing only in his mind.

HYLAS. It is undeniable.

PHILONOUS. But to make it still more plain: Is not *distance* a line turned endwise to the eye?

HYLAS. It is.

PHILONOUS. And can a line so situated be perceived by sight?

HYLAS. It cannot.

PHILONOUS. Doth it not therefore follow that distance is not properly and immediately perceived by sight?

HYLAS. It should seem so.

PHILONOUS. Again, is it your opinion that colours are at a distance?

HYLAS. It must be acknowledged, they are only in the mind.

PHILONOUS. But do not colours appear to the eye as coexisting in the same place with extension and figures?

HYLAS. They do.

PHILONOUS. How can you then conclude from sight, that figures exist without, when you acknowledge colours do not; the sensible appearance being the very same with regard to both?

HYLAS. I know not what to answer.

PHILONOUS. But allowing that distance was truly and immediately perceived by the mind, yet it would not thence follow it existed out of the mind. For whatever is immediately perceived is an idea: and can any *idea* exist out of the mind?

HYLAS. To suppose that, were absurd: but inform me, Philonous, can we perceive or know nothing beside our ideas?

PHILONOUS. As for the rational deducing of causes from effects, that is beside our inquiry. And by the senses you can best tell, whether you perceive anything which is not immediately perceived. And I ask you, whether the things immediately perceived, are other than your own sensations or ideas? You have indeed more than once, in the course of this conversation, declared yourself on those points; but you seem by this last question to have departed from what you then thought.

HYLAS. To speak the truth, Philonous, I think there are two kinds of objects, the one perceived immediately, which are likewise called *ideas*; the other are real things or external objects perceived by the mediation of ideas, which are their images and representations. Now I own, ideas do not exist without the mind; but the latter sort of objects do.* I am sorry I did not think of this distinction sooner; it would probably have cut short your discourse.

PHILONOUS. Are those external objects perceived by sense, or by some other faculty?

HYLAS. They are perceived by sense.

PHILONOUS. How! is there anything perceived by sense, which is not immediately perceived?

HYLAS. Yes, Philonous, in some sort there is. For example, when I look on a picture or statue of Julius Cæsar, I may be said after a manner to perceive him (though not immediately) by my senses.

PHILONOUS. It seems then, you will have our ideas, which alone are immediately perceived, to be pictures of external things: and that these also are perceived by sense, inasmuch as they have a conformity or resemblance to our ideas.

HYLAS. That is my meaning.

PHILONOUS. And in the same way that Julius Cæsar, in himself invisible, is nevertheless perceived by sight; real things in themselves imperceptible, are perceived by sense.

HYLAS. In the very same.

PHILONOUS. Tell me, Hylas, when you behold the picture of Julius Cæsar, do you see with your eyes any more than some colours and figures with a certain symmetry and composition of the whole?

HYLAS. Nothing else.

PHILONOUS. And would not a man, who had never known anything of Julius Cæsar, see as much?

HYLAS. He would.

PHILONOUS. Consequently he hath his sight, and the use of it, in as perfect a degree as you.

HYLAS. I agree with you.

PHILONOUS. Whence comes it then that your thoughts are directed to the Roman Emperor, and his are not? This cannot proceed from the sensations or ideas of sense by you then perceived; since you acknowledge you have no advantage over him in that respect. It should seem therefore to proceed from reason and memory: should it not?

HYLAS. It should.

PHILONOUS. Consequently it will not follow from that instance, that anything is perceived by sense which is not immediately perceived. Though I grant we may in one acceptation be said to perceive sensible things mediately by sense: that is, when from a frequently perceived connexion, the immediate perception of ideas by one sense suggests to the mind others perhaps belonging to another sense, which are wont to be connected with them. For instance, when I hear a coach drive along the streets, immediately I perceive only the sound; but from the experience I have had that such a sound is connected with a coach, I am said to hear the coach. It is nevertheless evident, that in truth and strictness, nothing can be *heard* but *sound*: and the coach is not then properly perceived by sense, but suggested from experience. So likewise when we are said to see a red-hot bar of iron; the solidity and heat of the iron are not the objects of sight, but suggested to the imagination by the colour and figure, which are properly perceived by that sense. In short, those things alone are actually and strictly perceived by any sense, which would have been perceived, in case that same sense had then been first conferred on us. As for other things, it is plain they are only suggested to the mind by experience grounded on former perceptions. But to return to your comparison of Cæsar's picture, it is plain, if you keep to that, you must hold the real things or archetypes of our ideas are not perceived by sense, but by some internal faculty of the soul, as reason or memory. I would therefore fain know, what arguments you can draw from reason for the existence of what you call *real things* or *material objects*. Or whether you remember to have seen them formerly as they are in themselves? or if you have heard or read of any one that did.

HYLAS. I see, Philonous, you are disposed to raillery; but that will never convince me.

PHILONOUS. My aim is only to learn from you, the way to come at the knowledge of *material beings*. Whatever we perceive, is perceived either immediately or mediately: by sense, or by reason and reflexion. But as you have excluded sense, pray shew me what reason you have to believe their existence; or what *medium* you can possibly make use of, to prove it either to mine or your own understanding.

HYLAS. To deal ingenuously, Philonous, now I consider the point, I do not find I can give you any good reason for it. But thus much seems pretty plain, that it is at least possible such things may really exist. And as long as there is no absurdity in supposing them, I am resolved to believe as I did, till you bring good reasons to the contrary.

PHILONOUS. What? is it come to this, that you only believe the existence of material objects, and that your belief is founded barely on the possibility of its being true? Then you will have me bring reasons against it: though another would think it reasonable, the proof should lie on him who holds the affirmative. And after all, this very point which you are now resolved to maintain without any reason, is in effect what you have more than once during this discourse seen good reason to give up. But to pass over all this; if I understand you rightly, you say our ideas do not exist without the mind; but that they are copies, images, or representations of certain originals that do.

HYLAS. You take me right.

PHILONOUS. They are then like external things.

HYLAS. They are.

PHILONOUS. Have those things a stable and permanent nature independent of our senses; or are they in a perpetual change, upon our producing any motions in our bodies, suspending, exerting, or altering our faculties or organs of sense.

HYLAS. Real things, it is plain, have a fixed and real nature, which remains the same, notwithstanding any change in our senses, or in the posture and motion of our bodies; which indeed may affect the ideas in our minds, but it were absurd to think they had the same effect on things existing without the mind.

PHILONOUS. How then is it possible, that things perpetually fleeting and variable as our ideas, should be copies or images of anything fixed and constant? Or in other words, since all sensible qualities, as size, figure, colour, &c. that is, our ideas are continually changing upon every alteration in the distance, medium, or instruments of sensation; how can any determinate material objects be properly represented or painted forth by several distinct things, each of which is so different from and unlike the rest? Or if you say it resembles some one only of our ideas, how shall we be able to distinguish the true copy from all the false ones?

HYLAS. I profess, Philonous, I am at a loss. I know not what to say to this.

PHILONOUS. But neither is this all. Which are material objects in themselves, perceptible or imperceptible?

HYLAS. Properly and immediately nothing can be perceived but ideas. All material things therefore are in themselves insensible, and to be perceived only by their ideas.

PHILONOUS. Ideas then are sensible, and their archetypes or originals insensible.

HYLAS. Right.

PHILONOUS. But how can that which is sensible be like that which is insensible? Can a real thing in itself *invisible* be like a *colour*; or a real thing which is not *audible*, be like a *sound*? In a word, can anything be like a sensation or idea, but another sensation or idea?

HYLAS. I must own, I think not.

PHILONOUS. Is it possible there should be any doubt in the point? Do you not perfectly know your own ideas?

HYLAS. I know them perfectly; since what I do not perceive or know, can be no part of my idea.

PHILONOUS. Consider therefore, and examine them, and then tell me if there be anything in them which can exist without the mind: or if you can conceive anything like them existing without the mind.

HYLAS. Upon inquiry, I find it is impossible for me to conceive or understand how anything but an idea can be like an idea. And it is most evident, that *no idea can exist without the mind*.

PHILONOUS. You are therefore by your principles forced to deny the reality of sensible things, since you made it to consist in an absolute existence exterior to the mind. That is to say, you are a downright *sceptic*. So I have gained my point, which was to shew your principles led to scepticism.

HYLAS. For the present I am, if not entirely convinced, at least silenced.

PHILONOUS. I would fain know what more you would require in order to a perfect conviction. Have you not had the liberty of explaining yourself all manner of ways? Were any little slips in discourse laid hold and insisted on? Or were you not allowed to retract or reinforce anything you had offered, as best served your purpose? Hath not everything you could say been heard and examined with all the fairness imaginable? In a word, have you not in every point been convinced out of your own mouth? And if you can at present discover any flaw in any of your former concessions, or think of any remaining subterfuge, any new distinction, colour, or comment whatsoever, why do you not produce it?

HYLAS. A little patience, Philonous. I am at present so amazed to see myself ensnared, and as it were imprisoned in the labyrinths you have drawn me into, that on the sudden it cannot be expected I should find my way out. You must give me time to look about me, and recollect myself.

PHILONOUS. Hark; is not this the college-bell?

HYLAS. It rings for prayers.

PHILONOUS. We will go in then if you please, and meet here again to-morrow morning. In the mean time you may employ your thoughts on this morning's discourse, and try if you can find any fallacy in it, or invent any new means to extricate yourself.

HYLAS. Agreed.

HYLAS. I beg your pardon, Philonous, for not meeting you sooner. All this morning my head was so filled with our late conversation, that I had not leisure to think of the time of the day, or indeed of anything else.

PHILONOUS. I am glad you were so intent upon it, in hopes if there were any mistakes in your concessions, or fallacies in my reasonings from them, you will now discover them to me.

HYLAS. I assure you, I have done nothing ever since I saw you, but search after mistakes and fallacies, and with that view have minutely examined the whole series of yesterday's discourse: but all in vain, for the notions it led me into, upon review appear still more clear and evident; and the more I consider them, the more irresistibly do they force my assent.

PHILONOUS. And is not this, think you, a sign that they are genuine, that they proceed from Nature, and are conformable to right reason? Truth and beauty are in this alike, that the strictest survey sets them both off to advantage. While the false lustre of error and disguise cannot endure being reviewed, or too nearly inspected.

HYLAS. I own there is a great deal in what you say. Nor can anyone be more entirely satisfied of the truth of those odd consequences, so long as I have in view the reasonings that lead to them. But when these are out of my thoughts, there seems on the other hand something so satisfactory, so natural and intelligible in the modern way of explaining things, that I profess I know not how to reject it.

PHILONOUS. I know not what way you mean.

HYLAS. I mean the way of accounting for our sensations or ideas.

PHILONOUS. How is that?

HYLAS. It is supposed the soul makes her residence in some part of the brain, from which the nerves take their rise, and are thence extended to all parts of the body: and that outward objects by the different impressions they make on the organs of sense, communicate certain vibrative motions to the nerves; and these being filled with spirits, propagate them to the brain or seat of the soul, which according to the various impressions or traces thereby made in the brain, is various affected with ideas.

PHILONOUS. And call you this an explication of the manner whereby we are affected with ideas?

HYLAS. Why not, Philonous, have you anything to object against it?

PHILONOUS. I would first know whether I rightly understand your hypothesis. You make certain traces in the brain to be the causes or occasions of our ideas. Pray tell me, whether by the *brain* you mean any sensible thing?

HYLAS. What else think you I could mean?

PHILONOUS. Sensible things are all immediately perceivable; and those things which are immediately perceivable, are ideas; and these exist only in the mind. Thus much you have, if I mistake not, long since agreed to.

HYLAS. I do not deny it.

PHILONOUS. The brain therefore you speak of, being a sensible thing, exists only in the mind. Now, I would fain know whether you think it reasonable to suppose, that one idea or thing existing in the mind, occasions all other ideas. And if you think so, pray how do you account for the origin of that primary idea or brain itself?

HYLAS. I do not explain the origin of our ideas by that brain which is perceivable to sense, this being itself only a combination of sensible ideas, but by another which I imagine.

PHILONOUS. But are not things imagined as truly in the mind as things perceived?

HYLAS. I must confess they are.

PHILONOUS. It comes therefore to the same thing; and you have been all this while accounting for ideas, by certain motions or impressions in the brain, that is, by some alterations in an idea, whether sensible or imaginable it matters not.

HYLAS. I begin to suspect my hypothesis.

PHILONOUS. Beside spirits, all that we know or conceive are our own ideas. When therefore you say, all ideas are occasioned by impressions in the brain, do you conceive this brain or no? If you do, then you talk of ideas imprinted in an idea, causing that same idea, which is absurd. If you do not conceive it, you talk unintelligibly, instead of forming a reasonable hypothesis.

HYLAS. I now clearly see it was a mere dream. There is nothing in it.

PHILONOUS. You need not be much concerned at it: for after all, this way of explaining things, as you called it, could never have satisfied any reasonable man. What connexion is there between a motion in the nerves, and the sensations of sound or colour in the mind? or how is it possible these should be the effect of that?

HYLAS. But I could never think it had so little in it, as now it seems to have.

PHILONOUS. Well then, are you at length satisfied that no sensible things have a real existence; and that you are in truth an arrant *sceptic*?

HYLAS. It is too plain to be denied.

PHILONOUS. Look! are not the fields covered with a delightful verdure? Is there not something in the woods and groves, in the rivers and clear springs that soothes, that delights, that transports the soul? At the prospect of the wide and deep ocean, or some huge mountain whose top is lost in the clouds, or of an old gloomy forest, are not our minds filled with a pleasing horror? Even in rocks and deserts, is there not an agreeable wildness? How sincere a pleasure is it to behold the natural beauties of the earth! To preserve and renew our relish for them, is not the veil of night alternately drawn over her face, and doth she not change her dress with the seasons? How aptly are the elements disposed? What variety and use in the meanest productions of Nature? What delicacy, what beauty, what contrivance in animal and vegetable bodies? How exquisitely are all things suited, as well to their particular ends, as to constitute apposite parts of the whole! And while they mutually aid and support, do they not also set off and illustrate each other? Raise now your thoughts from this ball of earth, to all those glorious luminaries that adorn the high arch of heaven. The motion and situation of the planets, are they not admirable for use and order? Were those (miscalled *erratic*) globes ever known to stray, in their repeated journeys through the pathless void? Do they not measure areas round the sun ever proportioned to the times? So fixed, so immutable are the laws by which the unseen Author of Nature actuates the universe. How vivid and radiant is the lustre of the fixed stars! How magnificent and rich that negligent profusion, with which they appear to be scattered throughout the whole azure vault! Yet if you take the telescope, it brings into your sight a new host of stars that escape the naked eye. Here they seem contiguous and minute, but to a nearer view immense orbs of light at various distances, far sunk in the abyss of space. Now you must call imagination to your aid. The feeble narrow sense cannot descry innumerable worlds revolving round the central fires; and in those worlds the energy of an all-perfect mind displayed in endless forms. But neither sense nor imagination are big enough to comprehend the boundless extent with all its glittering furniture. Though the labouring mind exert and strain each power to its utmost reach, there still stands out ungrasped a surplusage immeasurable. Yet all the vast bodies that compose this mighty frame, how distant and remote soever, are by some secret mechanism, some divine art and force linked in a mutual dependence and intercourse with each other, even with this earth, which was almost slipt from my thoughts, and lost in the crowd of worlds. Is not the whole system immense, beautiful, glorious beyond expression and beyond thought! What treatment then do those philosophers deserve, who would deprive these noble and delightful scenes of all reality? How should those principles be entertained, that lead us to think all the visible beauty of the creation a false imaginary glare? To be plain, can you expect this scepticism of yours will not be thought extravagantly absurd by all men of sense?

HYLAS. Other men may think as they please: but for your part you have nothing to reproach me with. My comfort is, you are as much a *sceptic* as I am.

PHILONOUS. There, Hylas, I must beg leave to differ from
you.

HYLAS. What! have you all along agreed to the premises, and
do you now deny the conclusion, and leave me to maintain
those paradoxes by myself which you led me into? This
surely is not fair.

PHILONOUS. I deny that I agreed with you in those notions
that led to scepticism. You indeed said, the reality of sensible things consisted in an *absolute existence* out of the
minds of spirits, or distinct from their being perceived. And
pursuant to this notion of reality, you are obliged to deny
sensible things any real existence: that is, according to your
own definition, you profess yourself a *sceptic*. But I neither
said nor thought the reality of sensible things was to be
defined after that manner. To me it is evident, for the
reasons you allow of, that sensible things cannot exist otherwise than in a mind or spirit. Whence I conclude, not that
they have no real existence, but that seeing they depend not
on my thought, and have an existence distinct from being
perceived by me, *there must be some other mind wherein
they exist.* As sure therefore as the sensible world really
exists, so sure is there an infinite omnipresent spirit who
contains and supports it.*

HYLAS. What! this is no more than I and all Christians hold;
nay, and all others too who believe there is a God, and that
he knows and comprehends all things.

PHILONOUS. Ay, but here lies the difference. Men commonly believe that all things are known or perceived by
God, because they believe the being of a God, whereas I on
the other side, immediately and necessarily conclude the
being of a God, because all sensible things must be perceived by him.

HYLAS. But so long as we all believe the same thing, what
matter is it how we come by that belief?

PHILONOUS. But neither do we agree in the same opinion.
For philosophers, though they acknowledge all corporeal
beings to be perceived by God, yet they attribute to them
an absolute subsistence distinct from their being perceived
by any mind whatever, which I do not. Besides, is there no

difference between saying, *there is a God, therefore he perceives all things*: and saying, *sensible things do really exist: and if they really exist, they are necessarily perceived by an infinite mind: therefore there is an infinite mind, or God.* This furnishes you with a direct and immediate demonstration, from a most evident principle, of the *being of a God.* Divines and philosophers had proved beyond all controversy, from the beauty and usefulness of the several parts of the creation, that it was the workmanship of God. But that setting aside all help of astronomy and natural philosophy, all contemplation of the contrivance, order, and adjustment of things, an infinite mind should be necessarily inferred from the bare existence of the sensible world, is an advantage peculiar to them only who have made this easy reflexion: that the sensible world is that which we perceive by our several senses; and that nothing is perceived by the senses beside ideas; and that no idea or archetype of an idea can exist otherwise than in a mind. You may now, without any laborious search into the sciences, without any subtlety of reason, or tedious length of discourse, oppose and baffle the most strenuous advocate for atheism. Those miserable refuges, whether in an eternal succession of unthinking causes and effects, or in a fortuitous concourse of atoms; those wild imaginations of Vanini,* Hobbes, and Spinoza; in a word the whole system of atheism, is it not entirely overthrown by this single reflexion on the repugnancy included in supposing the whole, or any part, even the most rude and shapeless of the visible world, to exist without a mind? Let any one of those abettors of impiety but look into his own thoughts, and there try if he can conceive how so much as a rock, a desert, a chaos, or confused jumble of atoms; how anything at all, either sensible or imaginable, can exist independent of a mind, and he need go no farther to be convinced of his folly. Can anything be fairer than to put a dispute on such an issue, and leave it to a man himself to see if he can conceive, even in thought, what he holds to be true in fact, and from a notional to allow it a real existence?*

HYLAS. It cannot be denied, there is something highly serviceable to religion in what you advance. But do you not think it looks very like a notion entertained by some eminent moderns,* of *seeing all things in God*?

PHILONOUS. I would gladly know that opinion; pray explain it to me.

HYLAS. They conceive that the soul being immaterial, is incapable of being united with material things, so as to perceive them in themselves, but that she perceives them by her union with the substance of God, which being spiritual is therefore purely intelligible, or capable of being the immediate object of a spirit's thought. Besides, the divine essence contains in it perfections correspondent to each created being; and which are for that reason proper to exhibit or represent them to the mind.

PHILONOUS. I do not understand how our ideas, which are things altogether passive and inert, can be the essence, or any part (or like any part) of the essence or substance of God, who is an impassive, indivisible, purely active being. Many more difficulties and objections there are, which occur at first view against this hypothesis; but I shall only add that it is liable to all the absurdities of the common hypotheses, in making a created world exist otherwise than in the mind of a spirit. Beside all which it hath this peculiar to itself; that it makes that material world serve to no purpose. And if it pass for a good argument against other hypotheses in the sciences, that they suppose Nature or the divine wisdom to make something in vain, or do that by tedious round-about methods, which might have been performed in a much more easy and compendious way, what shall we think of that hypothesis which supposes the whole world made in vain?

HYLAS. But what say you, are not you too of opinion that we see all things in God? If I mistake not, what you advance comes near it.

PHILONOUS. Few men think, yet all will have opinions. Hence men's opinions are superficial and confused. It is nothing strange that tenets, which in themselves are ever so different, should nevertheless be confounded with each other by those who do not consider them attentively. I shall not therefore be surprised, if some men imagine that I run into the enthusiasm of Malebranche, though in truth I am very remote from it. He builds on the most abstract general ideas, which I entirely disclaim. He asserts an absolute external world, which I deny. He maintains that we are deceived by our senses, and know not the real natures or the true forms and figures of extended beings; of all which I hold the direct contrary. So that upon the whole there are no principles more fundamentally opposite than his and mine. It must be owned* I entirely agree with what the holy Scripture saith, *that in God we live, and move, and have our being*. But that we see things in his essence after the manner above set forth, I am far from believing. Take here in brief my meaning. It is evident that the things I perceive are my own ideas, and that no idea can exist unless it be in a mind. Nor is it less plain that these ideas or things by me perceived, either themselves or their archetypes, exist independently of my mind, since I know myself not to be their author, it being out of my power to determine at pleasure, what particular ideas I shall be affected with upon opening my eyes or ears. They must therefore exist in some other mind, whose will it is they should be exhibited to me. The things, I say, immediately perceived, are ideas or sensations, call them which you will. But how can any idea or sensation exist in, or be produced by, anything but a mind or spirit? This indeed is inconceivable; and to assert that which is inconceivable, is to talk nonsense: Is it not?

HYLAS. Without doubt.

PHILONOUS. But on the other hand, it is very conceivable that they should exist in, and be produced by, a spirit; since this is no more than I daily experience in myself, inasmuch as I perceive numberless ideas; and by an act of my Will can form a great variety of them, and raise them up in my imagination: though it must be confessed, these creatures of the fancy are not altogether so distinct, so strong, vivid, and permanent, as those perceived by my senses, which latter are called *real things*. From all which I conclude, *there is a mind which affects me every moment with all the sensible impressions I perceive*. And from the variety, order, and manner of these, I conclude the Author of them to be *wise, powerful, and good, beyond comprehension.* Mark it well; I do not say, I see things by perceiving that which represents them in the intelligible substance of God. This I do not understand; but I say, the things by me perceived are known by the understanding, and produced by the will, of an infinite spirit. And is not all this most plain and evident? Is there any more in it, than what a little observation of our own minds, and that which passes in them not only enableth us to conceive, but also obligeth us to acknowledge?

HYLAS. I think I understand you very clearly; and own the proof you give of a Deity seems no less evident, than it is surprising. But allowing that God is the Supreme and Universal Cause of all things, yet may not there be still a third nature besides spirits and ideas? May we not admit a subordinate and limited cause of our ideas? In a word, may there not for all that be *matter*?

PHILONOUS. How often must I inculcate the same thing? You allow the things immediately perceived by sense to exist nowhere without the mind: but there is nothing perceived by sense, which is not perceived immediately: therefore there is nothing sensible that exists without the mind. The matter therefore which you still insist on, is something intelligible, I suppose; something that may be discovered by reason, and not by sense.

HYLAS. You are in the right.

PHILONOUS. Pray let me know what reasoning your belief of matter is grounded on; and what this matter is in your present sense of it.

HYLAS. I find myself affected with various ideas, whereof I know I am not the cause; neither are they the cause of themselves, or of one another, or capable of subsisting by themselves, as being altogether inactive, fleeting, dependent beings. They have therefore some cause distinct from me and them: of which I pretend to know no more, than that it is *the cause of my ideas*. And this thing, whatever it be, I call matter.

PHILONOUS. Tell me, Hylas, hath everyone a liberty to change the current proper signification annexed to a common name in any language? For example, suppose a traveller should tell you, that in a certain country men might pass unhurt through the fire; and, upon explaining himself, you found he meant by the word *fire* that which others call *water*: or if he should assert there are trees which walk upon two legs, meaning men by the term *trees*. Would you think this reasonable?

HYLAS. No; I should think it very absurd. Common custom is the standard of propriety in language. And for any man to affect speaking improperly, is to pervert the use of speech, and can never serve to a better purpose, than to protract and multiply disputes where there is no difference in opinion.

PHILONOUS. And doth not *matter*, in the common current acceptation of the word, signify an extended, solid, moveable, unthinking, inactive substance?

HYLAS. It doth.

PHILONOUS. And hath it not been made evident, that no such substance can possibly exist? And though it should be allowed to exist, yet how can that which is *inactive* be a *cause*; or that which is *unthinking* be a *cause of thought*? You may indeed, if you please, annex to the word *matter* a contrary meaning to what is vulgarly received; and tell me you understand by it an unextended, thinking, active being, which is the cause of our ideas. But what else is this, than to play with words, and run into that very fault you just now condemned with so much reason? I do by no means find fault with your reasoning in that you collect a cause from the phenomena; but I deny that the cause deducible by reason can properly be termed *matter*.

HYLAS. There is indeed something in what you say. But I am afraid you do not thoroughly comprehend my meaning. I would by no means be thought to deny that God or an Infinite Spirit is the supreme cause of all things. All I contend for, is, that subordinate to the supreme agent there is a cause of a limited and inferior nature, which concurs in the production of our ideas, not by any act of will or spiritual efficiency, but by that kind of action which belongs to matter, *viz. motion*.

PHILONOUS. I find, you are at every turn relapsing into your old exploded conceit, of a moveable and consequently an extended substance existing without the mind. What! Have you already forgot you were convinced, or are you willing I should repeat what has been said on that head? In truth this is not fair dealing in you, still to suppose the being of that which you have so often acknowledged to have no being. But not to insist farther on what has been so largely handled, I ask whether all your ideas are not perfectly passive and inert, including nothing of action in them?

HYLAS. They are.

PHILONOUS. And are sensible qualities anything else but ideas?

HYLAS. How often have I acknowledged that they are not?

PHILONOUS. But is not motion a sensible quality?

HYLAS. It is.

PHILONOUS. Consequently it is no action.

HYLAS. I agree with you. And indeed it is very plain, that when I stir my finger, it remains passive; but my will which produced the motion, is active.

PHILONOUS. Now I desire to know in the first place, whether motion being allowed to be no action, you can conceive any action besides volition: and in the second place, whether to say something and conceive nothing be not to talk nonsense: and lastly, whether having considered the premises, you do not perceive that to suppose any efficient or active cause of our ideas, other than *spirit*, is highly absurd and unreasonable?

HYLAS. I give up the point entirely. But though matter may not be a cause, yet what hinders its being an *instrument* subservient to the supreme agent in the production of our ideas?

PHILONOUS. An instrument, say you; pray what may be the figure, springs, wheels, and motions of that instrument?

HYLAS. Those I pretend to determine nothing of, both the substance and its qualities being entirely unknown to me.

PHILONOUS. What? You are then of opinion, it is made up of unknown parts, that it hath unknown motions, and an unknown shape.

HYLAS. I do not believe it hath any figure or motion at all, being already convinced, that no sensible qualities can exist in an unperceiving substance.

PHILONOUS. But what notion is it possible to frame of an instrument void of all sensible qualities, even extension itself?

HYLAS. I do not pretend to have any notion of it.

PHILONOUS. And what reason have you to think, this unknown, this inconceivable somewhat doth exist? Is it that you imagine God cannot act as well without it, or that you find by experience the use of some such thing, when you form ideas in your own mind?

HYLAS. You are always teasing me for reasons of my belief. Pray, what reasons have you not to believe it?

PHILONOUS. It is to me a sufficient reason not to believe the existence of anything, if I see no reason for believing it. But not to insist on reasons for believing, you will not so much as let me know what it is you would have me believe, since you say you have no manner of notion of it. After all, let me entreat you to consider whether it be like a philosopher, or even like a man of common sense, to pretend to believe you know not what, and you know not why.

HYLAS. Hold, Philonous. When I tell you matter is an *instrument*, I do not mean altogether nothing. It is true, I know not the particular kind of instrument; but however I have some notion of *instrument in general*, which I apply to it.

PHILONOUS. But what if it should prove that there is something, even in the most general notion of *instrument*, as taken in a distinct sense from *cause*, which makes the use of it inconsistent with the divine attributes?

HYLAS. Make that appear, and I shall give up the point.

PHILONOUS. What mean you by the general nature or notion of *instrument*?

HYLAS. That which is common to all particular instruments, composeth the general notion.

PHILONOUS. Is it not common to all instruments, that they are applied to the doing those things only, which cannot be performed by the mere act of our wills? Thus for instance, I never use an instrument to move my finger, because it is done by a volition. But I should use one, if I were to remove part of a rock, or tear up a tree by the roots. Are you of the same mind? Or can you shew any example where an instrument is made use of in producing an effect immediately depending on the will of the agent?

HYLAS. I own, I cannot.

PHILONOUS. How therefore can you suppose, that an all-perfect spirit, on whose will all things have an absolute and immediate dependence, should need an instrument in his operations, or not needing it make use of it? Thus it seems to me that you are obliged to own the use of a lifeless inactive instrument, to be incompatible with the infinite perfection of God; that is, by your own confession, to give up the point.

HYLAS. It doth not readily occur what I can answer you.

PHILONOUS. But methinks you should be ready to own the truth, when it hath been fairly proved to you. We indeed, who are beings of finite powers, are forced to make use of instruments. And the use of an instrument sheweth the agent to be limited by rules of another's prescription, and that he cannot obtain his end, but in such a way and by such conditions. Whence it seems a clear consequence, that the supreme unlimited agent useth no tool or instrument at all. The will of an omnipotent spirit is no sooner exerted than executed, without the application of means, which, if they are employed by inferior agents, it is not upon account of any real efficacy that is in them, or necessary aptitude to produce any effect, but merely in compliance with the laws of Nature, or those conditions prescribed to them by the first cause, who is himself above all limitation or prescription whatsoever.

HYLAS. I will no longer maintain that matter is an instrument. However, I would not be understood to give up its existence neither; since, notwithstanding what hath been said, it may still be an *occasion*.*

PHILONOUS. How many shapes is your matter to take? Or how often must it be proved not to exist, before you are content to part with it? But to say no more of this (though by all the laws of disputation I may justly blame you for so frequently changing the signification of the principal term) I would fain know what you mean by affirming that matter is an occasion, having already denied it to be a cause. And when you have shewn in what sense you understand *occasion*, pray in the next place be pleased to shew me what reason induceth you to believe there is such an occasion of our ideas.

HYLAS. As to the first point: by *occasion* I mean an inactive unthinking being, at the presence whereof God excites ideas in our minds.

PHILONOUS. And what may be the nature of that inactive unthinking being?

HYLAS. I know nothing of its nature.

PHILONOUS. Proceed then to the second point, and assign some reason why we should allow an existence to this in-active, unthinking, unknown thing.

HYLAS. When we see ideas produced in our minds after an orderly and constant manner, it is natural to think they have some fixed and regular occasions, at the presence of which they are excited.

PHILONOUS. You acknowledge then God alone to be the cause of our ideas, and that he causes them at the presence of those occasions.

HYLAS. That is my opinion.

PHILONOUS. Those things which you say are present to God, without doubt He perceives.

HYLAS. Certainly; otherwise they could not be to Him an occasion of acting.

PHILONOUS. Not to insist now on your making sense of this hypothesis, or answering all the puzzling questions and dif-ficulties it is liable to: I only ask whether the order and regularity observable in the series of our ideas, or the course of Nature, be not sufficiently accounted for by the wisdom and power of God; and whether it doth not dero-gate from those attributes, to suppose He is influenced, directed, or put in mind, when and what He is to act, by any unthinking substance. And lastly whether, in case I granted all you contend for, it would make anything to your pur-pose, it not being easy to conceive how the external or absolute existence of an unthinking substance, distinct from its being perceived, can be inferred from my allowing that there are certain things perceived by the mind of God, which are to Him the occasion of producing ideas in us.

HYLAS. I am perfectly at a loss what to think, this notion of *occasion* seeming now altogether as groundless as the rest.

PHILONOUS. Do you not at length perceive, that in all these different acceptations of *matter*, you have been only supposing you know not what, for no manner of reason, and to no kind of use?

HYLAS. I freely own myself less fond of my notions, since they have been so accurately examined. But still, methinks I have some confused perception that there is such a thing as *matter*.

PHILONOUS. Either you perceive the being of matter immediately, or mediately. If immediately, pray inform me by which of the senses you perceive it. If mediately, let me know by what reasoning it is inferred from those things which you perceive immediately. So much for the perception. Then for the matter itself, I ask whether it is object, *substratum*, cause, instrument, or occasion? You have already pleaded for each of these, shifting your notions, and making matter to appear sometimes in one shape, then in another. And what you have offered hath been disapproved and rejected by yourself. If you have anything new to advance, I would gladly hear it.

HYLAS. I think I have already offered all I had to say on those heads. I am at a loss what more to urge.

PHILONOUS. And yet you are loth to part with your old prejudice. But to make you quit it more easily, I desire that, beside what has been hitherto suggested, you will farther consider whether, upon supposition that matter exists, you can possibly conceive how you should be affected by it? Or supposing it did not exist, whether it be not evident you might for all that be affected with the same ideas you now are, and consequently have the very same reasons to believe its existence that you now can have?

HYLAS. I acknowledge it is possible we might perceive all things just as we do now, though there was no matter in the world; neither can I conceive, if there be matter, how it should produce any idea in our minds. And I do farther grant, you have entirely satisfied me, that it is impossible there should be such a thing as matter in any of the foregoing acceptations. But still I cannot help supposing that there is *matter* in some sense or other. What that is I do not indeed pretend to determine.

PHILONOUS. I do not expect you should define exactly the nature of that unknown being. Only be pleased to tell me, whether it is a substance: and if so, whether you can suppose a substance without accidents; or in case you suppose it to have accidents or qualities, I desire you will let me know what those qualities are, at least what is meant by matter's supporting them.

HYLAS. We have already argued on those points. I have no more to say to them. But to prevent any farther questions, let me tell you, I at present understand by *matter* neither substance nor accident, thinking nor extended being, neither cause, instrument, nor occasion, but something entirely unknown,* distinct from all these.

PHILONOUS. It seems then you include in your present notion of matter, nothing but the general abstract idea of *entity*.

HYLAS. Nothing else, save only that I super-add to this general idea the negation of all those particular things, qualities, or ideas that I perceive, imagine, or in anywise apprehend.

PHILONOUS. Pray where do you suppose this unknown matter to exist?

HYLAS. Oh Philonous! now you think you have entangled me; for if I say it exists in place, then you will infer that it exists in the mind, since it is agreed, that place or extension exists only in the mind: but I am not ashamed to own my ignorance. I know not where it exists; only I am sure it exists not in place. There is a negative answer for you: and you must expect no other to all the questions you put for the future about matter.

PHILONOUS. Since you will not tell me where it exists, be pleased to inform me after what manner you suppose it to exist, or what you mean by its *existence*.

HYLAS. It neither thinks nor acts, neither perceives, nor is perceived.

PHILONOUS. But what is there positive in your abstracted notion of its existence?

HYLAS. Upon a nice observation, I do not find I have any positive notion or meaning at all. I tell you again I am not ashamed to own my ignorance. I know not what is meant by its *existence*, or how it exists.

PHILONOUS. Continue, good Hylas, to act the same ingenuous part, and tell me sincerely whether you can frame a distinct idea of entity in general, prescinded from and exclusive of all thinking and corporeal beings, all particular things whatsoever.

HYLAS. Hold, let me think a little ... I profess, Philonous, I do not find that I can.* At first glance methought I had some dilute and airy notion of pure entity in abstract; but upon closer attention it hath quite vanished out of sight. The more I think on it, the more am I confirmed in my prudent resolution of giving none but negative answers, and not pretending to the least degree of any positive knowledge or conception of matter, its *where*, its *how*, its *entity*, or anything belonging to it.

PHILONOUS. When therefore you speak of the existence of matter, you have not any notion in your mind.

HYLAS. None at all.

PHILONOUS. Pray tell me if the case stands not thus: at first, from a belief of material substance you would have it that the immediate objects existed without the mind; then that their archetypes; then causes; next instruments; then occasions: lastly, *something in general*, which being interpreted proves *nothing*. So matter comes to nothing. What think you, Hylas, is not this a fair summary of your whole proceeding?

HYLAS. Be that as it will, yet I still insist upon it, that our not being able to conceive a thing, is no argument against its existence.

PHILONOUS. That from a cause, effect, operation, sign, or other circumstance, there may reasonably be inferred the existence of a thing not immediately perceived, and that it were absurd for any man to argue against the existence of that thing, from his having no direct and positive notion of it, I freely own. But where there is nothing of all this; where neither reason nor revelation induce us to believe the existence of a thing; where we have not even a relative notion of it; where an abstraction is made from perceiving and being perceived, from spirit and idea: lastly, where there is not so much as the most inadequate or faint idea pretended to: I will not indeed thence conclude against the reality of any notion or existence of anything: but my inference shall be, that you mean nothing at all: that you employ words to no manner of purpose, without any design or signification whatsoever. And I leave it to you to consider how mere jargon should be treated.

HYLAS. To deal frankly with you, Philonous, your arguments seem in themselves unanswerable, but they have not so great an effect on me as to produce that entire conviction, that hearty acquiescence which attends demonstration. I find myself still relapsing into an obscure surmise of I know not what, *matter*.

PHILONOUS. But are you not sensible, Hylas, that two things must concur to take away all scruple, and work a plenary assent in the mind? Let a visible object be set in never so clear a light, yet if there is any imperfection in the sight, or if the eye is not directed towards it, it will not be distinctly seen. And though a demonstration be never so well grounded and fairly proposed, yet if there is withal a stain of prejudice, or a wrong bias on the understanding, can it be expected on a sudden to perceive clearly and adhere firmly to the truth? No, there is need of time and pains: the attention must be awakened and detained by a frequent repetition of the same thing placed oft in the same, oft in different lights. I have said it already, and find I must still repeat and inculcate, that it is an unaccountable licence you take in pretending to maintain you know not what, for you know not what reason, to you know not what purpose. Can this be paralleled in any art or science, any sect or profession of men? Or is there anything so barefacedly groundless and unreasonable to be met with even in the lowest of common conversation? But perhaps you will still say, matter may exist, though at the same time you neither know what is meant by *matter*, or by its *existence*. This indeed is surprising, and the more so because it is altogether voluntary, you not being led to it by any one reason; for I challenge you to shew me that thing in Nature which needs matter to explain or account for it.

HYLAS. The reality of things cannot be maintained without supposing the existence of matter. And is not this, think you, a good reason why I should be earnest in its defence?

PHILONOUS. The reality of things! What things, sensible or intelligible?

HYLAS. Sensible things.

PHILONOUS. My glove, for example?

HYLAS. That or any other thing perceived by the senses.

PHILONOUS. But to fix on some particular thing; is it not a sufficient evidence to me of the existence of this *glove*, that I see it, and feel it, and wear it? Or if this will not do, how is it possible I should be assured of the reality of this thing, which I actually see in this place, by supposing that some unknown thing which I never did or can see, exists after an unknown manner, in an unknown place, or in no place at all? How can the supposed reality of that which is intangible, be a proof that anything tangible really exists? or of that which is invisible, that any visible thing, or in general of anything which is imperceptible, that a perceptible exists? Do but explain this, and I shall think nothing too hard for you.

HYLAS. Upon the whole, I am content to own the existence of matter is highly improbable; but the direct and absolute impossibility of it does not appear to me.

PHILONOUS. But granting matter to be possible, yet upon that account merely it can have no more claim to existence, than a golden mountain or a centaur.

HYLAS. I acknowledge it; but still you do not deny it is possible; and that which is possible, for aught you know, may actually exist.

PHILONOUS. I deny it to be possible; and have, if I mistake not, evidently proved from your own concessions that it is not. In the common sense of the word *matter*, is there any more implied, than an extended, solid, figured, moveable substance existing without the mind? And have not you acknowledged over and over, that you have seen evident reason for denying the possibility of such a substance?

HYLAS. True, but that is only one sense of the term *matter*.

PHILONOUS. But is it not the only proper genuine received sense? And if matter in such a sense be proved impossible, may it not be thought with good grounds absolutely impossible? Else how could anything be proved impossible? Or indeed how could there be any proof at all one way or other, to a man who takes the liberty to unsettle and change the common signification of words?

HYLAS. I thought philosophers might be allowed to speak more accurately than the vulgar, and were not always confined to the common acceptation of a term.

PHILONOUS. But this now mentioned is the common received sense among philosophers themselves. But not to insist on that, have you not been allowed to take matter in what sense you pleased? And have you not used this privilege in the utmost extent, sometimes entirely changing, at others leaving out or putting into the definition of it whatever for the present best served your design, contrary to all the known rules of reason and logic? And hath not this shifting unfair method of yours spun out our dispute to an unnecessary length; matter having been particularly examined, and by your own confession refuted in each of those senses? And can any more be required to prove the absolute impossibility of a thing, than the proving it impossible in every particular sense, that either you or anyone else understands it in?

HYLAS. But I am not so thoroughly satisfied that you have proved the impossibility of matter in the last most obscure abstracted and indefinite sense.

PHILONOUS. When is a thing shewn to be impossible?

HYLAS. When a repugnancy is demonstrated between the ideas comprehended in its definition.

PHILONOUS. But where there are no ideas, there no repugnancy can be demonstrated between ideas.

HYLAS. I agree with you.

PHILONOUS. Now in that which you call the obscure indefinite sense of the word *matter*, it is plain, by your own confession, there was included no idea at all, no sense except an unknown sense, which is the same thing as none. You are not therefore to expect I should prove a repugnancy between ideas where there are no ideas; or the impossibility of matter taken in an *unknown* sense, that is no sense at all. My business was only to shew, you meant *nothing*; and this you were brought to own. So that in all your various senses, you have been shewed either to mean nothing at all, or if anything, an absurdity. And if this be not sufficient to prove the impossibility of a thing, I desire you will let me know what is.

HYLAS. I acknowledge you have proved that matter is impossible; nor do I see what more can be said in defence of it. But at the same time that I give up this, I suspect all my other notions. For surely none could be more seemingly evident than this once was: and yet it now seems as false and absurd as ever it did true before. But I think we have discussed the point sufficiently for the present. The remaining part of the day I would willingly spend, in running over in my thoughts the several heads of this morning's conversation, and to-morrow shall be glad to meet you here again about the same time.

PHILONOUS. I will not fail to attend you.

THE THIRD DIALOGUE

PHILONOUS. Tell me, Hylas, what are the fruits of yesterday's meditation? Hath it confirmed you in the same mind you were in at parting? or have you since seen cause to change your opinion?

HYLAS. Truly my opinion is, that all our opinions are alike vain and uncertain. What we approve to-day, we condemn to-morrow. We keep a stir about knowledge, and spend our lives in the pursuit of it, when alas! we know nothing all the while: nor do I think it possible for us ever to know anything in this life. Our faculties are too narrow and too few. Nature certainly never intended us for speculation.

PHILONOUS. What! say you we can know nothing, Hylas?

HYLAS. There is not that single thing in the world, whereof we can know the real nature, or what it is in itself.

PHILONOUS. Will you tell me I do not really know what fire or water is?

HYLAS. You may indeed know that fire appears hot, and water fluid: but this is no more than knowing what sensations are produced in your own mind, upon the application of fire and water to your organs of sense. Their internal constitution, their true and real nature, you are utterly in the dark as to *that*.

PHILONOUS. Do I not know this to be a real stone that I stand on, and that which I see before my eyes to be a real tree?

HYLAS. *Know*? No, it is impossible you or any man alive should know it. All you know, is, that you have such a certain idea or appearance in your own mind. But what is this to the real tree or stone? I tell you, that colour, figure, and hardness, which you perceive, are not the real natures of those things, or in the least like them. The same may be said of all other real things or corporeal substances which compose the world. They have none of them anything in themselves, like those sensible qualities by us perceived.

We should not therefore pretend to affirm or know anything of them as they are in their own nature.

PHILONOUS. But surely, Hylas, I can distinguish gold, for
example, from iron: and how could this be if I knew not
what either truly was?

HYLAS. Believe me, Philonous, you can only distinguish between your own ideas. That yellowness, that weight, and
other sensible qualities, think you they are really in the
gold? They are only relative to the senses, and have no
absolute existence in Nature. And in pretending to distinguish the species of real things, by the appearances in
your mind, you may perhaps act as wisely as he that should
conclude two men were of a different species, because their
clothes were not of the same colour.

PHILONOUS. It seems then we are altogether put off with the
appearances of things, and those false ones too. The very
meat I eat, and the cloth I wear, have nothing in them like
what I see and feel.

HYLAS. Even so.

PHILONOUS. But is it not strange the whole world should be
thus imposed on, and so foolish as to believe their senses?
And yet I know not how it is, but men eat, and drink, and
sleep, and perform all the offices of life as comfortably and
conveniently, as if they really knew the things they are
conversant about.

HYLAS. They do so: but you know ordinary practice does not
require a nicety of speculative knowledge. Hence the vulgar
retain their mistakes, and for all that, make a shift to bustle
through the affairs of life. But philosophers know better
things.

PHILONOUS. You mean, they know that they *know nothing*.

HYLAS. That is the very top and perfection of human
knowledge.

PHILONOUS. But are you all this while in earnest, Hylas; and
are you seriously persuaded that you know nothing real in
the world? Suppose you are going to write, would you not
call for pen, ink, and paper, like another man; and do you
not know what it is you call for?

HYLAS. How often must I tell you, that I know not the real

nature of any one thing in the universe? I may indeed upon occasion make use of pen, ink, and paper. But what any one of them is in its own true nature, I declare positively I know not. And the same is true with regard to every other corporeal thing. And, what is more, we are not only ignorant of the true and real nature of things, but even of their existence. It cannot be denied that we perceive such certain appearances or ideas; but it cannot be concluded from thence that bodies really exist. Nay, now I think on it, I must agreeably to my former concessions farther declare, that it is impossible any real corporeal thing should exist in Nature.

PHILONOUS. You amaze me. Was ever anything more wild and extravagant than the notions you now maintain: and is it not evident you are led into all these extravagancies by the belief of *material substance*? This makes you dream of those unknown natures in everything. It is this occasions your distinguishing between the reality and sensible appearances of things. It is to this you are indebted for being ignorant of what everybody else knows perfectly well. Nor is this all: you are not only ignorant of the true nature of every thing, but you know not whether anything really exists, or whether there are any true natures at all; forasmuch as you attribute to your material beings an absolute or external existence, wherein you suppose their reality consists.* And as you are forced in the end to acknowledge such an existence means either a direct repugnancy, or nothing at all, it follows that you are obliged to pull down your own hypothesis of material substance, and positively to deny the real existence of any part of the universe. And so you are plunged into the deepest and most deplorable *scepticism* that ever man was. Tell me, Hylas, is it not as I say?

HYLAS. I agree with you. *Material substance* was no more than an hypothesis, and a false and groundless one too. I will no longer spend my breath in defence of it. But whatever hypothesis you advance, or whatsoever scheme of things you introduce in its stead, I doubt not it will appear every whit as false: let me but be allowed to question you upon it. That is, suffer me to serve you in your own kind, and I warrant it shall conduct you through as many perplexities and contradictions, to the very same state of scepticism that I myself am in at present.

PHILONOUS. I assure you, Hylas, I do not pretend to frame any hypothesis at all. I am of a vulgar cast, simple enough to believe my senses, and leave things as I find them. To be plain, it is my opinion, that the real things are those very things I see and feel, and perceive by my senses. These I know, and finding they answer all the necessities and purposes of life, have no reason to be solicitous about any other unknown beings. A piece of sensible bread, for instance, would stay my stomach better than ten thousand times as much of that insensible, unintelligible, real bread you speak of. It is likewise my opinion, that colours and other sensible qualities are on the objects. I cannot for my life help thinking that snow is white, and fire hot. You indeed, who by *snow* and *fire* mean certain external, unperceived, unperceiving substances, are in the right to deny whiteness or heat, to be affections inherent in them. But I, who understand by those words the things I see and feel, am obliged to think like other folks. And as I am no sceptic with regard to the nature of things, so neither am I as to their existence. That a thing should be really perceived by my senses, and at the same time not really exist, is to me a plain contradiction; since I cannot prescind or abstract, even in thought, the existence of a sensible thing from its being perceived. Wood, stones, fire, water, flesh, iron, and the like things, which I name and discourse of, are things that I know. And I should not have known them, but that I perceived them by my senses; and things perceived by the senses are immediately perceived; and things immediately perceived are ideas; and ideas cannot exist without the mind; their existence therefore consists in being perceived; when therefore they are actually perceived, there can be no doubt of their existence. Away then with all that scepticism, all those ridiculous philosophical doubts. What a jest is it for a philosopher to question the existence of sensible things, till he hath it proved to him from the veracity of God: or to pretend our knowledge in this point falls short of intuition or demonstration? I might as well doubt of my own being,* as of the being of those things I actually see and feel.

HYLAS. Not so fast, Philonous: you say you cannot conceive how sensible things should exist without the mind. Do you not?

PHILONOUS. I do.

HYLAS. Supposing you were annihilated, cannot you conceive it possible, that things perceivable by sense may still exist?

PHILONOUS. I can; but then it must be in another mind. When I deny sensible things an existence out of the mind, I do not mean my mind in particular, but all minds. Now it is plain they have an existence exterior to my mind, since I find them by experience to be independent of it. There is therefore some other mind wherein they exist, during the intervals between the times of my perceiving them: as likewise they did before my birth, and would do after my supposed annihilation. And as the same is true, with regard to all other finite created spirits; it necessarily follows, there is an *omnipresent eternal Mind*, which knows and comprehends all things, and exhibits them to our view in such a manner, and according to such rules as he himself hath ordained, and are by us termed the *Laws of Nature*.*

HYLAS. Answer me, Philonous. Are all our ideas perfectly inert beings? Or have they any agency included in them?

PHILONOUS. They are altogether passive and inert.

HYLAS. And is not God an agent, a being purely active?

PHILONOUS. I acknowledge it.

HYLAS. No idea therefore can be like unto, or represent the nature of God.

PHILONOUS. It cannot.

HYLAS. Since therefore you have no idea of the mind of God, how can you conceive it possible, that things should exist in his mind? Or, if you can conceive the mind of God without having an idea of it, why may not I be allowed to conceive the existence of matter, notwithstanding that I have no idea of it?

PHILONOUS. As to your first question; I own I have properly no idea, either of God or any other spirit; for these being active, cannot be represented by things perfectly inert, as our ideas are. I do nevertheless know, that I who am a spirit or thinking substance, exist as certainly, as I know my ideas exist. Farther, I know what I mean by the terms *I* and *myself*; and I know this immediately, or intuitively, though I do not perceive it as I perceive a triangle, a colour, or a sound. The mind, spirit or soul, is that indivisible unextended thing, which thinks, acts, and perceives. I say *indivisible*, because unextended; and *unextended*, because extended, figured, moveable things, are ideas; and that which perceives ideas, which thinks and wills, is plainly itself no idea, nor like an idea. Ideas are things inactive, and perceived: and spirits a sort of beings altogether different from them. I do not therefore say my soul is an idea, or like an idea. However, taking the word *idea* in a large sense, my soul may be said to furnish me with an idea, that is, an image, or likeness of God, though indeed extremely inadequate, For all the notion I have of God, is obtained by reflecting on my own soul heightening its powers, and removing its imperfections. I have therefore, though not an inactive idea, yet in myself some sort of an active thinking image of the Deity. And though I perceive Him not by sense, yet I have a notion of Him, or know Him by reflexion and reasoning. My own mind and my own ideas I have an immediate knowledge of; and by the help of these, do mediately apprehend the possibility of the existence of other spirits and ideas. Farther, from my own being, and from the dependency I find in myself and my ideas, I do by an act of reason, necessarily infer the existence of a God, and of all created things in the mind of God. So much for your first question. For the second: I suppose by this time you can answer it yourself. For you neither perceive matter objectively, as you do an inactive being or idea, nor know it, as you do yourself by a reflex act: neither do you mediately apprehend it by similitude of the one or the other: nor yet collect it by reasoning from that which you know immediately. All which makes the case of *matter* widely different from that of the *Deity*.

HYLAS. You say your own soul supplies you with some sort

of an idea or image of God. But at the same time you acknowledge you have, properly speaking, no idea of your own soul. You even affirm that spirits are a sort of beings altogether different from ideas. Consequently that no idea can be like a spirit. We have therefore no idea of any spirit. You admit nevertheless that there is spiritual substance, although you have no idea of it; while you deny there can be such a thing as material substance, because you have no notion or idea of it. Is this fair dealing? To act consistently, you must either admit matter or reject spirit. What say you to this?

PHILONOUS. I say in the first place, that I do not deny the existence of material substance, merely because I have no notion of it, but because the notion of it is inconsistent, or in other words, because it is repugnant that there should be a notion of it. Many things, for ought I know, may exist, whereof neither I nor any other man hath or can have any idea or notion whatsoever. But then those things must be possible, that is, nothing inconsistent must be included in their definition. I say secondly, that although we believe things to exist which we do not perceive; yet we may not believe that any particular thing exists, without some reason for such belief: but I have no reason for believing the existence of matter. I have no immediate intuition thereof: neither can I mediately from my sensations, ideas, notions, actions or passions, infer an unthinking, unperceiving, inactive substance, either by probable deduction, or necessary consequence. Whereas the being of myself, that is, my own soul, mind or thinking principle, I evidently know by reflexion. You will forgive me if I repeat the same things in answer to the same objections. In the very notion or definition of material substance, there is included a manifest repugnance and inconsistency. But this cannot be said of the notion of spirit. That ideas should exist in what doth not perceive, or be produced by what doth not act, is repugnant. But it is no repugnancy to say, that a perceiving thing should be the subject of ideas, or an active thing the cause of them. It is granted we have neither an immediate evidence nor a demonstrative knowledge of the existence of other finite spirits; but it will not thence follow that such spirits are on a foot with material substances: if to suppose the one be inconsistent, and it be not inconsistent to suppose the other; if the one can be inferred by no argument, and there is a probability for the other; if we see signs and effects indicating distinct finite agents like ourselves, and see no sign or symptom whatever that leads to a rational belief of matter. I say lastly, that I have a notion of spirit, though I have not, strictly speaking, an idea of it. I do not perceive it as an idea or by means of an idea, but know it by reflexion.

HYLAS. Notwithstanding all you have said, to me it seems, that according to your own way of thinking, and in consequence of your own principles, it should follow that you are only a system of floating ideas, without any substance to support them. Words are not to be used without a meaning. And as there is no more meaning in spiritual substance than in material substance, the one is to be exploded as well as the other.

PHILONOUS. How often must I repeat, that I know or am conscious of my own being; and that I myself am not my ideas, but somewhat else, a thinking active principle that perceives, knows, wills, and operates about ideas. I know that I, one and the same self, perceive both colours and sounds:* that a colour cannot perceive a sound, nor a sound a colour: that I am therefore one individual principle, distinct from colour and sound; and, for the same reason, from all other sensible things and inert ideas. But I am not in like manner conscious either of the existence or essence of matter. On the contrary, I know that nothing inconsistent can exist, and that the existence of matter implies an inconsistency. Farther, I know what I mean, when I affirm that there is a spiritual substance or support of ideas, that is, that a spirit knows and perceives ideas. But I do not know what is meant, when it is said, that an unperceiving substance hath inherent in it and supports either ideas or the archetypes of ideas. There is therefore upon the whole no parity of case between spirit and matter.

HYLAS. I own myself satisfied in this point. But do you in

earnest think, the real existence of sensible things consists in their being actually perceived? If so; how comes it that all mankind distinguish between them? Ask the first man you meet, and he shall tell you, *to be perceived* is one thing, and *to exist* is another.

PHILONOUS. I am content, Hylas, to appeal to the common sense of the world for the truth of my notion. Ask the gardener, why he thinks yonder cherry-tree exists in the garden, and he shall tell you, because he sees and feels it; in a word, because he perceives it by his senses. Ask him, why he thinks an orange-tree not to be there, and he shall tell you, because he does not perceive it. What he perceives by sense, that he terms a real being, and saith it *is*, or *exists*; but that which is not perceivable, the same, he saith, hath no being.

HYLAS. Yes, Philonous, I grant the existence of a sensible thing consists in being perceivable, but not in being actually perceived.

PHILONOUS. And what is perceivable but an idea? And can an idea exist without being actually perceived? These are points long since agreed between us.

HYLAS. But be your opinion never so true, yet surely you will not deny it is shocking, and contrary to the common sense of men. Ask the fellow, whether yonder tree hath an existence out of his mind: what answer think you he would make?

PHILONOUS. The same that I should myself, to wit, that it doth exist out of his mind. But then to a Christian it cannot surely be shocking to say, the real tree existing without his mind is truly known and comprehended by (that is, *exists in*) the infinite mind of God. Probably he may not at first glance be aware of the direct and immediate proof there is of this, inasmuch as the very being of a tree, or any other sensible thing, implies a mind wherein it is. But the point itself he cannot deny. The question between the materialists and me is not, whether things have a real existence out of the mind of this or that person, but whether they have an absolute existence, distinct from being perceived by God, and exterior to all minds. This indeed some heathens and philosophers have affirmed, but whoever entertains notions of the Deity suitable to the Holy Scriptures, will be of another opinion.

HYLAS. But according to your notions, what difference is there between real things, and chimeras formed by the imagination, or the visions of a dream, since they are all equally in the mind?

PHILONOUS. The ideas formed by the imagination are faint and indistinct; they have besides an entire dependence on the will. But the ideas perceived by sense, that is, real things, are more vivid and clear, and being imprinted on the mind by a spirit distinct from us, have not a like dependence on our will. There is therefore no danger of confounding these with the foregoing: and there is as little of confounding them with the visions of a dream, which are dim, irregular, and confused. And though they should happen to be never so lively and natural, yet by their not being connected, and of a piece with the preceding and subsequent transactions of our lives, they might easily be distinguished from realities. In short, by whatever method you distinguish *things* from *chimeras* on your own scheme, the same, it is evident, will hold also upon mine. For it must be, I presume, by some perceived difference, and I am not for depriving you of any one thing that you perceive.

HYLAS. But still, Philonous, you hold, there is nothing in the world but spirits and ideas. And this, you must needs acknowledge, sounds very oddly.

PHILONOUS. I own the word *idea*, not being commonly used for *thing*, sounds something out of the way. My reason for using it was, because a necessary relation to the mind is understood to be implied by that term; and it is now commonly used by philosophers, to denote the immediate objects of the understanding. But however oddly the proposition may sound in words, yet it includes nothing so very strange or shocking in its sense, which in effect amounts to no more than this, to wit, that there are only things perceiving, and things perceived; or that every unthinking being is necessarily, and from the very nature of its existence, perceived by some mind; if not by any finite created mind, yet certainly by the infinite mind of God, in whom *we live, and move, and have our being.* Is this as strange as to say, the sensible qualities are not on the objects: or, that we cannot be sure of the existence of things, or know anything of their real natures, though we both see and feel them, and perceive them by all our senses?

HYLAS. And in consequence of this, must we not think there are no such things as physical or corporeal causes; but that a spirit is the immediate cause of all the phenomena in Nature? Can there be anything more extravagant than this?

PHILONOUS. Yes, it is infinitely more extravagant to say, a thing which is inert, operates on the mind, and which is unperceiving, is the cause of our perceptions. Besides, that which to you, I know not for what reason, seems so extravagant, is no more than the Holy Scriptures assert in a hundred places. In them God is represented as the sole and immediate Author of all those effects, which some heathens and philosophers are wont to ascribe to Nature, matter, fate, or the like unthinking principle. This is so much the constant language of Scripture, that it were needless to confirm it by citations.

HYLAS. You are not aware, Philonous, that in making God the immediate author of all the motions in Nature, you make him the author of murder, sacrilege, adultery, and the like heinous sins.

PHILONOUS. In answer to that, I observe first, that the imputation of guilt is the same, whether a person commits an action with or without an instrument. In case therefore you suppose God to act by the mediation of an instrument, or occasion, called *matter*, you as truly make Him the author of sin as I, who think Him the immediate agent in all those operations vulgarly ascribed to Nature. I farther observe, that sin or moral turpitude doth not consist in the outward physical action or motion, but in the internal deviation of the will from the laws of reason and religion. This is plain, in that the killing an enemy in a battle, or putting a criminal legally to death, is not thought sinful, though the outward act be the very same with that in the case of murder. Since therefore sin doth not consist in the physical action, the making God an immediate cause of all such actions, is not making him the author of sin. Lastly, I have nowhere said that God is the only agent who produces all the motions in bodies. It is true, I have denied there are any other agents beside spirits: but this is very consistent with allowing to thinking rational beings, in the production of motions, the use of limited powers, ultimately indeed derived from God, but immediately under the direction of their own wills, which is sufficient to entitle them to all the guilt of their actions.

HYLAS. But the denying matter, Philonous, or corporeal substance; there is the point. You can never persuade me that this is not repugnant to the universal sense of mankind. Were our dispute to be determined by most voices, I am confident you would give up the point, without gathering the votes.

PHILONOUS. I wish both our opinions were fairly stated and submitted to the judgment of men who had plain common sense, without the prejudices of a learned education. Let me be represented as one who trusts his senses, who thinks he knows the things he sees and feels, and entertains no doubts, of their existence; and you fairly set forth with all your doubts, your paradoxes, and your scepticism about you, and I shall willingly acquiesce in the determination of any indifferent person.* That there is no substance wherein ideas can exist beside spirit, is to me evident. And that the objects immediately perceived are ideas, is on all hands agreed. And that sensible qualities are objects immediately perceived, no one can deny. It is therefore evident there can be no *substratum* of those qualities but spirit, in which they exist, not by way of mode or property, but as a thing perceived in that which perceives it. I deny therefore that there is any unthinking *substratum* of the objects of sense, and in that acceptation that there is any material substance. But if by *material substance* is meant only sensible body, that which is seen and felt (and the unphilosophical part of the world, I dare say, mean no more) then I am more certain of matter's existence than you, or any other philosopher, pretend to be. If there be anything which makes the generality of mankind averse from the notions I espouse, it is a misapprehension that I deny the reality of sensible things: but as it is you who are guilty of that and not I, it follows that in truth their aversion is against your notions, and not mine. I do therefore assert that I am as certain as of my own being, that there are bodies or corporeal substances (meaning the things I perceive by my senses), and that granting this, the bulk of mankind will take no thought about, nor think themselves at all concerned in the fate of those unknown natures, and philosophical quiddities, which some men are so fond of.

HYLAS. What say you to this? Since, according to you, men judge of the reality of things by their senses, how can a man be mistaken in thinking the moon a plain lucid surface, about a foot in diameter; or a square tower, seen at a distance, round; or an oar, with one end in the water, crooked?

PHILONOUS. He is not mistaken with regard to the ideas he actually perceives; but in the inferences he makes from his present perceptions. Thus in the case of the oar, what he immediately perceives by sight is certainly crooked; and so far he is in the right. But if he thence conclude, that upon taking the oar out of the water he shall perceive the same crookedness; or that it would affect his touch, as crooked things are wont to do: in that he is mistaken. In like manner, if he shall conclude from what he perceives in one station, that in case he advances toward the moon or tower, he should still be affected with the like ideas, he is mistaken. But his mistake lies not in what he perceives immediately and at present (it being a manifest contradiction to suppose he should err in respect of that) but in the wrong judgment he makes concerning the ideas he apprehends to be connected with those immediately perceived: or concerning the ideas that, from what he perceives at present, he imagines would be perceived in other circumstances. The case is the same with regard to the Copernican system. We do not here perceive any motion of the earth: but it were erroneous thence to conclude, that in case we were placed at as great a distance from that, as we are now from the other planets, we should not then perceive its motion.

HYLAS. I understand you; and must needs own you say things plausible enough: but give me leave to put you in mind of one thing. Pray, Philonous, were you not formerly as positive that matter existed, as you are now that it does not?

PHILONOUS. I was. But here lies the difference. Before, my positiveness was founded without examination, upon prejudice; but now, after inquiry, upon evidence.

HYLAS. After all, it seems our dispute is rather about words than things. We agree in the thing, but differ in the name. That we are affected with ideas from without is evident; and it is no less evident, that there must be (I will not say archetypes, but) powers without the mind, corresponding to those ideas. And as these powers cannot subsist by themselves, there is some subject of them necessarily to be admitted, which I call *matter*, and you call *spirit*. This is all the difference.

PHILONOUS. Pray, Hylas, is that powerful being, or subject of powers, extended?

HYLAS. It hath not extension; but it hath the power to raise in you the idea of extension.

PHILONOUS. It is therefore itself unextended.

HYLAS. I grant it.

PHILONOUS. Is it not also active?

HYLAS. Without doubt: otherwise, how could we attribute powers to it?

PHILONOUS. Now let me ask you two questions: *first*, whether it be agreeable to the usage either of philosophers or others, to give the name *matter* to an unextended active being? And *secondly*, whether it be not ridiculously absurd to misapply names contrary to the common use of language?

HYLAS. Well then, let it not be called matter, since you will have it so, but some *third nature* distinct from matter and spirit. For, what reason is there why you should call it spirit? does not the notion of spirit imply, that it is thinking as well as active and unextended?

PHILONOUS. My reason is this: because I have a mind to have some notion or meaning in what I say; but I have no notion of any action distinct from volition, neither can I conceive volition to be anywhere but in a spirit: therefore when I speak of an active being, I am obliged to mean a spirit. Beside, what can be plainer than that a thing which hath no ideas in itself, cannot impart them to me; and if it hath ideas, surely it must be a spirit. To make you comprehend the point still more clearly if it be possible: I assert as well as you, that since we are affected from without, we must allow powers to be without in a being distinct from ourselves. So far we are agreed. But then we differ as to the kind of this powerful being. I will have it to be spirit, you matter, or I know not what (I may add too, you know not what) third nature. Thus I prove it to be spirit. From the effects I see produced, I conclude there are actions; and because actions, volitions; and because there are volitions, there must be a will. Again, the things I perceive must have an existence, they or their archetypes, out of my mind: but being ideas, neither they nor their archetypes can exist otherwise than in an understanding: there is therefore an understanding. But will and understanding constitute in the strictest sense a mind or spirit. The powerful cause therefore of my ideas, is in strict propriety of speech a *spirit*.

HYLAS. And now I warrant you think you have made the point very clear, little suspecting that what you advance leads directly to a contradiction. Is it not an absurdity to imagine any imperfection in God?

PHILONOUS. Without doubt.

HYLAS. To suffer pain is an imperfection.

PHILONOUS. It is.

HYLAS. Are we not sometimes affected with pain and uneasiness by some other being?

PHILONOUS. We are.

HYLAS. And have you not said that being is a spirit, and is not that spirit God?

PHILONOUS. I grant it.

HYLAS. But you have asserted, that whatever ideas we perceive from without, are in the mind which affects us. The ideas therefore of pain and uneasiness are in God; or in other words, God suffers pain: that is to say, there is an imperfection in the Divine Nature, which you acknowledged was absurd. So you are caught in a plain contradiction.

PHILONOUS. That God knows or understands all things, and that He knows among other things what pain is, even every sort of painful sensation, and what it is for His creatures to suffer pain, I make no question. But that God, though He knows and sometimes causes painful sensations in us, can Himself suffer pain, I positively deny. We who are limited and dependent spirits, are liable to impressions of sense, the effects of an external agent, which being produced against our wills, are sometimes painful and uneasy. But God, whom no external being can affect, who perceives nothing by sense as we do, whose will is absolute and independent, causing all things, and liable to be thwarted or resisted by nothing; it is evident, such a being as this can suffer nothing, nor be affected with any painful sensation, or indeed any sensation at all. We are chained to a body, that is to say, our perceptions are connected with corporeal motions. By the Law of our Nature we are affected upon every alteration in the nervous parts of our sensible body: which sensible body rightly considered, is nothing but a complexion of such qualities or ideas, as have no existence distinct from being perceived by a mind: so that this connexion of sensations with corporeal motions, means no more than a correspondence in the order of Nature between two sets of ideas, or things immediately perceivable. But God is a pure spirit, disengaged from all such sympathy or natural ties. No corporeal motions are attended with the sensations of pain or pleasure in his mind. To know everything knowable is certainly a perfection; but to endure, or suffer, or feel any thing by sense, is an imperfection. The former, I say, agrees to God, but not the latter. God knows or hath ideas; but His ideas are not convey'd to Him by sense,* as ours are. Your not distinguishing where there is so manifest a difference, makes you fancy you see an absurdity where there is none.

HYLAS. But all this while you have not considered, that the quantity of matter hath been demonstrated to be proportional to the gravity of bodies. And what can withstand demonstration?

PHILONOUS. Let me see how you demonstrate that point.

HYLAS. I lay it down for a principle, that the moments or quantities of motion in bodies, are in a direct compounded reason of the velocities and quantities of matter contained in them. Hence, where the velocities are equal, it follows, the moments are directly as the quantity of matter in each. But it is found by experience, that all bodies (bating the small inequalities, arising from the resistance of the air) descend with an equal velocity; the motion therefore of descending bodies, and consequently their gravity, which is the cause or principle of that motion, is proportional to the quantity of matter: which was to be demonstrated.

PHILONOUS. You lay it down as a self-evident principle, that the quantity of motion in any body, is proportional to the velocity and *matter* taken together: and this is made use of to prove a proposition, from whence the existence of *matter* is inferred. Pray is not this arguing in a circle?

HYLAS. In the premise I only mean, that the motion is proportional to the velocity, jointly with the extension and solidity.

PHILONOUS. But allowing this to be true, yet it will not thence follow, that gravity is proportional to *matter*, in your philosophic sense of the word; except you take it for granted, that unknown *substratum*, or whatever else you call it, is proportional to those sensible qualities; which to suppose, is plainly begging the question. That there is magnitude and solidity, or resistance, perceived by sense, I readily grant; as likewise that gravity may be proportional to those qualities, I will not dispute. But that either these qualities as perceived by us, or the powers producing them do exist in a *material substratum*; this is what I deny, and you indeed affirm, but notwithstanding your demonstration, have not yet proved.

HYLAS. I shall insist no longer on that point. Do you think however, you shall persuade me the natural philosophers have been dreaming all this while; pray what becomes of all their hypotheses and explications of the phenomena, which suppose the existence of matter?

PHILONOUS. What mean you, Hylas, by the phenomena?

HYLAS. I mean the appearances which I perceive by my senses.

PHILONOUS. And the appearances perceived by sense, are they not ideas?

HYLAS. I have told you so a hundred times.

PHILONOUS. Therefore, to explain the phenomena, is to shew how we come to be affected with ideas, in that manner and order wherein they are imprinted on our senses. Is it not?

HYLAS. It is.

PHILONOUS. Now if you can prove, that any philosopher hath explained the production of any one idea in our minds by the help of *matter*, I shall for ever acquiesce, and look on all that hath been said against it as nothing: but if you cannot, it is in vain to urge the explication of phenomena. That a being endowed with knowledge and will, should produce or exhibit ideas, is easily understood. But that a being which is utterly destitute of these faculties should be able to produce ideas, or in any sort to affect an intelligence, this I can never understand. This I say, though we had some positive conception of matter, though we knew its qualities, and could comprehend its existence, would yet be so far from explaining things, that it is itself the most inexplicable thing in the world. And yet for all this, it will not follow, that philosophers have been doing nothing; for by observing and reasoning upon the connexion of ideas, they discover the laws and methods of Nature, which is a part of knowledge both useful and entertaining.

HYLAS. After all, can it be supposed God would deceive all mankind? Do you imagine, he would have induced the whole world to believe the being of matter, if there was no such thing?

PHILONOUS. That every epidemical opinion arising from prejudice, or passion, or thoughtlessness, may be imputed to God, as the Author of it, I believe you will not affirm. Whatsoever opinion we father on him, it must be either because he has discovered it to us by supernatural revelation, or because it is so evident to our natural faculties, which were framed and given us by God, that it is impossible we should withhold our assent from it. But where is the revelation? or where is the evidence that extorts the belief of matter? Nay, how does it appear, that matter taken for something distinct from what we perceive by our senses, is thought to exist by all mankind, or indeed by any except a few philosophers, who do not know what they would be at? Your question supposes these points are clear; and when you have cleared them, I shall think myself obliged to give you another answer. In the mean time let it suffice that I tell you, I do not suppose God has deceived mankind at all.

HYLAS. But the novelty, Philonous, the novelty! There lies the danger. New notions should always be discountenanced; they unsettle men's minds, and nobody knows where they will end.

PHILONOUS. Why the rejecting a notion that hath no foundation either in sense or in reason, or in divine authority, should be thought to unsettle the belief of such opinions as are grounded on all or any of these, I cannot imagine. That innovations in government and religion, are dangerous, and ought to be discountenanced, I freely own. But is there the like reason why they should be discouraged in philosophy? The making anything known which was unknown before, is an innovation in knowledge: and if all such innovations had been forbidden, men would* have made a notable progress in the arts and sciences. But it is none of my business to plead for novelties and paradoxes. That the qualities we perceive, are not on the objects: that we must not believe our senses: that we know nothing of the real nature of things, and can never be assured even of their existence: that real colours and sounds are nothing but certain unknown figures and motions: that motions are in themselves neither swift nor slow: that there are in bodies absolute extensions, without any particular magnitude or figure: that a thing stupid, thoughtless and inactive, operates on a spirit: that the least particle of a body, contains innumerable extended parts. These are the novelties, these are the strange notions which shock the genuine uncorrupted judgment of all mankind; and being once admitted, embarrass the mind with endless doubts and difficulties. And it is against these and the like innovations, I endeavour to vindicate common sense. It is true, in doing this, I may perhaps be obliged to use some *ambages*,* and ways of speech not common. But if my notions are once thoroughly understood, that which is most singular in them, will in effect be found to amount to no more than this: that it is absolutely impossible, and a plain contradiction to suppose, any unthinking being should exist without being perceived by a mind. And if this notion be singular, it is a shame it should be so at this time of day, and in a Christian country.

HYLAS. As for the difficulties other opinions may be liable to, those are out of the question. It is your business to defend your own opinion. Can anything be plainer, than that you are for changing all things into ideas? You, I say, who are not ashamed to charge me with *scepticism*. This is so plain, there is no denying it.

PHILONOUS. You mistake me. I am not for changing things into ideas, but rather ideas into things; since those immediate objects of perception, which according to you, are only appearances of things, I take to be the real things themselves.

HYLAS. Things! you may pretend what you please; but it is certain, you leave us nothing but the empty forms of things, the outside only which strikes the senses.

PHILONOUS. What you call the empty forms and outside of things, seems to me the very things themselves. Nor are they empty or incomplete otherwise, than upon your supposition, that matter is an essential part of all corporeal things. We both therefore agree in this, that we perceive only sensible forms: but herein we differ, you will have them to be empty appearances, I real beings. In short you do not trust your senses, I do.

HYLAS. You say you believe your senses; and seem to applaud yourself that in this you agree with the vulgar. According to you therefore, the true nature of a thing is discovered by the senses. If so, whence comes that disagreement? Why is not the same figure, and other sensible qualities, perceived all manner of ways? and why should we use a microscope, the better to discover the true nature of a body, if it were discoverable to the naked eye?

PHILONOUS. Strictly speaking, Hylas, we do not see the same object that we feel; neither is the same object perceived by the microscope, which was by the naked eye. But in case every variation was thought sufficient to constitute a new kind or individual, the endless number or confusion of names would render language impracticable. Therefore to avoid this as well as other inconveniencies which are obvious upon a little thought, men combine together several ideas, apprehended by divers senses, or by the same sense at different times, or in different circumstances, but observed however to have some connexion in Nature, either with respect to co-existence or succession; all which they refer to one name, and consider as one thing. Hence it follows that when I examine by my other senses a thing I have seen, it is not in order to understand better the same object which I had perceived by sight, the object of one sense not being perceived by the other senses. And when I look through a microscope, it is not that I may perceive more clearly what I perceived already with my bare eyes, the object perceived by the glass being quite different from the former. But in both cases my aim is only to know what ideas are connected together; and the more a man knows of the connexion of ideas, the more he is said to know of the nature of things. What therefore if our ideas are variable; what if our senses are not in all circumstances affected with the same appearances? It will not thence follow, they are not to be trusted, or that they are inconsistent either with themselves or anything else, except it be with your preconceived notion of (I know not what) one single, unchanged, unperceivable, real nature, marked by each name: which prejudice seems to have taken its rise from not rightly understanding the common language of men speaking of several distinct ideas, as united into one thing by the mind. And indeed there is cause to suspect several erroneous conceits of the philosophers are owing to the same original: while they began to build their schemes, not so much on notions as words, which were framed by the vulgar, merely for conveniency and dispatch in the common actions of life, without any regard to speculation.

HYLAS. Methinks I apprehend your meaning.

PHILONOUS. It is your opinion, the ideas we perceive by our senses are not real things, but images, or copies of them. Our knowledge therefore is no farther real, than as our ideas are the true representations of those originals. But as these supposed originals are in themselves unknown, it is impossible to know how far our ideas resemble them; or whether they resemble them at all. We cannot therefore be sure we have any real knowledge. Farther, as our ideas are perpetually varied, without any change in the supposed real things, it necessarily follows they cannot all be true copies of them: or if some are, and others are not, it is impossible to distinguish the former from the latter. And this plunges us yet deeper in uncertainty. Again, when we consider the point, we cannot conceive how any idea, or anything like an idea, should have an absolute existence out of a mind: nor consequently, according to you, how there should be any real thing in Nature. The result of all which is, that we are thrown into the most hopeless and abandoned *scepticism*. Now give me leave to ask you, *first*, whether your referring ideas to certain absolutely existing unperceived substances, as their originals, be not the source of all this *scepticism*? *Secondly*, whether you are informed, either by sense or reason, of the existence of those unknown originals? And in case you are not, whether it be not absurd to suppose them? *Thirdly*, whether, upon inquiry, you find there is anything distinctly conceived or meant by the *absolute or external existence of unperceiving substances*? *Lastly*, whether the premises considered, it be not the wisest way to follow Nature, trust your senses, and laying aside all anxious thought about unknown natures or substances, admit with the vulgar those for real things, which are perceived by the senses?

HYLAS. For the present, I have no inclination to the answering part. I would much rather see how you can get over what follows. Pray are not the objects perceived by the senses of one, likewise perceivable to others present? If there were an hundred more here, they would all see the garden, the trees, and flowers as I see them. But they are not in the same manner affected with the ideas I frame in my imagination. Does not this make a difference between the former sort of objects and the latter?

PHILONOUS. I grant it does. Nor have I ever denied a difference between the objects of sense and those of imagination. But what would you infer from thence? You cannot say that sensible objects exist unperceived, because they are perceived by many.

HYLAS. I own, I can make nothing of that objection: but it hath led me into another. Is it not your opinion that by our senses we perceive only the ideas existing in our minds?

PHILONOUS. It is.

HYLAS. But the same idea which is in my mind, cannot be in yours, or in any other mind. Doth it not therefore follow from your principles, that no two can see the same thing? And is not this highly absurd?

PHILONOUS. If the term *same* be taken in the vulgar acceptation, it is certain (and not at all repugnant to the principles I maintain) that different persons may perceive the same thing; or the same thing or idea exist in different minds. Words are of arbitrary imposition; and since men are used to apply the word *same* where no distinction or variety is perceived, and I do not pretend to alter their perceptions, it follows, that as men have said before, *several saw the same thing*, so they may upon like occasions still continue to use the same phrase, without any deviation either from propriety of language, or the truth of things. But if the term *same* be used in the acceptation of philosophers, who pretend to an abstracted notion of identity, then, according to their sundry definitions of this notion (for it is not yet agreed wherein that philosophic identity consists), it may or may not be possible for divers persons to perceive the same thing. But whether philosophers shall think fit to call a thing the *same* or no, is, I conceive, of small importance. Let us suppose several men together, all endued with the same faculties, and consequently affected in like sort by their senses, and who had yet never known the use of language; they would without question agree in their perceptions. Though perhaps, when they came to the use of speech, some regarding the uniformness of what was perceived, might call it the *same* thing: others especially regarding the diversity of persons who perceived, might choose the denomination of different things. But who sees not that all the dispute is about a word? to wit, whether what is perceived by different persons, may yet have the term *same* applied to it? Or suppose a house, whose walls or outward shell remaining unaltered, the chambers are all pulled down, and new ones built in their place; and that you should call this the *same*, and I should say it was not the *same* house: would we not for all this perfectly agree in our thoughts of the house, considered in itself? and would not all the difference consist in a sound? If you should say, we differed in our notions; for that you superadded to your idea of the house the simple abstracted idea of identity, whereas I did not; I would tell you I know not what you mean by that *abstracted idea of identity*; and should desire you to look into your own thoughts, and be sure you understood yourself . . . Why so silent, Hylas? Are you not yet satisfied, men may dispute about identity and diversity, without any real difference in their thoughts and opinions, abstracted from names? Take this farther reflexion with you: that whether matter be allowed to exist or no, the case is exactly the same as to the point in hand. For the materialists themselves acknowledge what we immediately perceive by our senses, to be our own ideas. Your difficulty therefore, that no two see the same thing, makes equally against the materialists and me.

HYLAS. But they suppose an external archetype,* to which referring their several ideas, they may truly be said to perceive the same thing.

PHILONOUS. And (not to mention your having discarded those archetypes) so may you suppose an external archetype on my principles; *external*, I mean, to your own mind; though indeed it must be supposed to exist in that mind which comprehends all things; but then this serves all the ends of identity, as well as if it existed out of a mind. And I am sure you yourself will not say, it is less intelligible.

HYLAS. You have indeed clearly satisfied me, either that there is no difficulty at bottom in this point; or if there be, that it makes equally against both opinions.

PHILONOUS. But that which makes equally against two contradictory opinions, can be a proof against neither.

HYLAS. I acknowledge it. But after all, Philonous, when I consider the substance of what you advance against *scepticism*, it amounts to no more than this. We are sure that we really see, hear, feel; in a word, that we are affected with sensible impressions.

PHILONOUS. And how are we concerned any farther? I see this *cherry*, I feel it, I taste it: and I am sure *nothing* cannot be seen, or felt, or tasted: it is therefore *real*. Take away the sensations of softness, moisture, redness, tartness, and you take away the cherry. Since it is not a being distinct from sensations; a *cherry*, I say, is nothing but a congeries of sensible impressions, or ideas perceived by various senses: which ideas are united into one thing (or have one name given them) by the mind; because they are observed to attend each other. Thus when the palate is affected with such a particular taste, the sight is affected with a red colour, the touch with roundness, softness, &c. Hence, when I see, and feel, and taste, in sundry certain manners, I am sure the *cherry* exists, or is real; its reality being in my opinion nothing abstracted from those sensations. But if by the word *cherry* you mean an unknown nature distinct from all those sensible qualities, and by its existence something distinct from its being perceived; then indeed I own, neither you nor I, nor any one else can be sure it exists.*

HYLAS. But what would you say, Philonous, if I should bring the very same reasons against the existence of sensible things in a mind, which you have offered against their existing in a material *substratum*?

PHILONOUS. When I see your reasons, you shall hear what I have to say to them.

HYLAS. Is the mind extended or unextended?

PHILONOUS. Unextended, without doubt.

HYLAS. Do you say the things you perceive are in your mind?

PHILONOUS. They are.

HYLAS. Again, have I not heard you speak of sensible impressions?

PHILONOUS. I believe you may.

HYLAS. Explain to me now, O Philonous! how it is possible there should be room for all those trees and houses to exist in your mind. Can extended things be contained in that which is unextended? Or are we to imagine impressions made on a thing void of all solidity? You cannot say objects are in your mind, as books in your study: or that things are imprinted on it, as the figure of a seal upon wax. In what sense therefore are we to understand those expressions? Explain me this if you can: and I shall then be able to answer all those queries you formerly put to me about my *substratum*.

PHILONOUS. Look you, Hylas, when I speak of objects as existing in the mind or imprinted on the senses; I would not be understood in the gross literal sense, as when bodies are said to exist in a place, or a seal to make an impression upon wax. My meaning is only that the mind comprehends or perceives them; and that it is affected from without, or by some being distinct from itself. This is my explication of your difficulty; and how it can serve to make your tenet of an unperceiving material *substratum* intelligible, I would fain know.

HYLAS. Nay, if that be all, I confess I do not see what use can be made of it. But are you not guilty of some abuse of language in this?

PHILONOUS. None at all: it is no more than common custom, which you know is the rule of language, hath authorized: nothing being more usual, than for philosophers to speak of the immediate objects of the understanding as things existing in the mind. Nor is there anything in this, but what is conformable to the general analogy of language; most part of the mental operations being signified by words borrowed from sensible things; as is plain in the terms *comprehend, reflect, discourse*, &c. which being applied to the mind, must not be taken in their gross original sense.

HYLAS. You have, I own, satisfied me in this point: but there still remains one great difficulty, which I know not how you will get over. And indeed it is of such importance, that if you could solve all others, without being able to find a solution for this, you must never expect to make me a proselyte to your principles.

PHILONOUS. Let me know this mighty difficulty.

HYLAS. The Scripture account of the Creation, is what appears to me utterly irreconcileable with your notions. Moses tells us of a Creation: a Creation of what? of ideas? No certainly, but of things, of real things, solid corporeal substances. Bring your principles to agree with this, and I shall perhaps agree with you.

PHILONOUS. Moses mentions the sun, moon, and stars, earth and sea, plants and animals: that all these do really exist, and were in the beginning created by God, I make no question. If by *ideas*, you mean fictions and fancies of the mind, then these are no ideas. If by *ideas*, you mean immediate objects of the understanding, or sensible things which cannot exist unperceived, or out of a mind, then these things are ideas. But whether you do, or do not call them *ideas*, it matters little. The difference is only about a name. And whether that name be retained or rejected, the sense, the truth and reality of things continues the same. In common talk, the objects of your senses are not termed *ideas* but *things*. Call them so still: provided you do not attribute to them any absolute external existence, and I shall never quarrel with you for a word. The Creation therefore I allow to have been a creation of things, of *real* things. Neither is this in the least inconsistent with my principles, as is evident from what I have now said; and would have been evident to you without this, if you had not forgotten what had been so often said before. But as for solid corporeal substances, I desire you to shew where Moses makes any mention of them; and if they should be mentioned by him, or any other inspired writer, it would still be incumbent on you to shew those words were not taken in the vulgar acceptation, for things falling under our senses, but in the philosophic acceptation, for matter, or an unknown quiddity, with an absolute existence. When you have proved these points, then (and not till then) may you bring the authority of Moses into our dispute.

HYLAS. It is in vain to dispute about a point so clear. I am content to refer it to your own conscience. Are you not satisfied there is some peculiar repugnancy between the Mosaic account of the Creation, and your notions?

PHILONOUS. If all possible sense, which can be put on the first chapter of *Genesis*, may be conceived as consistently with my principles as any other, then it has no peculiar repugnancy with them. But there is no sense you may not as well conceive, believing as I do. Since, beside spirits, all you conceive are ideas; and the existence of these I do not deny. Neither do you pretend they exist without the mind.

HYLAS. Pray let me see any sense you can understand it in.

PHILONOUS. Why, I imagine that if I had been present at the Creation, I should have seen things produced into being; that is, become perceptible, in the order described by the sacred historian. I ever before believed the Mosaic account of the Creation, and now find no alteration in my manner of believing it. When things are said to begin or end their existence, we do not mean this with regard to God, but His creatures. All objects are eternally known by God, or which is the same thing, have an eternal existence in his mind: but when things before imperceptible to creatures, are by a decree of God, made perceptible to them; then are they said to begin a relative existence, with respect to created minds. Upon reading therefore the Mosaic account of the Creation, I understand that the several parts of the world became gradually perceivable to finite spirits, endowed with proper faculties; so that whoever such were present, they were in truth perceived by them. This is the literal obvious sense suggested to me, by the words of the Holy Scripture: in which is included no mention or no thought, either of *substratum*, instrument, occasion, or absolute existence. And upon inquiry, I doubt not, it will be found, that most plain honest men, who believe the Creation, never think of those things any more than I. What metaphysical sense you may understand it in, you only can tell.

HYLAS. But, Philonous, you do not seem to be aware, that

you allow created things in the beginning, only a relative, and consequently hypothetical being: that is to say, upon supposition there were men to perceive them, without which they have no actuality of absolute existence, wherein Creation might terminate. Is it not therefore according to you plainly impossible, the Creation of any inanimate creatures should precede that of man? And is not this directly contrary to the Mosaic account?

PHILONOUS. In answer to that I say, *first*, created beings might begin to exist in the mind of other created intelligences, beside men. You will not therefore be able to prove any contradiction between Moses and my notions, unless you first shew, there was no other order of finite created spirits in being before man. I say farther, in case we conceive the Creation, as we should at this time a parcel of plants or vegetables of all sorts, produced by an invisible power, in a desert where nobody was present: that this way of explaining or conceiving it, is consistent with my principles, since they deprive you of nothing, either sensible or imaginable: that it exactly suits with the common, natural, undebauched notions of mankind: That it manifests the dependence of all things on God; and consequently hath all the good effect or influence, which it is possible that important article of our faith should have in making men humble, thankful, and resigned to their Creator. I say moreover, that in this naked conception of things, divested of words, there will not be found any notion of what you call the *actuality of absolute existence*. You may indeed raise a dust with those terms, and so lengthen our dispute to no purpose. But I entreat you calmly to look into your own thoughts, and then tell me if they are not an useless and unintelligible jargon.

HYLAS. I own, I have no very clear notion annexed to them. But what say you to this? Do you not make the existence of sensible things consist in their being in a mind? And were not all things eternally in the mind of God? Did they not therefore exist from all eternity, according to you? And how could that which was eternal, be created in time? Can anything be clearer or better connected than this?

PHILONOUS. And are not you too of opinion, that God knew all things from eternity?

HYLAS. I am.

PHILONOUS. Consequently they always had a being in the Divine Intellect.

HYLAS. This I acknowledge.

PHILONOUS. By your own confession therefore, nothing is new, or begins to be, in respect of the mind of God. So we are agreed in that point.

HYLAS. What shall we make then of the Creation?

PHILONOUS. May we not understand it to have been entirely in respect of finite spirits; so that things, with regard to us, may properly be said to begin their existence, or be created, when God decreed they should become perceptible to intelligent creatures, in that order and manner which he then established, and we now call the laws of Nature? You may call this a *relative*, or *hypothetical existence* if you please. But so long as it supplies us with the most natural, obvious, and literal sense of the Mosaic history of the Creation; so long as it answers all the religious ends of that great article; in a word, so long as you can assign no other sense or meaning in its stead; why should we reject this? Is it to comply with a ridiculous sceptical humour of making everything nonsense and unintelligible? I am sure you cannot say, it is for the glory of God. For allowing it to be a thing possible and conceivable, that the corporeal world should have an absolute subsistence extrinsical to the mind of God, as well as to the minds of all created spirits: yet how could this set forth either the immensity or omniscience of the Deity, or the necessary and immediate dependence of all things on him? Nay, would it not rather seem to derogate from those attributes?

HYLAS. Well, but as to this decree of God's, for making things perceptible: what say you, Philonous, is it not plain, God did either execute that decree from all eternity, or at some certain time began to will what he had not actually willed before, but only designed to will. If the former, then there could be no Creation or beginning of existence in finite things. If the latter, then we must acknowledge something new to befall the Deity; which implies a sort of change: and all change argues imperfection.

PHILONOUS. Pray consider what you are doing. Is it not evident, this objection concludes equally against a creation in any sense; nay, against every other act of the Deity, discoverable by the light of Nature? None of which can we conceive, otherwise than as performed in time, and having a beginning. God is a being of transcendent and unlimited perfections: his nature therefore is incomprehensible to finite spirits. It is not therefore to be expected, that any man, whether *materialist* or *immaterialist*, should have exactly just notions of the Deity, his attributes, and ways of operation. If then you would infer anything against me, your difficulty must not be drawn from the inadequateness of our conceptions of the Divine Nature, which is unavoidable on any scheme; but from the denial of matter, of which there is not one word, directly or indirectly, in what you have now objected.

HYLAS. I must acknowledge, the difficulties you are concerned to clear, are such only as arise from the non-existence of matter, and are peculiar to that notion. So far you are in the right. But I cannot by any means bring myself to think there is no such peculiar repugnancy between the Creation and your opinion; though indeed where to fix it, I do not distinctly know.

PHILONOUS. What would you have! do I not acknowledge a two-fold state of things, the one ectypal or natural, the other archetypal and eternal? The former was created in time; the latter existed from everlasting in the mind of God. Is not this agreeable to the common notions of divines? or is any more than this necessary in order to conceive the Creation? But you suspect some peculiar repugnancy, though you know not where it lies. To take away all possibility of scruple in the case, do but consider this one point. Either you are not able to conceive the Creation on any hypothesis whatsoever; and if so, there is no ground for dislike or complaint against my particular opinion on that score: or you are able to conceive it; and if so, why not on my principles, since thereby nothing conceivable is taken

away? You have all along been allowed the full scope of
sense, imagination, and reason. Whatever therefore you
could before apprehend, either immediately or mediately
by your senses, or by ratiocination from your senses; whatever you could perceive, imagine or understand, remains
still with you. If therefore the notion you have of the Creation by other principles be intelligible, you have it still upon
mine; if it be not intelligible, I conceive it to be no notion at
all; and so there is no loss of it. And indeed it seems to me
very plain, that the supposition of matter, that is, a thing
perfectly unknown and inconceivable, cannot serve to
make us conceive anything. And I hope, it need not be
proved to you, that if the existence of matter doth not make
the Creation conceivable, the Creation's being without
it inconceivable, can be no objection against its non-
existence.

HYLAS. I confess, Philonous, you have almost satisfied me in
this point of the Creation.

PHILONOUS. I would fain know why you are not quite satisfied. You tell me indeed of a repugnancy between the Mosaic history and immaterialism: but you know not where it
lies. Is this reasonable, Hylas? Can you expect I should
solve a difficulty without knowing what it is? But to pass by
all that, would not a man think you were assured there is no
repugnancy between the received notions of materialists
and the inspired writings?

HYLAS. And so I am.

PHILONOUS. Ought the historical part of Scripture to be
understood in a plain obvious sense, or in a sense which is
metaphysical, and out of the way?

HYLAS. In the plain sense, doubtless.

PHILONOUS. When Moses speaks of herbs, earth, water, &c.
as having been created by God; think you not the sensible
things, commonly signified by those words, are suggested to
every unphilosophical reader?

HYLAS. I cannot help thinking so.

PHILONOUS. And are not all ideas, or things perceived by
sense, to be denied a real existence by the doctrine of the
materialists?

HYLAS. This I have already acknowledged.

PHILONOUS. The Creation therefore, according to them, was not the creation of things sensible, which have only a relative being, but of certain unknown natures, which have an absolute being, wherein Creation might terminate.

HYLAS. True.

PHILONOUS. Is it not therefore evident, the asserters of matter destroy the plain obvious sense of Moses, with which their notions are utterly inconsistent; and instead of it obtrude on us I know not what, something equally unintelligible to themselves and me?

HYLAS. I cannot contradict you.

PHILONOUS. Moses tells us of a Creation. A Creation of what? of unknown quiddities, of occasions, or *substratums*? No certainly; but of things obvious to the senses. You must first reconcile this with your notions, if you expect I should be reconciled to them.

HYLAS. I see you can assault me with my own weapons.

PHILONOUS. Then as to *absolute existence*; was there ever known a more jejune notion than that? Something it is, so abstracted and unintelligible, that you have frankly owned you could not conceive it, much less explain anything by it. But allowing matter to exist, and the notion of absolute existence to be as clear as light; yet was this ever known to make the Creation more credible? Nay hath it not furnished the *atheists* and *infidels* of all ages, with the most plausible argument against a Creation? That a corporeal substance, which hath an absolute existence without the minds of spirits, should be produced out of nothing by the mere will of a spirit, hath been looked upon as a thing so contrary to all reason, so impossible and absurd, that not only the most celebrated among the ancients, but even divers modern and Christian philosophers have thought matter coeternal with the Deity. Lay these things together, and then judge you whether materialism disposes men to believe the creation of thing.

HYLAS. I own, Philonous, I think it does not. This of the Creation is the last objection I can think of; and I must needs own it hath been sufficiently answered as well as the rest. Nothing now remains to be overcome, but a sort of unaccountable backwardness that I find in myself toward your notions. .

PHILONOUS. When a man is swayed, he knows not why, to one side of a question; can this, think you, be anything else but the effect of prejudice, which never fails to attend old and rooted notions? And indeed in this respect I cannot deny the belief of matter to have very much the advantage over the contrary opinion, with men of a learned education.

HYLAS. I confess it seems to be as you say.

PHILONOUS. As a balance therefore to this weight of prejudice, let us throw into the scale the great advantages that arise from the belief of immaterialism, both in regard to religion and human learning. The being of a God, and incorruptibility of the soul, those great articles of religion, are they not proved with the clearest and most immediate evidence? When I say the being of a *God*, I do not mean an obscure general cause of things, whereof we have no conception, but *God*, in the strict and proper sense of the word. A being whose spirituality, omnipresence, providence, omniscience, infinite power and goodness, are as conspicuous as the existence of sensible things, of which (notwithstanding the fallacious pretences and affected scruples of *sceptics*) there is no more reason to doubt, than of our own being. Then with relation to human sciences; in natural philosophy, what intricacies, what obscurities, what contradictions, hath the belief of matter led men into! To say nothing of the numberless disputes about its extent, continuity, homogeneity, gravity, divisibility, &c. do they not pretend to explain all things by bodies operating on bodies, according to the laws of motion? and yet, are they able to comprehend how any one body should move another? Nay, admitting there was no difficulty in reconciling the notion of an inert being with a cause; or in conceiving how an accident might pass from one body to another; yet by all their strained thoughts and extravagant suppositions, have they been able to reach the mechanical production of any one animal or vegetable body? Can they account by the laws of motion, for sounds, tastes, smells, or colours, or for the regular course of things? Have they accounted by physical principles for the aptitude and contrivance, even of the most inconsiderable parts of the universe? But laying aside matter and corporeal causes, and admitting only the efficiency of an all-perfect mind, are not all the effects of Nature easy and intelligible? If the phenomena are nothing else but *ideas*; God is a *spirit*, but matter an unintelligent, unperceiving being. If they demonstrate an unlimited power in their cause; God is active and omnipotent, but matter an inert mass. If the order, regularity, and usefulness of them, can never be sufficiently admired; God is infinitely wise and provident, but matter destitute of all contrivance and design. These surely are great advantages in *physics*. Not to mention that the apprehension of a distant Deity, naturally disposes men to a negligence in their *moral* actions, which they would be more cautious of, in case they thought Him immediately present, and acting on their minds without the interposition of matter, or unthinking second causes. Then in *metaphysics*; what difficulties concerning entity in abstract, substantial forms, hylarchic principles, plastic natures, substance and accident, principle of individuation, possibility of matter's thinking, origin of ideas, the manner how two independent substances, so widely different as *spirit* and *matter*, should mutually operate on each other?* What difficulties, I say, and endless disquisitions concerning these and innumerable other the like points, do we escape by supposing only spirits and ideas? Even the *mathematics* themselves, if we take away the absolute existence of extended things, become much more clear and easy; the most shocking paradoxes and intricate speculations in those sciences, depending on the infinite divisibility of finite extension, which depends on that supposition. But what need is there to insist on the particular sciences? Is not that opposition to all science whatsoever, that phrensy of the ancient and modern *sceptics*, built on the same foundation? Or can you produce so much as one argument against the reality of corporeal things, or in behalf of that avowed utter ignorance of their natures, which doth not suppose their reality to consist in an external absolute existence? Upon this supposition indeed, the objections from the change of colours in a pigeon's neck, or the appearances of a broken oar in the water, must be allowed to have weight. But those and the like objections vanish, if we do not maintain the being of absolute external originals, but place the reality of things in ideas, fleeting indeed, and changeable; however not changed at random, but according to the fixed order of Nature. For herein consists that constancy and truth of things, which secures all the concerns of life, and distinguishes that which is *real* from the irregular visions of the fancy.

HYLAS. I agree to all you have now said, and must own that nothing can incline me to embrace your opinion, more than the advantages I see it is attended with. I am by nature lazy; and this would be a mighty abridgement in knowledge. What doubts, what hypotheses, what labyrinths of amusement, what fields of disputation, what an ocean of false learning, may be avoided by that single notion of *immaterialism*?

PHILONOUS. After all, is there anything farther remaining to be done? You may remember you promised to embrace that opinion, which upon examination should appear most agreeable to common sense, and remote from *scepticism*. This by your own confession is that which denies matter, or the absolute existence of corporeal things. Nor is this all; the same notion has been proved several ways, viewed in different lights, pursued in its consequences, and all objections against it cleared. Can there be a greater evidence of its truth? or is it possible it should have all the marks of a true opinion, and yet be false?

HYLAS. I own myself entirely satisfied for the present in all respects. But what security can I have that I shall still continue the same full assent to your opinion, and that no unthought-of objection or difficulty will occur hereafter?

PHILONOUS. Pray, Hylas, do you in other cases, when a point is once evidently proved, withhold your assent on account of objections or difficulties it may be liable to? Are the difficulties that attend the doctrine of incommensurable quantities, of the angle of contact, of the asymptotes to curves or the like, sufficient to make you hold out against mathematical demonstration? Or will you disbelieve the providence of God, because there may be some particular things which you know not how to reconcile with it? If there are difficulties attending immaterialism, there are at the same time direct and evident proofs for it. But for the existence of matter, there is not one proof, and far more numerous and insurmountable objections lie against it. But where are those mighty difficulties you insist on? Alas! you know not where or what they are; something which may possibly occur hereafter. If this be a sufficient pretence for withholding your full assent, you should never yield it to any proposition, how free soever from exceptions, how clearly and solidly soever demonstrated.

HYLAS. You have satisfied me, Philonous.

PHILONOUS. But to arm you against all future objections, do but consider, that which bears equally hard on two contradictory opinions, can be a proof against neither. Whenever therefore any difficulty occurs, try if you can find a solution for it on the hypothesis of the *materialists*. Be not deceived by words; but sound your own thoughts. And in case you cannot conceive it easier by the help of *materialism*, it is plain it can be no objection against *immaterialism*. Had you proceeded all along by this rule, you would probably have spared yourself abundance of trouble in objecting; since of all your difficulties I challenge you to shew one that is explained by matter; nay, which is not more unintelligible with, than without that supposition, and consequently makes rather *against* than *for* it. You should consider in each particular, whether the difficulty arises from the *non-existence of matter*. If it doth not, you might as well argue from the infinite divisibility of extension against the divine prescience, as from such a difficulty against *immaterialism*. And yet upon recollection I believe you will find this to have been often, if not always the case. You should likewise take heed not to argue on a *petitio principii*.* One is apt to say, the unknown substances ought to be esteemed real things, rather than the ideas in our minds: and who can tell but the unthinking external substance may concur as a cause or instrument in the production of our ideas? But is not this proceeding on a supposition that there are such external substances? And to suppose this, is it not begging the question? But above all things you should beware of imposing on yourself by that vulgar sophism, which is called *ignoratio elenchi.** You talked often as if you thought I maintained the non-existence of sensible things: whereas in truth no one can be more thoroughly assured of their existence than I am: and it is you who doubt; I should have said, positively deny it. Everything that is seen, felt, heard, or any way perceived by the senses, is on the principles I embrace, a real being, but not on yours. Remember, the matter you contend for is an unknown somewhat (if indeed it may be termed *somewhat*) which is quite stripped of all sensible qualities, and can neither be perceived by sense, nor apprehended by the mind. Remember, I say, that it is not any object which is hard or soft, hot or cold, blue or white, round or square, &c. For all these things I affirm do exist. Though indeed I deny they have an existence distinct from being perceived; or that they exist out of all minds whatsoever. Think on these points; let them be attentively considered and still kept in view. Otherwise you will not comprehend the state of the question; without which your objections will always be wide of the mark, and instead of mine, may possibly be directed (as more than once they have been) against your own notions.

HYLAS. I must needs own, Philonous, nothing seems to have kept me from agreeing with you more than this same *mistaking the question*. In denying matter, at first glimpse I am tempted to imagine you deny the things we see and feel; but upon reflexion find there is no ground for it. What think you therefore of retaining the name *matter*, and applying it to sensible things? This may be done without any change in your sentiments: and believe me it would be a means of reconciling them to some persons, who may be more shocked at an innovation in words than in opinion.

PHILONOUS. With all my heart: retain the word *matter*, and apply it to the objects of sense, if you please, provided you do not attribute to them any subsistence distinct from their being perceived. I shall never quarrel with you for an expression. *Matter*, or *material substance*, are terms introduced by philosophers; and as used by them, imply a sort of independency, or a subsistence distinct from being perceived by a mind: but are never used by common people; or if ever, it is to signify the immediate objects of sense. One would think therefore, so long as the names of all particular things, with the terms *sensible*, *substance*, *body*, *stuff*, and the like, are retained, the word *matter* should be never missed in common talk. And in philosophical discourses it seems the best way to leave it quite out; since there is not perhaps any one thing that hath more favoured and strengthened the depraved bent of the mind toward *atheism*, than the use of that general confused term.

HYLAS. Well but, Philonous, since I am content to give up the notion of an unthinking substance exterior to the mind, I think you ought not to deny me the privilege of using the word *matter* as I please, and annexing it to a collection of sensible qualities subsisting only in the mind. I freely own there is no other substance in a strict sense, than *spirit*. But I have been so long accustomed to the term *matter*, that I know not how to part with it. To say, there is no *matter* in the world, is still shocking to me. Whereas to say, there is no *matter*, if by that term be meant an unthinking substance existing without the mind: but if by *matter* is meant some sensible thing, whose existence consists in being perceived, then there is *matter*: this distinction gives it quite another turn: and men will come into your notions with small difficulty, when they are proposed in that manner. For after all, the controversy about *matter* in the strict acceptation of it, lies altogether between you and the philosophers; whose principles, I acknowledge, are not near so natural, or so agreeable to the common sense of mankind, and Holy Scripture, as yours. There is nothing we either desire or shun, but as it makes, or is apprehended to make some part of our happiness or misery. But what hath happiness or misery, joy or grief, pleasure or pain, to do with absolute existence, or with unknown entities, abstracted from all relation to us? It is evident, things regard us only as they are pleasing or displeasing: and they can please or displease, only so far forth as they are perceived. Farther therefore we are not concerned; and thus far you leave things as you found them. Yet still there is something new in this doctrine. It is plain, I do not now think with the philosophers, nor yet altogether with the vulgar. I would know how the case stands in that respect: precisely, what you have added to, or altered in my former notions.

PHILONOUS. I do not pretend to be a setter-up of *new notions*. My endeavours tend only to unite and place in a clearer light that truth, which was before shared between the vulgar and the philosophers: the former being of opinion, that *those things they immediately perceive are the real things*; and the latter, that *the things immediately perceived, are ideas which exist only in the mind*. Which two notions put together, do in effect constitute the substance of what I advance.*

HYLAS. I have been a long time distrusting my senses; methought I saw things by a dim light, and through false glasses. Now the glasses are removed, and a new light breaks in upon my understanding. I am clearly convinced that I see things in their native forms; and am no longer in pain about their unknown natures or absolute existence. This is the state I find myself in at present: though indeed the course that brought me to it, I do not yet thoroughly comprehend. You set out upon the same principles that Academics, Cartesians, and the like sects, usually do; and for a long time it looked as if you were advancing their philosophical *scepticism*; but in the end your conclusions are directly opposite to theirs.

PHILONOUS. You see, Hylas, the water of yonder fountain, how it is forced upwards, in a round column, to a certain height; at which it breaks and falls back into the basin from whence it rose: its ascent as well as descent, proceeding from the same uniform law or principle of *gravitation*. Just so, the same principles which at first view lead to *scepticism*, pursued to a certain point, bring men back to common sense.

EXPLANATORY NOTES

The Preface

6 this was omitted from *B*, the 1734 edition, but its sentiments are sufficiently to the point to merit inclusion.

Introduction

7 *Introduction*: both Locke and Berkeley start their major work with a long attack on what they take to be the source of the errors of their opponents. In both cases, this purging of error is meant to clear the way for a correct empiricism. In both cases, the real contribution of these supposedly important preliminaries is unclear. Locke attacks 'innate ideas'. On the one hand, it is plain why an empiricist should wish to prove that we have no other source of knowledge except experience and, therefore, that we have no innate knowledge. On the other hand, Locke's way of attacking innate ideas seems to concern itself entirely with the genesis of our ideas, not with their justification and hardly to engage with the role given to a priori truth and reasoning as it is found in Descartes, Spinoza, or Plato. Locke's attack seems hardly relevant to the real issues between rationalism and empiricism. In a similar way, it is, from a certain perspective, clear why someone who believes that *esse est percipi* should want to insist that our genuine concepts operate by closely reflecting experience and should not be built up into 'abstract' structures. But his attack on abstract ideas, apart from refuting an eccentric account of generality he finds in Locke, hardly seems to relate to anything else in the history of philosophy. Neither Locke nor Berkeley had captured the source of their opponents' 'errors' in the way they thought they had. By the same token, by failing to analyse correctly what they were against, they also failed to express what constitutes a proper empiricism, as they understood it. This has been a perennial problem for empiricism. Hume thought one could simply say that all ideas are faded impressions, then had to admit that we could have an idea of a shade we had never experienced, thereby admitting a kind of a priori structure in colour perception that his empiricism did not allow. And, in the twentieth century, the failure to contrive a

plausible version of the verification principle is another instance of the same difficulty.

In Berkeley's case, the unclarity has its roots in a confusion about whether the offending abstractness is a feature of the ideas as psychological phenomena, or whether it is a feature of their contents—that they are ideas *of* improperly abstract conceptions. The attack on Locke is an attack on the former, for its burden is that there could not be an actual psychological episode of the kind Locke appears to say abstract ideas are. Furthermore, Berkeley explicitly exonerates his opponents of claiming to conceive *of* impossibly abstract things, for he says, at s. 7: 'It is agreed on all hands, that the qualities or modes of things do never really exist each of them apart by itself . . .' Thus it is only to the account of the conceiving that he objects, not to their idea of what is conceived of. This is the opposite of what he requires if abstraction is to be the source of our false conceptions of matter and mind-independence, for these are the contents of conceptions, not the psychological vehicle of them. Equally, when he attacks those who believe numbers are objects for being deceived by abstraction, it is the object of the conception, not the mode of conceiving he is calling abstract.

An at least partial resolution of this problem can be found in Berkeley's imagistic theory of thought, according to which concepts are just images and the image is or contains the content of the concept. The image is, for Berkeley, identical with (a facet of) the thing it is an image of, so the distinction between conceiving and its object is dissolved. I discuss in section (vii) of the Introduction how the imagistic theory is supposed to function in the argument for immaterialism, and what its weaknesses are as a theory of concepts: and, in section (viii), why, though a failure as such a theory, it may not be so bad as a theory of certain kinds of conceptual content.

7 *But no sooner . . . comprehend*: a classic instance of this is the first of Descartes's *Meditations*.

   It is said . . . things: e.g. in Locke, *Essay*, I. I. 5; 4. 3. 6.

8 *principles . . . philosophy*: Jessop, in his edition, says: 'The chief of the impugned principles are—that there are abstract "ideas"; that "ideas" can be copies of what is by definition unperceivable; that the corporeal exists independently of any mental apprehension whatever; that the corporeal has causal power, i.e. originates change; and that mind is, or would be if our knowing were adequate, an "idea", i.e. an object of the same general kind, on

the same plane, as the objects of sense. There are derivative principles, such as the untrustworthiness of the senses, and the infinite divisibility of matter.' This is a useful list, but it should be remembered that the error of abstraction is meant to underlie all the rest: see s. 6.

15 *such an idea*: there are those, such as Yolton, who deny that Locke's ideas are images and say that they are more like ideas in our intellectualist sense. It is hard to see what is the difficulty Locke has in mind if it is not that of forming these very strange images—the concept or definition of a triangle does not seem attended with any problem.

16 *triangle*: in *C* this section ended here; the remainder was added in *B*.

19 *'Tis . . . impracticable*: This shows how odd is Berkeley's concept of an idea. What is a definition of if not an idea or concept? If Berkeley were to reply that it is of the meaning of a word, what notion are we to have of meaning that does not reintroduce the problem?

communicating . . . language: the doctrine of this paragraph has proved popular with modern philosophers who wish to emphasize the emotive meaning of words and Wittgensteinian approaches to 'meaning as use', not reference. Whether or not these approaches have any merit in their own right, I do not think they are much help to Berkeley. He is struggling with the problem of generality and this resides as much in emotive effect or other kinds of standards of usage as it does in reference. (The concept of a *rule*, which involves generality, is much discussed in connection with Wittgenstein.) It is no help to say that we may be 'affected with the promise of a *good thing*, though we have no idea what it is', for we must have the concept of a *good thing* even if we have no *picture* of what particular good it is: and it is the concept we should be interested in.

22 *many . . . words*: for example, Hobbes, *Leviathan*, 1. 4; Locke, *Essay*, 3. 10.

Part I

24 *Part I*: the main text is called 'Part I' because Berkeley had intended to write a second part dealing with the nature of spirit: indeed he claims that he did 'make considerable progress in it', but lost it on a journey in Italy and could not be bothered rewriting it. I cannot believe that Berkeley is not telling the truth, but it is also almost impossible to believe that any interest-

ing ideas he may have had on spirit would not have found their way into *Alciphron*, which concerns the philosophy of religion, or *Siris'* eccentric metaphysical meditations. He was prepared to rework the *Theory of Vision* into the *Theory of Vision Vindicated*, and the *Three Dialogues* were composed because the *Principles* had escaped notice. It is incredible that he should not have found some vehicle for publishing any ideas on spirit with which he was at all satisfied.

In Berkeley's argument of ss. 1–5, the first two sections summarize his system, and from the last half sentence of s. 2 to the end of s. 3 is a rather forced appeal to intuition to support that system. In s. 4 he has to face the fact that it is an 'opinion strangely prevailing' that 'sensible objects have an existence ... distinct from their being perceived ...' That there should be such a prevailing opinion is particularly strange as it is based on a 'manifest contradiction'. He explains it in s. 5 as the seductive power of abstract ideas.

It is not surprising that few were influenced by Berkeley's arguments on reading the *Principles*. The blunt appeal to intuition is not convincing. It does not seem 'evident', as he claims, that the 'ideas imprinted on sense ... cannot exist otherwise than in a mind perceiving them', nor that the existence of the table *consists in* the actual and possible experiences one might have of it (though, of course, its existence does *imply* the availability of such experiences). And the argument that the mind-independence of sensible qualities is a manifest contradiction seems to rest on precisely that ambiguity in Locke's use of 'idea' for which so many criticized him. The word 'idea' normally means, roughly, 'thought', and thoughts are mind-dependent, but 'idea' as used by Locke to mean 'whatever is the *object* of the understanding when a man thinks', does not seem to have this implication. Nor is it obvious, as he implies, that a sensory *idea*—that is, a sensory *object*—is the same as a *sensation*.

The appeal to the danger of abstract ideas shows, however, that there is a deeper rationale to Berkeley's intuition. As the last sentence of s. 5 makes clear, a non-abstract—that is, an imagistic—conception of an object will represent it as it would be if perceived from a certain perspective, so that all conception is in terms of what a perception would be like. This line of argument is developed in ss. 22–4. The Introduction, and ss. 1–5, ss. 22–4 of the main text constitute a more or less complete argument. See Editor's Introduction, (vii) and (viii).

24 *operations of the mind*: some commentators have been worried by the fact that Berkeley does not believe that operations of the mind give rise to ideas, but only to *notions*, for activities cannot be caught in the 'still frame' of an idea. They are, however, *objects* of human knowledge and ideas in the loose sense that Berkeley occasionally allows. See ss. 27, 35–40, 142 for *notions*.

26 *perception of it*: following this, *A* adds: 'In truth the object and the sensation are the same thing, and cannot therefore be abstracted from each other.'

To be convinced . . . perceived: this sentence exhibits Berkeley's imagism. The task one is asked to try to perform cannot be simply a verbal-conceptual one, for it is difficult to see what one would there be trying to do, except forming a straightforward sentence; the task is that of concentrating to see whether one can form a certain kind of image.

27 *there can be . . . ideas*: again, this seems to rely on the ambiguity of the term 'idea'.

an idea can be like nothing but an idea: I discuss this maxim in the Editor's Introduction, section vc. The gloss Berkeley here gives it—'a colour or figure can be like nothing but another colour or figure'—shows that it can be multiply ambiguous. The gloss suggests the innocuous 'a quality can be like nothing but the same kind of quality'. Then there is the stronger 'anything (or, perhaps, any *quality*) which is an object of a mental activity can be like nothing but something which is also the object of a mental activity'. Third, 'the indubitably subjective content of a mental state (for example, a sensation) could be like nothing that was not also the subjective content of a mental state'. The first and the third of these are, I think, uncontroversial, but the second is what is required and it seems to beg the question and/or cash in on the ambiguity of Locke's use of 'idea'. I suggest in the Editor's Introduction, however, ways in which, by the use of the *assimilation argument*, one could get from the third to the second.

There is a somewhat different ambiguity in the argument at the end of s. 8. A colour *qua* quality could never be invisible, but it could be invisible *qua* having a certain ontological location. Thus a red patch could be invisible because it qualified an area of physical space and not an area of a visual field, but *qua* red it would be just like the red that qualifies a visual field.

Some there are: Locke, *Essay*, 2. 8.

28 *extension . . . inconceivable*: on the one hand, this is again an appeal to imagism. On the other hand, the thought that matter cannot be purely formal or geometrical and must possess some quality at least analogous to a secondary quality is one that it is difficult to abandon. See Robinson, *Matter and Sense*, ch. 7.

great and small, swift and slow: it is natural to object that these are relative terms and not objective sizes. That there is no such thing as objective size can be got from the argument about the mite in the first *Dialogue* (see Editor's Introduction, vi) and, perhaps, from the arguments in s. 12 and s. 13 that number and unity are subjective, for this would make any metric for size subjective.

materia prima: Aristotle, like most of the ancients, believed that there are four elements, earth, fire, air, and water, each element possessing two qualities; for example, fire is hot and dry, earth hot and wet, etc. He also believed that these elements could transform into each other, so that if its wetness were replaced by dryness, a portion of earth would be transformed into fire. Furthermore, he believed that when anything changed, something must underlie that change and persist through it. In the case of elemental change there is no more basic describable kind of thing to underlie it, so what underlies elemental change must be a bare, characterless materiality, called 'prime matter'. It cannot exist on its own and is a pure potentiality for being some determinate element or other. Some scholars now deny that Aristotle believed in prime matter. For the text and a thorough discussion, see C. J. F. Williams's translation of and commentary on *De Generatione et Corruptione* in the Clarendon Aristotle series.

29 *That number . . . respects*: the argument is that, because counting is concept-relative, then there are no objective facts about number. So, because something may be *one* word and *four* letters it is neither one nor four objectively. From this it would seem to follow that, if the individuation of objects is sortal-relative (that is, kind- or concept-relative) then the individuation of objects is mind-dependent. If, in Quine's words, there is 'no entity without identity', this would make their existence mind-dependent. The move from sortal-relativity to mind-dependence would not be valid if there were natural kinds in the world. The crucial premiss in Berkeley's argument is that there cannot be natural kinds *if* there are alternative ways of individuating—something cannot naturally *be* both *one word*

and *four letters*, for it cannot be both one and four. This raises the kind of issues discussed in, for example, David Wiggins, *Sameness and Substance*.

Unity . . . mind: Locke says this at *Essay*, 2. 7. 7; 2. 16. 1.

30 *Though it must be confessed . . . object*: the argument in s. 14 has two parts. First, it says that the argument from illusion is just as applicable to primary qualities as to secondary. Second it takes that argument as showing that the qualities to which it is applied 'have no existence in matter, or without the mind'. The first claim is correct, the second copies a mistake of Locke's (*Essay*, 2. 8. 21). The argument from illusion only shows that *those instances of the quality of which we are directly aware* exist only in the mind, not that there are no other instances outside the mind. Locke is, therefore, wrong to use the argument to show that secondary qualities are essentially subjective. In the middle of s. 15, Berkeley more or less recognizes this point, and has to fall back on previous arguments.

It is said: Locke, *Essay*, 2. 8. 19; 2. 23. 2; 1. 4. 8.

31 *how . . . to know this?*: ss. 18–20 state the epistemological argument against an external world. Once it is agreed that we are not directly aware of such a world, then belief in it cannot be justified from perception. So it must be from reason, but the possibility of total hallucination shows that there is no necessary connection which could form the foundation of such reasoning. In s. 19, however, Berkeley considers what we would now call an *argument to the best explanation* for positing a world. He has no objection to this as a kind of argument but thinks it will not do in this context. He does not argue, as he does in s. 25, that the physical world would be a useless supposition because, as nothing but a will can really cause anything, a physical world could not be the explanation of our experience. His argument is more sophisticated and does not depend on the doctrine that all causation is will. It rests on the fact that it appears wholly unintelligible why bodies should give rise specifically to experience, even if they are causally active with respect to each other. It has been remarked, at least from Locke, that there is no way that the production of conscious states can be made intelligible from the perspective of physical science. Most of the strategies for doing so are reductionist, such as behaviourism and functionalism, and, in the view of most other philosophers, simply deny the reality of consciousness.

33 *say somewhat of them*: this is done, ss. 85–134.

33 *nobody by to perceive them*: resumption of the strategy from s. 5.
    Notice the extremely psychologistic conception of conceivability
    in s. 22 and s. 24. The argument in s. 23 is extensively discussed
    in the Editor's Introduction. To see s. 23 as a development of s.
    5, see Peacocke, in Foster and Robinson (eds.). He argues that
    all imagining is as from a viewpoint and that it is, therefore,
    problematic whether one can form an empirical conception
    of how the object is *in itself*, independently of all perceptual
    perspectives.

34 *no such thing contained in them*: it is more plausible to say that
    visual ideas do not include power than that tactile ones do not.

35 *Though it must . . . words*: the last sentence of this section was
    inserted only in *B*.

36 *enables us . . . benefit of life*: this is a point at which Berkeley can
    be seen not to have been aware of a major problem for idealism
    or phenomenalism. The laws of nature are stated in terms of the
    behaviour of *physical objects and events* not in terms of ideas. It
    is the fundamental principle of analytical phenomenalism that
    statements about the former can be analysed into statements
    about the latter. If this were possible then it would be possible
    to reinterpret the laws of nature as being about ideas. If the
    analysis were impossible then one would have to accept that
    physical *concepts* were basic to natural laws, even if the things
    they applied to were nothing more than collections of ideas. This
    marks a major distinction of types of idealism. As a matter of
    fact, the attempt to analyse physical concepts in terms of ideas is
    generally agreed to have been unsuccessful. That we cannot
    eliminate or analyse our physical concepts is a major feature of
    Kantian Idealism.

40 *things rather than ideas*: following naturally from the previous
    note, we can say that Berkeley fails to notice the need for a more
    developed account of what makes a set of ideas into a
    physical thing, and, hence, fails to notice the problems in such a
    construction.

43 *continual creation*: the doctrine of continuous creation is the
    orthodox doctrine. For example, St Thomas Aquinas, *Summa
    Theologiae*, pt. I, q. 104, art. 1.

44 *infinite and shapeless*: this is an interesting *reductio* on the con-
    cept of matter. It could be reconstructed as follows:

        1. Matter, if physically real, is infinitely divisible.

2. Any real feature of a physical or empirical reality is representable in perception.

3. Any perceptual representation has finite extent (i.e. is not infinitely small). Therefore

4. Any real feature of a physical or empirical reality is of positive finite extent. Therefore

5. Any piece of matter, if physically real, consists of an infinite number of finitely large pieces.

6. Anything infinite is formless (for to have form is to be bounded, which contradicts infinity). Therefore

7. All pieces of matter are infinite and formless.

I suppose the argument can be avoided if one distinguishes between being empirically infinitely divisible, so there are an infinity of actual physical parts, and being mathematically so divisible, as is any continuum. The parts of the former would have to be empirically real and so, perhaps, in principle perceptible by some possible sense: but the parts of a continuum are mere points and not real in the same sense, and, certainly, not necessarily perceptible by anything. In fact, in a way similar to Zeno's paradoxes, Berkeley is trying to generate a boundless infinite out of the delimited infinite of the continuum.

45 *think with the learned, and speak with the vulgar*: Jessop notes that this tag is quoted by Bacon in *De Augmentis Scientiarum* (5. 4) and is from the sixteenth-century Italian, Augustinus Niphus.

46 *schoolmen ... modern philosophers*: amongst the medievals, Jessop cites Thomas Bradwardine (*c.*1290–1349), Nicholas d'Autrecourt (fourteenth cent.), and Algazel (1059–1111) as having held doctrines like this. Amongst the moderns, Descartes, *Principia* 1. 28; Malebranche, *Recherche*, 6. 2. 3; Samuel Clarke, *Discourse on the Being and Attributes of God*.

53 *in whom we live, move, and have our being*: Acts 17: 28.

54 *unknown occasion ... will of God*: an occasion, in this sense, is contrasted with a cause. Some Cartesians—for example, Malebranche—believed that mind and matter could not interact, so God produced the appropriate 'interactive' effects directly. The state of the material world (presumably of the brain) being the *occasion* for His acting directly on mind, and the state of a mind (for example, an act of will) being the *occasion* of his acting directly on the brain to produce the willed behaviour.

59 *Some there are*: Jessop cites Malebranche, *Entretiens sur la métaphysique*, and Bayle, *Dictionaire historique*, s.v. 'Zenon', n. H, and s.v. 'Phyrron', n. B.

62 *archetypes*: prototypes or models for other derivative instances or copies.

63 *that of other spirits by reason*: Berkeley's system only overcomes scepticism if we have grounds for believing in the ideas had by others and not ourselves. The victim of a Cartesian evil demon, or the 'brain in a vat' being fed coherent hallucinatory experiences by the wicked scientist, can be sure of the existence of their own ideas, but are wrong in believing that they are part of a real, intersubjective world. This comes down to the problem of other minds, for, if the other bodies we seem to experience do have the appropriate experiences associated with them, as we assume they do, then the world is, by Berkelian standards, a real one. As God is directly responsible for our perceptions of other bodies there is no causal necessity for there to be other human minds associated with them. Everything then turns on having a proof that the spirit who causes our experiences is not, in this respect, a deceiver. It is fair to say that Berkeley does not give this problem the attention it deserves, talking as if, once he has argued that our experiences must be caused by God, he has solved all difficulties. He does not recognize the independence of the problem of other minds. See also note on s. 147.

64 *must be in another mind*: this is not strictly consistent with the doctrine of s. 3, which allows a hypothetical existence to unperceived objects. The fact that everything exists in God's mind has led some scholars to distinguish between *idealism*, according to which objects are made up solely of actual ideas and are guaranteed their permanent existence by their permanent presence, in archetypal form, in God's mind: and *phenomenalism*, according to which objects consist of actual ideas and the truth of counterfactuals about what experiences people *would have* or *would have had* under appropriate circumstances. The question then arises whether Berkeley was an idealist, in this strict sense, or a phenomenalist who held that God guaranteed the truth of the counterfactuals; or whether he inconsistently oscillated between the two. This question is nicely dealt with by Urmson in his *Berkeley*. He argues that there is no inconsistency in the text, and that Berkeley's idealism is a form of theistic phenomenalism. Indeed, it is not clear why the archetypal existence of the ideas in the mind of God need be different from His

possessing the appropriate intentions with respect to His creatures' experiences.

65 *uncreated and coeternal*: the eternity of matter was the most common view amongst the Greeks, because they found the notion of creation from nothing unintelligible. For example, Aristotle, *De Caelo*, 2. 1, 283^{b}26 ff.

Mind . . . sustains all things: Berkeley never gives attention to the obvious possibility of a pagan Berkelianism, according to which different spirits might be responsible for providing the experiences associated with different objects. The sun could then have its own spirit which provides us with our sun-appropriate experiences: in general, different parts of nature would have their ruling spirit. This was the kind of Berkelianism supported by the more romantically Irish Yeats.

66 *Socinians*: early unitarians, denying the Trinity and the divinity of Jesus.

67 *Time . . . succession of ideas in our minds*: in his second letter to Johnson, Berkeley says that the succession of ideas *constitutes* time and is not simply its metric. Issues connected with time, space, the continuum, or infinity are among the most intractable in philosophy. One problem with Berkeley's theory is that it would seem to be necessary that the individual ideas whose succession makes up time must themselves have duration or less than an infinite number of them could not possess temporal extent. Time cannot, therefore *consist in* the succession of ideas for they must possess it individually. The natural response is that the individual ideas possess the minimal discernible time interval, like the *minima visibilia* that are supposed to make up space. The difficulty with this is that it is hard to think of any positive extent or duration without it making sense to think that there must be within it a half of that extent or duration.

the soul always thinks: Descartes believed that the soul always thinks. He needed this because of his view that consciousness (i.e. thought) is the essence of mind, so it can never lack it. See his 'Response to the Fifth Set of Objections'. Berkeley had added to this section in manuscript the following

> Sure I am that shou'd anyone tell me there is a time wherein a spirit actually exists without perceiving, or an idea without being perceiv'd, or that there is a 3rd sort of being which exists tho it neither wills nor perceives nor is perceived, his words would have no other effect on my mind than if he talk'd in an

unknown language. Tis indeed an easie matter for a man to say the mind exists without thinking, but to conceive a meaning that may correspond to those sounds, or to frame a notion of a spirit's existence abstracted from its thinking, this seems to me impossible, and I suspect that even they who are the stiffest abetters of that tenent might abate somewhat of their firmness wou'd they but lay aside the words and calmly attending to their own thoughts examine what they meant by them.

68 *a man to be happy or an object good*: the argument of this section is that if there are no abstract ideas, then there is no role for conceptual analysis. This is, at least, a natural conclusion: notice that the examples given of happiness, goodness, justice, and virtue are typical of the things that Plato tries to define. Presumably Platonic forms are paradigms of abstract ideas. Berkeley argues that, with his ontology, to strive to provide necessary and sufficient conditions for the application of a concept, when we know perfectly well in practice how to apply it, is pure pedantry. On the other hand, it is unclear why a proper definition of general ideas, as he conceives of them, is not just as necessary as for general ideas conceived of as abstract.

69 *but of late ... insensible particles*: see Locke's *real essences*; *Essay*, 3. 3. 15 ff.

70 *some are ... for pronouncing universal*: in this and the following section Berkeley does not merely reject a realist interpretation of science but doubts the existence of exceptionless scientific laws, even in the operational sense. In some ways, his view of natural law is Aristotelian—things happen 'usually or for the most part' rather than universally. His belief in the irreducibility of teleological explanation is also Aristotelian. This 'reactionary' aspect of Berkeley's philosophy of science is developed at length in *Siris*.

71 *Those men*: this section in *A* begins: 'It appears from section 66, etc. that the steady, consistent methodes of nature, may not be unfitly styled the *language* of its *Author*, whereby he discovers his *attributes* to our view, and directs us how to act for the convenience and felicity of life. And to me, those men ...'

72 *The best key ... admired treatise*: *A* has instead, 'The best grammar of the kind we are speaking of, will easily be acknowledged to be a treatise of mechanics, demonstrated and applied to nature, by a philosopher of a neighbouring nation whom all the

world admire. I shall not take upon me to make remarks, on the performance of that extraordinary person: only some things he has advanced, so directly opposite to the doctrine we have hitherto laid down, that we should be wanting, in the regard due to the authority of so great a man, did we not take some notice of them. In the entrance of that justly admired treatise . . .' The treatise referred to here and in *B* is Newton's *Principia*. Berkeley discusses the topics of these sections more fully in *De Motu*. The reference in *A* to Newton as a philosopher 'of a neighbouring nation' is often cited as evidence that Berkeley thought of himself as Irish. By contrast, when, slightly over a century later, the Duke of Wellington was asked whether he, being born in Ireland, of Anglo-Irish family, considered himself Irish, replied 'not everything born in a stable is a horse'.

75 *experiment*: the 'bucket experiment' is one of two thought experiments that Newton employed to show that space was absolute not relative. Imagine a bucket containing water and suspended by a rope. Now imagine the bucket spinning—say turning it until the rope becomes tense and letting it go. At first the bucket will turn leaving the water stationary, but, as a result of friction, the water will start to turn with the bucket, until it is fully turning with the bucket and so stationary with respect to it. Centrifugal force will make the water higher at the edge, with a trough in the middle. Now suppose that the bucket is the only thing in the physical universe. It will not be spinning with respect to anything, but, as the state of the water shows, it is spinning. Hence it is moving through absolute, not relative, space. In the other thought experiment we imagine two metal spheres joined by a taut rope. If the spheres begin to spin round each other tension increases in the rope. If they are alone in the physical universe, they are not moving with respect to anything, yet the increased tension shows they are moving, hence they, too, are moving in absolute space.

As far as I am aware, no one has answered these arguments satisfactorily. Mach claimed that we do not know that these phenomena would occur in an otherwise empty universe, but as neither the centrifugal force nor the tension are caused by the gravitational pull of other bodies, the assumption is reasonable. Berkeley's answer seems unsatisfactory, for he denies that the water is moving and so, presumably, believes its surface must remain flat in any world where nothing else exists. This is probably not the line he should have taken, for the experiment can be turned to his advantage, by using it to show that there is no adequate account of autonomous physical space. The experiments show that the relational view is defective and the standard objections show that absolute space is impossible. Physical theory seems to require that the bucket should spin. If space is not absolute then the idea of its spinning cannot be explained by reference to its relationship to other *possible* objects, for to say that it would be moving relative to *something at p* presupposes an independent identity of that point. The notion of the rotation of a single object round its own axis makes clear sense in a visual or phenomenal field. So, without absolute space, only by reference to what it would be experientially like can the phenomena Newton cites make sense. *If* absolute space is a defective conception then space must be a construct from experience. (I am grateful to my colleague Barry Dainton for explaining the experiments.)

76 *dilemma to which several ... employed their thoughts*: in entry 298 of the *Philosophical Commentaries* Berkeley says that Locke, More, and Raphson 'seem to make God extended'.

77 *difficiles nugae*: Latin for 'difficult trivialities'.

79 *To study them for their own sake*: the question of whether numbers need to be treated as entities in their own right—Platonism about numbers—is still a very live issue. Practising mathematicians are often Platonists, Gödel being a striking example. For a modern defence of realism, see Bob Hale, *Abstract Objects* (Oxford: Blackwell, 1987). Berkeley's position seems to be a mixture of extreme nominalism, which turns numbers into numerals, and the reduction of numbers to sets, so that 'five', for example, stands for any group of five things. The former theory is wholly incapable of dealing with the necessity of mathematical truth, for signs are ruled only by convention, or, derivatively, by the laws of nature which govern the things they are signs of, but arithmetical truths are not contingent in either of these ways.

82 *no such thing as the ten-thousandth part of an inch:* Berkeley's argument here shows that he has not properly worked out the difference between the physical and the phenomenal. The use of microscopes and other instruments gives a perfectly good sense to the notion of a ten-thousandth of an inch as a part of the physical world. The 'idea' that represents that size when someone views through a microscope will not be one ten-thousandth the size of the 'idea' he has when viewing an inch-long object in a normal way. There may be no sense to the idea of one ten-

thousandth of a visual field. One response to this problem is to deny that the microscopic is a real part of the physical world. It exists only as a theoretical device for prediction and explanation. It is difficult to reconcile this with the fact that magnification comes in degrees and Berkeley would not want to say that what is seen through an ordinary magnifying glass is unreal. The only consistent position is to treat the physical ontology, both at the ordinary and scientific levels, as a necessary mode of interpreting experience, which interpretation has a conceptual structure of its own, not necessarily intelligible directly in terms of the properties of ideas. This, of course, would be difficult to fit with everything Berkeley says about abstraction.

84 *it being impossible*: following this, *A* also has: 'And whatever mathematicians may think of fluxions or the differential calculus and the like, a little reflection will show them, that in working by these methods, they do not conceive or imagine lines or surfaces less than what are perceivable to sense. They may, indeed, call those little and almost insensible quantities infinitesimals or infinitesimals of infinitesimals, if they please: but at bottom this is all, they being in truth finite, nor does the solution of problems require the supposing any other. But this will be most clearly made out hereafter.'

87 *we understand the meaning of the word*: this criterion of meaningfulness, namely that we take ourselves to understand the words, is too liberal for Berkeley's other purposes, as it would allow in most abstractions.

It must not . . . : *A* starts less abruptly: 'The natural immortality of the soul is a necessary consequence of the foregoing doctrine. But before we attempt to prove this, it is fit that we explain the meaning of that tenet. It must not . . .'

88 *we may not . . . verbal concern*: this second half of s. 142 was added in *B*.

89 *retire . . . meaning*: in *A*, instead of 'retire' to the end, there is: 'depart from some received prejudices and modes of speech, and retiring into themselves attentively consider their own meaning. But the difficulties arising on this head demand a more particular disquisition, than suits the designs of this treatise.'

90 *who works all in all*: I Corinthians 12: 6

by whom all things consist: Colossians 1: 17.

90 *other persons*: this reinforces the point made in the note to page
    64. Berkeley takes the evidence for other human minds as
    unproblematic even though such minds are not directly respon-
    sible for the ideas we perceive of their bodies.

    upholding all things by . . . his Power: Hebrews 1: 3.

94 *Manichean heresy*: to which St Augustine subscribed before his
    conversion to Catholic orthodoxy. It held that there was an evil
    god as well as a good one. It was partly reaction against this
    heresy that led Augustine to emphasize that evil has no positive
    existence and is a mere absence of good.

THREE DIALOGUES

In *A* and *B* the subtitle reads: 'The design of which is plainly to
demonstrate the reality and perfection of human knowledge,
the incorporeal nature of the soul, and the immediate providence of a Deity: in opposition to sceptics and atheists. Also, to
open a method for rendering the sciences more easy, useful, and
compendious.'

The *Three Dialogues* were written because the *Principles* had
failed to make an impact. There is, therefore, a similarity between Berkeley's reasons for writing them and Hume's for following up his *Treatise* with the *Enquiries*. In both cases the
author had not taken enough care in the original work to present
shocking doctrine in the most digestible form. The argument of
the *Principles* had rested too much on the essentially obscure
attack on abstract ideas. The *Dialogues* begins from issues in the
philosophy of perception with which his readers were familiar
and which seemed intuitively easy to understand. The overall
structure of the argument can be represented as follows.

  1. All sensible qualities, both primary and secondary, exist as
     ideas—that is, in the mind.
  2. Nothing can be like an idea but an idea. Therefore
  3. All sensible qualities, both primary and secondary, exist
     only in the mind.

There are then various arguments, mainly in the *Second Dialogue*, to show that conceptions of matter that try to do without
imputing sensible qualities to it, are vacuous.

The argument for (1) divides into two parts; first a proof that
secondary qualities exist as ideas, then the same for primary
qualities. This argument, however, takes place under the shadow

of a confusion, namely that proving that a quality exists in the mind shows that it exists in that form only. See note on s. 15 of the *Principles*. As they are originally presented, therefore, the arguments for (1) are taken to be arguments for (3), from which (1) is not thought to differ. It is when Hylas realizes that refuting naïve realism is not equivalent to refuting representative realism that Philonous is obliged to employ (2) to complete the argument.

The form of representative realism that Philonous is trying to controvert at that stage is not Lockean representative realism, but one that holds that the external world possesses both primary and secondary qualities (that is, (2a) not (2b) of my Editor's Introduction) for the distinction in status between primary and secondary qualities has already been attacked. The subargument which does this is

1. Secondary qualities do not/cannot exist outside the mind.
2. Primary qualities cannot be conceived to exist without secondary qualities. Therefore
3. Neither primary nor secondary qualities exist outside the mind.

The second premiss of the second argument is less general and less important to Berkeley's system than the second premiss of the first.

103 *The Preface*: this was omitted from *C*.

First Dialogue

107 *Philonous*: from the Greek, meaning 'lover of mind'.

Hylas: from the Greek, meaning 'matter'.

109 *my denial . . . your affirmation*: the scepticism of the ancient sceptics, such as Pyrrho (*c*.365–*c*.275 BC), was founded on the belief that every reason for believing a proposition could be matched by an equally good one for not believing it. So one was supposed to suspend belief and this detachment from caring about the truth was meant to bring peace of mind. The discussion here follows the move to a more modern sense of the term, in which scepticism is doubting *or denying* the reality of fundamental objects of belief, such as God or the external world. The thought that scepticism is engendered by the way our sense-contents stand as a 'veil of perception' between the subject and the world is modern not classical.

112 *But is not . . . heat . . . pain?*: Berkeley here uses what I call, in the Editor's Introduction, the *assimilation argument* against a naïve realist theory of the perception of heat.

   1. Great heat is identical to pain.
   2. Pain is mind-dependent: it is not possible for an unperceiving thing to have pain.
   3. Material substance is not a perceiving thing. Therefore
   4. Material substance is not a subject of pain. Therefore
   5. Material substance is not a subject of heat.

To avoid the conclusion Hylas decides that great heat causes pain but is not identical with it. Philonous' reply is that as, when being burnt, we have one, painful, sensation, the pain and the heat must be one idea. He probably should have said that they are features of one and the same idea, like the shape and colour of a visual datum, which can be discerned by *selective attention* (see my Editor's Introduction (vii)). Then when Hylas argues that very moderate heat has neither pain nor pleasure with it, Philonous could have replied that if a feature F is ever a feature of a kind of idea which possesses another feature G which is essentially mind-dependent then any idea of which F is a feature will be mind-dependent: an idea cannot move in and out of being mind-dependent as it acquires other features. Instead, Philonous resorts to the argument from illusion to clinch the case against heat. This same strategy—*assimilation* followed by *illusion*—is used against naïve realism about taste and smell.

118 *as to sounds*: the strategy against sound is entirely different from those used so far; it is the *causal argument* against naïve realism. Hylas' response involves the first use in the dialogue of the primary–secondary quality distinction in the manner of Locke and contemporary science. The experiment with the bell in a near-vacuum was performed by Otto von Guericke (1602–86), who was also the inventor of the air-pump.

120 *the case of colours*: the strategy against colour is the argument from illusion, putting most stress on the generation of 'unreal' colours, like the illusory purple of mountains and blue of the sky, and the differences of colour under microscopic perception. He cites the ordinary variations of perceptible colour of objects in passing. Newton's experiments with prisms and light had taken place about fifty years before Berkeley wrote the *Dialogues*.

126 *Is it your opinion . . . ? It is*: this is a very strange view—or appears to be. Hylas appears to agree that the *very same* instances of shape as those we see are in the external world,

though not the same instances of colour; though the shapes are, it would seem, nothing but the outlines of the colours. I discuss this in the Editor's Introduction (iv). This view is not simply strange in itself, but it is odd that it should be mentioned in this context, where Hylas has just referred to contemporary philosophers, who propounded not this *primary quality direct realism*, but *Lockean representative realism*. Perhaps by 'very figure and extension' Berkeley does not mean very same *instance*, but *specifically* just like: the contrast is with the suggestion soon to follow that objects possess extension with no specific magnitude (or, presumably, form). The argument based on the difference in perception between mites and men which follows can be interpreted (as I do in the Editor's Introduction) as an argument against the possibility of extension existing as real and unperceived: but Philonous compares it to the argument used to show that we do not perceive heat directly. This suggests that the 'mite' argument is against a direct realist account of the perception of shape, which requires that Hylas is propounding primary quality direct realism. Most probably, there is confusion being caused—once again—by the uncertainty about what the argument from illusion proves. If Hylas is following Locke's apparent principle that any proof that we do not perceive a given quality directly is *ipso facto* a proof that that quality does not exist outside the mind, then the hypothesis that primary qualities exist outside the mind will entail that we perceive them directly. Given that it has already been proved that we do not perceive secondary qualities directly, this is *primary quality direct realism*.

127 *mite*: I discuss the 'mite' argument in the Editor's Introduction (vi).

128 *Odd . . . oddness*: this was the extent of this speech in the first two editions, the rest was added in *C*.

129 *time measured . . . in our minds?*: see discussion of time in *Principles*, s. 98.

132 *Let me think . . . I do not find that I can*: this remark and some in the preceding passage only make sense if 'frame the idea' means 'form an image': it is difficult to see what the problem would be in thinking the concepts in any other sense.

133 *distinguish the object from the sensation*: this and the following argument concerning substratum are discussed in the Editor's Introduction, sect. (v*b*)

139 *a contradiction . . . conceiving a thing which is unconceived?*: see
     Introduction (v) and the second note on *Principles*, p. 33.

141 *the . . . object you . . . perceive, exists at a distance*: this is dealt
     with in greater detail in *Essay Towards a New Theory of Vision*
     and *Theory of Vision Vindicated*.

143 *ideas do not exist without the mind . . . objects do*: it is from this
     point that the discussion is directed unequivocally against rep-
     resentative realism, though against the form that allows second-
     ary qualities to be possessed by matter. He has three arguments
     against, two of them serious and one extremely weak. The first is
     epistemological—that we could not come to know of the exist-
     ence of an external world. This is discussed more satisfactorily at
     Principles, ss. 18–20. The second is the weak claim, 'things per-
     petually fleeting and variable as our ideas [could not be] copies
     or images of any thing fixed or constant'. The third is the prin-
     ciple that 'an idea can be like nothing but an idea', which is
     discussed at length in the Editor's Introduction, s. (vc).

Second Dialogue

152 *infinite omnipresent spirit who . . . supports it*: see second note on
     the *Principles*, p. 65. See also note on *Principles*, p. 64.

153 *Vanini, Hobbes, and Spinoza*: that Hobbes, famous for the
     Leviathan, was a materialist is uncontroversial. Spinoza, in his
     Ethics, identifies the world with God, because it is a necessary
     being. It is a permanent matter of controversy whether he was
     a materialist who called the physical world 'God' or whether
     he really believed that the world as a whole was both physical
     and conscious. Vanini was an Italian priest burned for atheism
     in 1606.

     to allow it a real existence?: Berkeley's point remains a good one.
     Naturalistic explanations of the order in the world—for
     example, the Darwinian explanation of order in living creatures
     that Butler and Paley cited in their natural theology—can
     overturn the traditional arguments, but not Berkeley's; for, with-
     out matter, there could not be a naturalistic explanation of
     the world.

154 *a notion entertained by some eminent moderns*: this is
     Malebranche's view.

155 *Few men think . . . It must be owned*: this part of the speech was
     added in *C*.

160 *occasion*: see the note on *Principles*, p. 54.

163 *something entirely unknown*: the concepts of matter discussed from here to the end, which deny it all positive known features and put it outside space and time, can be compared with Kant's *noumenon*; it is an utterly unknowable, non-mental place-holder.

164 *I do not find that I can*: another instance in which the peculiarity of Hylas' efforts to think suggest that the ideas must be images.

Third Dialogue

171 *external existence, wherein . . . reality consists*: this is another instance, like that discussed at *Principles*, p. 36, where Berkeley is unaware of the degree of autonomy of physical concepts. If Putnam, Kripke, and other modern philosophers are correct, natural-kind substance names—such as 'water', 'salt', 'tiger'—operate by designating the *real essences* or scientific structure of the kinds of things in question; they do not have a proper *nominal essence*, or determinate verbal definition. (For these terms, see Locke's *Essay*, 3.6.) The internal structures are not known by ordinary perception. All this could be true of our physical concepts even if internal structures had a purely theoretical or hypothetical existence, as an idealist or phenomenalist requires. Berkeley talks as if it were not part of our ordinary concept of the physical that it possessed properties that are hidden from normal perception and are essential to it. He does not need to claim this—though any empiricist will insist that the content of any microscopic description will be constrained by, and given sense by, its relation to experience.

　　None of this has a very direct connection with scepticism. For this, see note on *Principles*, p. 63. The discussion moves rather uneasily between knowing the real nature of things and knowing whether they exist at all.

173 *might as well doubt of my own being*: see *Principles*, ibid. Berkeley does need a proof of the goodness of God before he can overcome scepticism of the 'evil demon' or 'brain in a vat' kind.

　　Laws of Nature: at *Principles*, s. 30 Berkeley had said that the laws of nature govern the ordering of *ideas* and here it is *physical things*. For why this makes a difference, see note on that passage (p. 36).

176 *perceive both colours and sounds:* the theory that the self is merely a collection of ideas was defended by Hume, but he never seemed to get to grips with the point Berkeley makes here.

No 'bundle theorist' has ever satisfactorily explained the relation between the contents of the different senses and faculties that constitutes their being experienced as belonging to the same subject. As this 'unity of apperception' (in Kant's phrase) had been remarked on by Aristotle (*De Anima*, 425^{b}12) as well as used explicitly by Berkeley to reject the bundle theory, it is strange that it has not received more serious attention.

180 *Let me be represented . . . determination of any indifferent person*: what follows is an illuminating argument. It runs:

1. *It is evident that* only minds have ideas.
2. *It is on all hands agreed that* all objects of immediate perception are ideas.
3. *No one can deny that* sensible qualities are objects of immediate perception. Therefore
4. Sensible qualities exist only in minds.

The argument is valid. Point (3) states the common-sense or naïve realist theory of perception. It looks, therefore, as if common sense is committed to idealism. But the flaw is that (1) and (2) equivocate between the natural and the Lockean sense of 'idea'. In the normal sense, it is evident that only minds have ideas, but it is agreed only amongst Lockean philosophers to call everything the mind concerns itself with, an 'idea', as opposed to some other kind of thing.

It is worth considering whether a serious argument can be brought for the Lockean conflation of all the objects of the mind with ideas, as normally understood. By 'serious argument' I mean, at least, one that does not rest simply on taking the expression 'in the mind' in an overly literal way. A more serious reason would probably start from the claim that the mind can relate to something as an object of thought only if there is some kind of mental representation of it which is 'in the mind' in the more literal sense. If this is augmented with the doctrine that mental representations are images, with the understanding that images neither have, nor are vehicles for, anything with intrinsic intentionality, then one has the Lockean doctrine. The latter requirement—the absence of intrinsic intentionality—is derived from the nominalist reaction against Aristotle. Aristotle believed that thought was accompanied by images, but the capacity of a psychological episode to possess the defining properties of thought depended not on the images but on the forms which the images made available: the intellect abstracts the forms from the images, which are the vehicles whereby the forms are made available to consciousness. Forms, which are, when thought, universals, are paradigms of abstract ideas. The rejection of such abstraction in favour of a nominalist particularism—the rejection of all universal or non-particular entities—leaves one with images pure and simple. In brief, Locke's conception of an idea can be derived by combining the thought that a mental act requires a mental vehicle with the insistence that that vehicle is entirely particular in its nature. This is at one with the failures of imagism to deal with thought; see the discussion of *Principles* s. 23 in the Editor's Introduction.

184 *ideas . . . not conveyed to Him by sense*: this looks suspiciously close to allowing God to have abstract ideas. The spirit of Berkeley's general theory is that sensible objects have only their sensible form—there is not some refined intellectual version of the same content. Berkeley is careful not to attribute God's possession of archetypal versions of the ideas to His being pure intellect, without sensation, for that would prompt the response that our intellect is, as such, immaterial, and should be able to grasp qualities in their intellectual form. But he does put it down to God's being wholly active—that is, pure will, and his account of the human self is that it is, in itself, just will (see A. C. Lloyd in Foster and Robinson (eds.)). The point is that Berkeley's need to deny that God has experiences of a certain kind whilst allowing Him the knowledge that would go with those experiences forces him to allow that the objects of our cognition can take a non-perceptual form; and that it is difficult to see what objection there could in principle be to allowing a similar kind of cognition to the human spirit, which is an image of the divine.

187 *men would*: there is a dispute amongst scholars whether a 'not' was omitted from all three editions (which is one's immediate reaction to the sense) or whether there is irony in the mode of expression.

188 *ambages*: circumlocutions, dark or obscure language.

192 *they suppose an external archetype*: Hylas has the important point that we make sense of the world not just as a bundle of sensible features, but as objects and that, therefore, an understanding of object concepts is required. This fits in with much modern conceptual analysis. Berkeley, like Locke and the empiricists in general, before the development of 'logical empiricism' in the twentieth century, regards this as a species of scholasticism: given that we know that objects are no more than

collections of ideas and are not united by real occult entities such as *forms*, or possessed of Scotus's mysterious 'this-ness' then working out necessary and sufficient conditions for the applications of concepts is pure pedantry.

193 *neither you nor I . . . can be sure it exists*: Berkeley is failing again to notice the scope given for scepticism by the importance to his system of intersubjectivity. See note on *Principles*, p. 63.

203 *substantial forms . . . on each other*: these topics are taken from the scholastics, the Cambridge Platonists, Locke, and Descartes. It is fair to remark that Berkeley failed to deliver Part II of the *Principles*, which would have explained the nature of spirit—the major metaphysical lacuna in his own system.

205 *petitio principii*: the fallacy of begging the question.

206 *ignoratio elenchi*: the fallacy of missing the point.

207 *which two notions . . . constitute the substance of what I advance*: this is a valuable way of looking at Berkeley's system, but Philonous' way of describing it as placing 'in a clearer light that truth, which was before shared between the vulgar and the philosophers' is a little disingenuous. The vulgar and the philosophers had incompatible positions, namely naïve and representative realism. Berkelian idealism is formed by melding the direct theory of perception from the former with the latter's belief that the objects of the mind are purely mental. This is more the production of a new system by compromise, rather than exposing a shared truth. Berkelianism is not so much pure common sense, as the best one can do for common sense, in the light of the arguments of the philosophers. One is forced to choose between the direct intuition that what we are aware of is the world itself and the somewhat more metaphysical conviction of its absolute mind-independence. Berkeley very plausibly judges that the former is more essential to being at home in the world.

INDEX

abstract ideas xix, xxvii–xxxiii, 7–23, 25–6, 29, 59, 67–8, 77, 79, 81–2, 88–9, 131, 155, 209–10, 220, 224, 231
Academics 208
accidents 30, 137, 138
act–object analysis xxi, 132–6
agency, power 34, 36, 51–2, 68–9, 71, 89, 174
Alciphron 212
Algazel 217
animal minds 12
Aquinas, St Thomas 216
archetypes 155, 164, 192
argument to best explanation 215
Aristotle xii, xix, 20, 28, 219, 220, 230
assimilation argument xix, xxiv, 112–15, 117, 118, 213
associationism xxx
astronomy 49
atheism xiii, 59, 65, 84–5, 94, 153, 201, 207
atomism xi
attraction 69, 70
Augustine, St 224
Augustinus Niphus 217
Autrecourt, N. d' 217
Ayer, A. J. xxxv

Bacon, Sir F. 217
Bayle, P. 218
beauty 148, 150–1
Boyle, R. xi
Bradley, F. xxxvi
Bradwardine, T. 217
brain 148–9
'bucket experiment' 75, 221–2

Cambridge Platonists 232
causal argument (against direct realism) xix, 118–20, 124–5

causation xxiii, 36–7, 46, 52, 68, 70–1, 157, 179
chimeras 178
Clarke, S. 217
colour xx, 9–10, 27, 67, 120–6, 133–4, 135, 136, 169, 213, 226
concepts, *see* abstract ideas
Copernican system 45, 181
Creation, the 151, 195–201

Dainton, B. 222
deism xiii
Descartes, R. xi, xii, xxviii, 209, 210, 219, 232
direct realism xiv, xix, 111–25
distance, perception of 41, 141
dreams 31, 140, 178
Duns Scotus 232

Einstein, A. xxxvi
empiricism 209–10
Epicureans 65
Essay towards a New Theory of Vision x, xxix, 212, 228
esse est percipi vel percipere xiv, xxxiv, 25–7, 63, 84, 112, 172, 209
extension 9, 13, 27–8, 30, 44, 67, 79–80, 126–30, 131, 132, 133, 134, 185

fatalism 65
fire 216
force (Newtonian) 73
forms 231
Foster, J. xxxvi
free will 48

Galileo xi
general ideas 13
geometry 79–84

God ix, xii, xvii, 6, 8, 32, 46, 51–2, 55–6, 57, 70–1, 76, 90–5, 110, 132, 152–7, 159, 161, 173–4, 177, 178–9, 196, 198–9, 201–3, 225, 229, 231
Gödel, K. 222
goodness 68
gravity 129, 233–4
Guericke, O. von 226

happiness 68
heat and cold xx, 29, 112–16, 127, 130, 169, 226
Hegel, F. xxxvi
Hobbes, T. xiii, xxviii, 65, 153, 211
Hume, D. xiii, xvii, xviii, xxxiii–xxxv, xxxvi, 209, 224, 229

identity 191–2, 214
ignoratio elenchi 209
illusion, argument from xix, 115–16, 117, 118, 126–30
imagination 11, 36, 37, 155, 178, 190–1
imagism xviii, xxxii, 213
  see also abstract ideas
immortality of soul 87
infinite divisibility 79–82
infinitesimals 83, 223
innate ideas 209
instrument, matter as 159–60, 164
intellect, pure 132

jaundice 123
Jessop, T. E. 210, 217, 218
Johnson, Dr S. (lexicographer) xxxvi
Johnson, S. (American divine) 219

Kant, I. xxv, 216, 229, 230
knowledge 61
Kripke, S. 229

language 9, 13, 18–21, 45–6, 60, 189, 194

Leibniz, G. ix
light 124, 135, 136
Lindsay, A. D. xxxv
Lloyd, A. C. 231
Locke, J. ix–xiii, xvi, xx, xxviii, xxxv, 12, 14–15, 27–30, 142–7, 209, 210, 211, 212, 215, 220, 222, 227, 232

Mach, E. xxxvi, 221
Malebranche, N. xi, 155, 217, 218, 228
Manicheanism 94
mathematics 48, 68, 76–84, 131, 203
matter:
  as supposed cause of ideas 156–7, 182–3, 205–6
  as supposed occasion for ideas 54–5, 160–2, 164, 201
  Locke's theory of 27
  role in science 185–6
memory 143
microscopes 122
Mill, J. S. xxxv
miracles 48, 51, 60
momentum 185
morality 68, 89, 203
More, H. 222
motion 9, 27–8, 66, 67, 69, 72, 128–9, 132
  absolute and relative 72–6, 130–1
  as intermediate cause of sensation 157–8, 202–3

naïve realism, *see* direct realism
natural science 45, 68–76, 202–3
nature:
  laws of 36, 70–2, 160, 186
  order in 141, 204
'new philosophy' xi, xiii, 148–50
  see also atomism; natural science
Newton, Sir I. xi, xiii, 221
  his *Principia* 72, 75
nominalism xxvii–xxxii, 230, 231

notions xxxiv, 63, 87, 88, 109, 164,
165, 175, 213
number 29, 77–9

Ockham xxviii

pain xx, 40, 52, 54, 90, 94, 112–15,
130, 136, 183–4, 226
pan-psychism ix
passivity:
of ideas 34, 158
of mind in perception 135
petitio principii 205
phantasm xii
Philosophical Commentaries x,
xxxiv
place 66, 73
Plato 209, 220
pleasure xx, 68, 90, 114–15, 130
Popper, K. xxxvi
primary qualities xi, xv, xvi,
27–30, 34, 56, 126, 130, 133
primary quality direct realism xv,
126–33, 226–7
Principles, Pt. II 211
providence 50, 65, 205
Putnam, H. 229
Pyrrho 225

Quine, W. V. O. 214

Raphson, J. 222
rationalism 209
real essences 220, 229
reason 31, 63, 85, 132, 143, 165,
174
relations 63, 88
religion and immaterialism
59–61, 85, 87, 153, 202
representative realism xiv, xv,
xviii, xxiii, 9–15, 142–7, 225,
227
resurrection of Christ 66
revelation 165, 187
Russell, B. xxxv

scepticism xii, xvii, 6, 7, 62–4, 85,

107, 109–10, 146, 150, 151,
169–70, 188, 190, 193, 202,
204, 208
schoolmen xii, 17, 20, 43
Scripture 59–60, 92, 155, 178, 179,
195–7, 207
secondary qualities xi, xv, xx, xxi,
27–8, 29–30, 43, 56, 125–6,
130, 133, 139
self, the 24, 86–7, 174, 175–6
sensation 25, 67, 86, 133, 136,
155
sense data xii
shape 126–8, 133–4, 169
sight 41–2, 135, 141
sin, God not responsible for
179–80
Siris 212, 220
smell 118, 135, 202
Socinians 66
solidity 129, 185
soul 6, 24, 35, 65, 67, 86, 87, 88,
154, 174
sounds 118–19, 202
space 72, 76
Spinoza, B. ix, 153, 210
spirit xxxiv, 24, 26, 32, 35, 37–8,
51, 55, 63, 67, 84, 85–9, 129,
140, 152, 203
as sole efficient cause 69, 70,
71, 155, 158, 179
as sole substance 26, 85
Sprigge, T. xxxvi
structural representative realism
xvi
substratum xi–xii, xxii, 56, 136–7,
180, 185, 201

taste 29, 116–17, 202
time 66–7, 72
touch 41

understanding 35
uniformity of nature 36–7, 48, 51,
71
unity 29, 77–8

Vanini 153
'veil of perception' xi
velocity 185
verification principle 210
Vienna Circle xxxv
virtue 87, 95, 110, 132

Wellington, Duke of 221

will xxiii, 35, 70, 89, 134–5, 155,
    158, 180, 186
Wittgenstein, L. 211

Yeats, W. B. 219
Yolton, J. W. 211

Zeno 217

A SELECTION OF   OXFORD WORLD'S CLASSICS

THOMAS AQUINAS	**Selected Philosophical Writings**
FRANCIS BACON	**The Essays**
WALTER BAGEHOT	**The English Constitution**
GEORGE BERKELEY	**Principles of Human Knowledge** and **Three Dialogues**
EDMUND BURKE	**A Philosophical Enquiry into the Origin of Our Ideas of the Sublime and Beautiful** **Reflections on the Revolution in France**
CONFUCIUS	**The Analects**
ÉMILE DURKHEIM	**The Elementary Forms of Religious Life**
FRIEDRICH ENGELS	**The Condition of the Working Class in England**
JAMES GEORGE FRAZER	**The Golden Bough**
SIGMUND FREUD	**The Interpretation of Dreams**
THOMAS HOBBES	**Human Nature** and **De Corpore Politico** **Leviathan**
JOHN HUME	**Selected Essays**
NICCOLO MACHIAVELLI	**The Prince**
THOMAS MALTHUS	**An Essay on the Principle of Population**
KARL MARX	**Capital** **The Communist Manifesto**
J. S. MILL	**On Liberty and Other Essays** **Principles of Political Economy** and **Chapters on Socialism**
FRIEDRICH NIETZSCHE	**Beyond Good and Evil** **The Birth of Tragedy** **On the Genealogy of Morals** **Twilight of the Idols**

A SELECTION OF   OXFORD WORLD'S CLASSICS

THOMAS PAINE   **Rights of Man, Common Sense, and Other
                         Political Writings**

JEAN-JACQUES ROUSSEAU   **The Social Contract
                         Discourse on the Origin of Inequality**

ADAM SMITH   **An Inquiry into the Nature and Causes of
                         the Wealth of Nations**

MARY WOLLSTONECRAFT   **A Vindication of the Rights of Woman**

Bhagavad Gita

The Bible Authorized King James Version
With Apocrypha

Dhammapada

Dharmasūtras

The Koran

The Pañcatantra

The Sauptikaparvan (from the Mahabharata)

The Tale of Sinuhe and Other Ancient Egyptian Poems

Upaniṣads

ANSELM OF CANTERBURY	**The Major Works**
THOMAS AQUINAS	**Selected Philosophical Writings**
AUGUSTINE	**The Confessions** **On Christian Teaching**
BEDE	**The Ecclesiastical History**
HEMACANDRA	**The Lives of the Jain Elders**
KĀLIDĀSA	**The Recognition of Śakuntalā**
MANJHAN	**Madhumalati**
ŚĀNTIDEVA	**The Bodhicaryàvatàra**

A SELECTION OF   OXFORD WORLD'S CLASSICS

Classical Literary Criticism

The First Philosophers: The Presocratics
  and the Sophists

Greek Lyric Poetry

Myths from Mesopotamia

APOLLODORUS   The Library of Greek Mythology

APOLLONIUS OF RHODES   Jason and the Golden Fleece

APULEIUS   The Golden Ass

ARISTOPHANES   Birds and Other Plays

ARISTOTLE   The Nicomachean Ethics
                       Physics
                       Politics

BOETHIUS   The Consolation of Philosophy

CAESAR   The Civil War
                       The Gallic War

CATULLUS   The Poems of Catullus

CICERO   Defence Speeches
                       The Nature of the Gods
                       On Obligations
                       The Republic and The Laws

EURIPIDES   Bacchae and Other Plays
                       Medea and Other Plays
                       Orestes and Other Plays
                       The Trojan Women and Other Plays

GALEN   Selected Works

HERODOTUS   The Histories

HOMER   The Iliad
                       The Odyssey

A SELECTION OF   **OXFORD WORLD'S CLASSICS**

HORACE	The Complete Odes and Epodes
JUVENAL	The Satires
LIVY	The Dawn of the Roman Empire
	The Rise of Rome
MARCUS AURELIUS	The Meditations
OVID	The Love Poems
	Metamorphoses
	Sorrows of an Exile
PETRONIUS	The Satyricon
PLATO	Defence of Socrates, Euthyphro, and Crito
	Gorgias
	Phaedo
	Republic
	Symposium
PLAUTUS	Four Comedies
PLUTARCH	Greek Lives
	Roman Lives
	Selected Essays and Dialogues
PROPERTIUS	The Poems
SOPHOCLES	Antigone, Oedipus the King, and Electra
STATIUS	Thebaid
SUETONIUS	Lives of the Ceasars
TACITUS	Agricola and Germany
	The Histories
VIRGIL	The Aeneid
	The Eclogues and Georgics

A SELECTION OF OXFORD WORLD'S CLASSICS

JANE AUSTEN	Emma
	Mansfield Park
	Persuasion
	Pride and Prejudice
	Sense and Sensibility
MRS BEETON	Book of Household Management
LADY ELIZABETH BRADDON	Lady Audley's Secret
ANNE BRONTË	The Tenant of Wildfell Hall
CHARLOTTE BRONTË	Jane Eyre
	Shirley
	Villette
EMILY BRONTË	Wuthering Heights
SAMUEL TAYLOR COLERIDGE	The Major Works
WILKIE COLLINS	The Moonstone
	No Name
	The Woman in White
CHARLES DARWIN	The Origin of Species
CHARLES DICKENS	The Adventures of Oliver Twist
	Bleak House
	David Copperfield
	Great Expectations
	Nicholas Nickleby
	The Old Curiosity Shop
	Our Mutual Friend
	The Pickwick Papers
	A Tale of Two Cities
GEORGE DU MAURIER	Trilby
MARIA EDGEWORTH	Castle Rackrent

A SELECTION OF **OXFORD WORLD'S CLASSICS**

GEORGE ELIOT
Daniel Deronda
The Lifted Veil and Brother Jacob
Middlemarch
The Mill on the Floss
Silas Marner

SUSAN FERRIER
Marriage

ELIZABETH GASKELL
Cranford
The Life of Charlotte Brontë
Mary Barton
North and South
Wives and Daughters

GEORGE GISSING
New Grub Street
The Odd Woman

THOMAS HARDY
Far from the Madding Crowd
Jude the Obscure
The Mayor of Casterbridge
The Return of the Native
Tess of the d'Urbervilles
The Woodlanders

WILLIAM HAZLITT
Selected Writings

JAMES HOGG
The Private Memoirs and Confessions of a
    Justified Sinner

JOHN KEATS
The Major Works
Selected Letters

CHARLES MATURIN
Melmoth the Wanderer

WALTER SCOTT
The Antiquary
Ivanhoe
Rob Roy

MARY SHELLEY
Frankenstein
The Last Man

A SELECTION OF   OXFORD WORLD'S CLASSICS

ROBERT LOUIS   Kidnapped and Catriona
STEVENSON   The Strange Case of Dr Jekyll and
                         Mr Hyde and Weir of Hermiston
                      Treasure Island

BRAM STOKER   Dracula

WILLIAM MAKEPEACE   Vanity Fair
THACKERAY

OSCAR WILDE   Complete Shorter Fiction
                      The Major Works
                      The Picture of Dorian Gray

DOROTHY WORDSWORTH   The Grasmere and Alfoxden Journals

WILLIAM WORDSWORTH   The Major Works

The Oxford World's Classics Website

www.worldsclassics.co.uk

- Information about new titles
- Explore the full range of Oxford World's Classics
- Links to other literary sites and the main OUP webpage
- Imaginative competitions, with bookish prizes
- Peruse the Oxford World's Classics Magazine
- Articles by editors
- Extracts from Introductions
- A forum for discussion and feedback on the series
- Special information for teachers and lecturers

www.worldsclassics.co.uk

American Literature

British and Irish Literature

Children's Literature

Classics and Ancient Literature

Colonial Literature

Eastern Literature

European Literature

History

Medieval Literature

Oxford English Drama

Poetry

Philosophy

Politics

Religion

The Oxford Shakespeare

A complete list of Oxford Paperbacks, including Oxford World's Classics, Oxford Shakespeare, Oxford Drama, and Oxford Paperback Reference, is available in the UK from the Academic Division Publicity Department, Oxford University Press, Great Clarendon Street, Oxford OX2 6DP.

In the USA, complete lists are available from the Paperbacks Marketing Manager, Oxford University Press, 198 Madison Avenue, New York, NY 10016.

Oxford Paperbacks are available from all good bookshops. In case of difficulty, customers in the UK can order direct from Oxford University Press Bookshop, Freepost, 116 High Street, Oxford OX1 4BR, enclosing full payment. Please add 10 per cent of published price for postage and packing.